TALES FOR THE COMMON PEOPLE

AND

OTHER CHEAP REPOSITORY TRACTS

TALES FOR THE COMMON PEOPLE

AND

OTHER CHEAP REPOSITORY TRACTS

Selected, with an introduction and notes
by Clare MacDonald Shaw

TRENT EDITIONS

Published by Trent Editions, 2002

Trent Editions
Department of English and Media Studies
The Nottingham Trent University
Clifton Lane
Nottingham NG11 8NS

Printed in Great Britain by Goaters Limited, Nottingham
ISBN 1 84233 062 4

Contents

Introduction

Hannah More's choice of the title *Tales for the Common People* strikes modern readers as arrogant in its assumption of class distinctions. In our nominally egalitarian system we find the companion title, *Stories for the Middle Ranks of Society*, similarly disturbing. But historians warn against making easy assumptions about social divisions in late eighteenth-century Britain. Instead of relying on concepts of opposition between the working class and the middle class, we might consider an older social model, founded on religious belief, of the different orders of society as links in the chain of being.[1] In this system of thought the controlling metaphor is one of connection and interdependence rather than hostile division; we are to imagine finely graduated levels within these orders rather than two opposed camps; More shows in her tales how appropriate or unsuitable social behaviour results in the swift rise or fall of the individual within the system.

Such a metaphor would be comforting in the 1790s to those in the middle ranks, given the conflicting evidence from the French Revolution of violent division in the body politic. As post-revolutionary England suffered from the effects of the war with France there was widespread fear of the radical influence of Tom Paine, whose *Rights of Man* appeared in 1791-2. Extremist Jacobin infiltrators were thought to be undermining the system; treason and subversion were suspected in the educated classes, and the poor might too readily be incited to riot, especially when the hard winters of 1794 and 1795 threatened famine. Those who believed in the established order, like Hannah More and her friends, set about defending it. Unlike Tom Paine and Mary Wollstonecraft, who asserted human rights and proposed radical change in the system, she urged readers at all levels to concentrate on their duties towards each other, repairing and strengthening the social fabric.

The tales in this edition formed part of her plan; they show how the individual should act on Biblical authority, both for the benefit of others and in order to achieve peace of mind and respect within a stable community. Fortunately for the reader, characters like Black Giles the poacher and rat-catcher, his wife Tawney Rachel the fortune-teller, and Sinful Sally the prostitute dramatically fail to live up to these expectations. Their histories form part of a series of more than a hundred little pamphlets or chapbooks issued by the Cheap Repository under More's editorial guidance, most of which are unsigned and undated. Although there were other contributing authors, she complained of having to supply much of the writing herself, and her biographer M.G. Jones lists fifty of the tracts as 'ascribed to More'.[2] The founding of the Repository was a remarkable cultural project to indoctrinate the nation by the monthly dissemination of ideologically correct material disguised as entertaining stories and ballads. The system was in operation between 1795 and 1798, though the *Cheap Repository Tracts* were reprinted in various forms for decades after it closed. The division of some narratives into the controversial categories of *Tales for the Common People* and *Stories for the Middle Ranks of Society* occurred when More republished them in 1801.

The Cheap Repository experiment managed to be at the same time politically counter-revolutionary and morally radical. It was driven by the new spirit of Evangelical awakening within the Church of England; its supporters were determined to reform the national character and to arm it against vice and sedition. The ten tales and four ballads printed here show how More makes quick progress in writing persuasive fiction. The early history of *Tom White* is bland and episodic in comparison with the more subtle psychological analysis of motivation in later tales like *Tawney Rachel* and *Hester Wilmot*. Her developing skill in narrative construction and her experiments in voice show what she might have achieved had her view of religious propriety allowed her to give more licence to the villains and less space to the virtuous, or to admit that human nature is not clearly divisible into these categories.

At this point it seems appropriate to consider the *Tales* in the context of her other work, and to examine the way in which, from modest beginnings, and at a time when women's opportunities for self-development were severely restricted, she achieved fame and influence as a writer and reformer.

Outline of More's life and work

She was born in 1745 in Stapleton, Gloucestershire, the fourth of the five daughters of Jacob More, schoolmaster, and his wife Mary (neé Grace). The girls were educated by their father for a career in teaching. When the eldest daughter opened a school for young ladies in Bristol, her sisters attended until they were old enough to take part in teaching and management. The school was successful and achieved lasting renown.

After accepting a proposal of marriage from William Turner in 1767 when she was twenty-three, More gave up her professional and financial share in the school, but her middle-aged suitor twice postponed the ceremony. The long delay caused friends to advise her in 1773 to break the engagement and to accept his compensating offer of £200 a year for the disruption to her career and the pain and social embarrassment caused. She decided to remain single, rejecting other proposals. The annual allowance gave her a degree of independence; she was able to travel between Bristol and London for many years.

Living in London in the 1770s, she developed friendships in several social circles. She was welcomed by the Bluestockings, a group of women who were interested in the arts and other intellectual pursuits; they included Anna Laetitia Barbauld. Elizabeth Montagu, Mrs Vesey, Elizabeth Carter and Hester Chapone. She made the acquaintance of influential men in the literary and artistic establishment, including Dr Johnson, Sir Joshua Reynolds, Edmund Burke and Horace Walpole. Friendship with David Garrick, the famous actor, and Eva, his wife, turned her mind to the theatre. She had earlier written dramatic dialogues for use in schools, including *A Search after Happiness*, first published in 1773. Now she tried her hand at writing drama in the current style; *The Inflexible Captive: a Tragedy* (1774), was staged in Bath. *Percy* (1777) was a success at Covent Garden, but her third play failed.

During the 1770s and 1780s she also developed her interest in poetry, publishing narrative, reflective and satiric verse. The best of this work includes *Sensibility* (1782), *Florio: A Tale for Fine Gentlemen and Ladies, The Bas Bleu, or Conversation* (1786) and her forthright and moving abolitionist poem *Slavery* (1788). Having lived in Bristol, a major port, she had first-hand experience of British involvement in the cruel trade.

As her literary reputation grew, she began to make her mark in aristocratic society, but letters to her sisters record a growing dissatisfaction with the frivolity of fashionable pursuits and the emptiness of worldly fame. After the death of Garrick in 1779 she had lived in seclusion with his wife, writing and giving serious reflection to her purpose in life. Her religious commitment, already shown in the *Sacred Dramas* of 1782, was renewed by an experience of spiritual awakening which also transformed her interest in political issues. She began to address the upper classes directly at a time when events in France helped to focus their attention on the need for self-reformation. *Thoughts on the Importance of the Manners of the Great* appeared in 1788, and *An Estimate of the Religion of the Fashionable World* in 1790.

Among her friends in the later 1780s was John Newton, the former slave-trader captain who had undergone conversion, and the Evangelical reformer and abolitionist William Wilberforce. In this new stage of her life she spent more time near Bristol, setting up with the help of her sister Martha (Patty) a chain of Sunday Schools in the Mendip Hills in order to provide religious education for the poor, many of whom proved in the early stages to be resistant or openly hostile. The project was difficult and expensive, though Wilberforce gave the sisters financial help. More's letters reporting to him on the foundation of the schools were reprinted with her sister's *Journals* in 1859, providing detailed and lively accounts of her battles with the 'heathen' villagers and landlords.[3] Sunday Schools would play a central part in the Cheap Repository Tracts.

Her acquaintances in the early 1790s included several bishops and influential members of the aristocracy. Observing the effects of the French Revolution, they feared that the extreme revolutionary fervour of the Jacobins would infect the lower orders of British society. As More had first-hand knowledge of the lives of the poor from administering her Sunday Schools, the Bishop of London asked her to write 'some little thing' to quell the dangerous tendencies which were being inflamed by radical writings. She declined, but in 1792 published the anti-Jacobin pamphlet *Village Politics* in which a dialogue between Jack Anvil the Blacksmith and Tom Hod the Mason sets out the argument for and against revolt.[4] As More strongly believed that the social order was ordained by God, the conservative view must win. However, she did not think it inconsistent to believe that a divinely-appointed system should need considerable reform.

With the support of Evangelical friends in the Church of England she began to organize the Cheap Repository project – her ambitious plan to flood the country with chapbooks that would advance the cause of moral rather than political revolution by teaching the lower and middle orders of society their respective duties rather than their rights. Eye-catching woodcuts might mislead customers into thinking that the new chapbooks were no different from the 'vile trash' which they replaced in the pedlar's pack. But to make sure of a large readership, many were bought by middle-class supporters of the scheme for distribution to the masses.

The Cheap Repository Tracts – some written by More, some by her sisters and friends – were issued monthly between 1795 and 1797, with a few in 1798. They included all the tales and ballads reprinted in this edition, although the title *Tales for the Common People* was not used until 1801, when More reorganized most of her own tracts for publication in her second *Collected Works*, dividing them into *Tales* or *Stories for the Middle Ranks of Society*, and separating the prose works from the ballads. Further details of the complex publication and distribution of the Tracts, and of their social influence, are given later in this introduction and in the bibliography and notes on the texts.

Other works written by More in the 1790s include *Remarks on the Speech of M. Dupont made in the National Convention of France* (1793), and her major work, *Strictures on the Modern System of Female Education* (1799), which proved highly influential and was frequently reprinted. This book should be compared with Mary Wollstonecraft's *Vindication of the Rights of Woman* (1792); the writers are politically opposed, but share a concern for developing the moral and intellectual capacities of women and ensuring that a more rational system of education will allow them to take on social responsibilities instead of wasting their lives in the exercise of superficial accomplishments and the pursuits of vanity and idleness.

The success of More's writing allowed her to build in 1801 a new house, Barley Wood, to be shared by her sisters for a life of quiet retreat. However, she had made enemies as a result of her intrusion into religious and political affairs, which were regarded by the more conservative clergy as the preserve of men. Although she always invited the support of local ministers in setting up her Sunday Schools or promoting the chapbooks, some were suspicious of her crusading zeal in the cause of religion, which smacked to them of Dissent, especially of Methodism. Wesley's followers had growing support in the country, threatening the complacency of the Established, but unreformed, Church of England.

Although More denied such accusations, regarding herself as a staunch Anglican and suspecting Methodists of excessive spiritual enthusiasm, she tried to import some of their religious energy into her Sunday Schools.[5] Knowing that children found it difficult to learn the formal Church Catechism, she wrote an alternative version for the very young. This little booklet, smaller than a child's hand, is innocently called *Questions and Answers for the Mendip and Sunday Schools* (1795) but a cleric might have seen it as a woman's attempt to rewrite part of the Church liturgy; in her schools she could be indoctrinating a new generation, advancing religiously radical views. This theme of Catechism as the basis of Christian learning is repeatedly stressed in the Tales. In *Black Giles, Part Two* she shows how the minister might combine testing on the Commandments with simpler questions for slow or reluctant learners. Her *Questions and Answers* gives young children a quick-fire test in short words.[6]

The resentment of some of the clergy and other traditionalists broke out in a pamphlet war, known as the Blagdon Controversy, which lasted from 1801 to 1803. The immediate cause was the question of More's involvement in the dismissal of the curate of Blagdon, Mr Bere, after a dispute over the unorthodox and over-zealous conduct of one of her Sunday School teachers. Pamphlets full of invective were issued by her supporters and detractors; some of these make specific reference to the Cheap Repository Tracts as evidence of her influence. A few titles are listed in the Bibliography, but there were twenty-three angry exchanges in all, and the language was often not clerical.

Being attacked in this public manner for several years was painful to More; a woman's reputation and her sense of propriety were threatened by such exposure, but she continued to work. Developing the theories on women's education put forward in *Strictures,* she set out in *Hints Towards Forming the Character of a Young Princess* (1805) her opinion of the training suitable for a woman of the highest rank who would have access to power. This was well-received at court, and her advice was taken. Princess Charlotte, the subject of the treatise, died young, but the book might have influenced the education of Queen Victoria.

In 1808, reverting to analysis of middle-class mores, she published *Cælebs in Search of a Wife.* Although this is a didactic work, it is lightly disguised as fiction. Cœlebs (Latin for 'bachelor') travels the country in search of the ideal wife. He tests many candidates, who all prove morally or intellectually inadequate, until he finds Lucilla. While retaining the correct degree of feminine modesty, she has a disciplined mind, engages herself in constructive charity work, is devout and self-denying. Jane Austen, in a letter to her sister, made it clear that she was not looking forward to reading this book; she wrote, 'I do not like the Evangelicals'.[7] Readers who know More's lighter satires of the 1780s, or who respond to the touches of humour in the *Tales,* might wonder what happened to her old spirit and wit in the later work, but serious Evangelical commitment at this time recognized the sacrifice of authorial levity as essential to the expression of God's purpose. The darker tones of Austen's *Mansfield Park* (1814), which takes religious commitment and the role of the Church in the community as a central theme, reflect the developing influence of writers like More on the national consciousness.

In another letter Austen notes that some new acquaintance are reading More's latest work 'with delight' – presumably her *Practical Piety* of 1811.[8] This work became a popular manual for the application of religion to everyday life; readers of the *Tales* will find similarly detailed analysis of motives and actions in both Parts of the *History of Hester Wilmot.* To respond to More's religious writings we might need to adjust our vision. Society today concerns itself with the material welfare of the body. We give close attention to matters of diet and physical exercise, and punish the flesh according to unattainable ideals of perfection; we discuss issues of nutrition, purity and contamination with a similar absorption to that displayed in Evangelical writings relating to the health of the spirit. Our sense of urgency comes from an awareness of the brevity of life; for most Evangelicals an eternity of hell began at death for unregenerate souls. An apocalyptic sense of doom infects readers of the more extreme examples of their writing, but, except in death-bed scenes, Hannah More practised restraint. De Quincey gives an account of watching the actress Mrs Siddons talking about religion by the hour with More without understanding the profound ideological differences which lay between them, for instance on the inefficacy of repentance alone to guarantee redemption.[9] More believed that for the salvation of the soul a moment of sudden and overwhelming recognition of sin and saving grace is required – the moment of conversion recorded in simple terms in the Cheap Repository Tracts printed here, for example in the lives of Tom White, Betty Brown, Hester Wilmot and her parents, and the black slave, Yamba. Clearly the Shepherd of Salisbury Plain and his wife, like Patient Joe, are among the elect, but Black Giles and Tawney Rachel have chosen the path to damnation. Sinful Sally, like Giles, repents at the last moment, but both have tested Providence; it may be too late to receive grace.

More continued to write on questions of ethics and religion; her later books included *Christian Morals* (1813), *An Essay on the Character and Writings of St Paul* (1815) and *Moral Sketches of Prevailing Opinions and Manners* (1819), in which she advised fathers on the part they should play in bringing up sons.

When her *Collected Works* were brought out by Cadell and Davies in 1818, much enlarged since 1801, the publishers also issued separately a two-volume set of the *Tales for the Common People* and *Stories for the Middle Ranks of Society*, which had retained their popularity with the public. The old narratives were still on sale at Hatchards and other bookshops, in versions of the three-volume anthology first issued by Rivington in 1798 after the Cheap Repository project was closed down. The cheaper separate tracts were still sold by Evans, who was granted joint printing rights at that time. The sober 1818 edition was clearly intended for the middle-class library; it had dispensed with the woodcuts. It is worth remembering that the *Tales* were available to and affordable by all classes of society from 1795 up to the Victorian period.

Concerned by the renewed threat of sedition and riot in the difficult years after Waterloo, More issued in 1819 a selection of her old and new tracts with some revised versions. *Village Politics* (1792) is updated as *The*

Village Disputants. There is some interesting material for the social historian here; in 'The Delegate' she shows a radical party representative creating unrest among workers – an early treatment of a theme developed by Gaskell and Dickens – but these tracts were not added to the popular collections. She continued to write and publish in her later years, outliving all her sisters. Being regarded by the public as an oracle, she received a constant stream of visitors – eighty in one week, she complained.[10]

Because of failing health and the thieving ways of her unredeemed servants, she left old home for Bristol, where she died in 1833. After her death her works continued to be reprinted though much of the Victorian period. The pious but not entirely reliable *Memoirs of the Life and Correspondence of Mrs. Hannah More* by William Roberts appeared in 1834, establishing her as an Evangelical saint. It contains much essential material, though Roberts cut and edited the letters to an extent that displeased one of her friends. His uncritical celebration of her life caused a hostile reaction to her cult among some readers.

Annals of the poor: More's village Sunday Schools in relation to the *Tales*
More would have considered the development of Sunday Schools to be one of her major achievements because of their unremitting work towards the salvation of souls. In the late eighteenth century the Sunday School movement, founded by Robert Raikes in 1780, was being greatly expanded across the country by the initiative and cooperation of benevolent members of the middle class, who were concerned, like More, that religious principles were not being inculcated in the young, or that illiteracy prevented the reading of the Bible. Although the schools recruited children, their parents and other parishioners were often welcomed into the fold. More and her sister Patty, with the encouragement of their friend Wilberforce, resolved in 1789 to set up mainly at their own expense a school in Cheddar and, later, a circuit of schools in the Mendip villages which, to their eyes, were full of 'heathen' fellow-creatures in need of missionary redemption. Wilberforce, a member the Evangelical reforming group which became known as the Clapham Sect, supplied additional funds. From More's letters to him we have a clear impression of the difficulties involved in this exercise. She later put these experiences to good use, recording characters and incidents in her *Tales*, where the local Sunday School is often the catalyst for reform within the community

Writing to Wilberforce from Cheddar in 1789, she describes her attempt to propitiate the 'chief despot of the village, who is very rich and very brutal', so that he would not obstruct the experiment, but when she enters 'the monster's den' this member of the class of 'rich savages'

> begged I would not think of bringing any religion into the country; it
> was the worst thing in the world for the poor, for it made them lazy
> and useless. In vain did I represent to him that they would be more
> industrious as they were better principled.

She made eleven more of these canvassing visits, trying to rent suitable
properties for use as schools, showing a devious and worldly side of her
nature which ensured success at some cost to her conscience. Instead of
mentioning religion, she appealed to self-interest:

> the petty tyrants I stroked and tamed, the ugly children I fondled, the
> pointers and spaniels I caressed, the cyder I commended. After these
> irresistible flatteries, I inquired of each if he could recommend to me
> a house; and said that I had a little plan which I hoped would secure
> their orchards from being robbed, their rabbits from being shot, their
> poultry from being stolen, and which might lower the poor-rates.[11]

The common crimes she lists here are among those practised by Black
Giles the poacher, whose Tale is included in this book. It is clear that
these squires and rich farmers colluded with the neglectful Church; in
many remote parishes they could claim the services of a curate but, as
More reports, had not done so in the fear that their tithes would be
increased. This selfish practice had left their tenants without moral guidance,
even in some cases without access to burial services. Though her sister
pitied the hard hearts of these ignorant 'rich poor wretches', drunk every
day before dinner and 'plunged in such vices as make me think London
a virtuous place', More's sterner approach to sin convinced her that they
too needed education; they and their more civilized counterparts are
addressed and informed of their social duties in her *Stories for the Middle
Ranks of Society* – for example, in *The Two Wealthy Farmers* and *The History
of Mr Fantom*.

The sisters' commitment to the project involved financial risk. More
gave details of the cost of renting good properties with gardens, adapting
them by taking down walls and adding windows in order to accommodate
a great number of children. On taking out a seven-year lease for one of
these, at six and a half guineas a year, she wrote 'There's courage for you'.
The schools, which were to become central to the life of the community,
held evening classes in reading as well as lessons in practical skills and
Sunday meetings, so a full-time master or mistress had to be appointed;
More says in her letter that she has 'written to different manufacturing

towns for a mistress'. A respectable local women of good Christian judgement could be trusted to undertake the religious teaching on Sundays; however, such women might have been influenced by dissenting sects. More admits to appointing one such: 'I am afraid she must be called a methodist.' Rumours of infiltration of the Church by Methodist supporters began to spread, though it was not until 1800 that unease among the clergy led to pamphlet attacks on the sisters.

Her opinion of the clergy in other local parishes puts their resentment into context: 'Mr G is intoxicated about six times a week, and very frequently is prevented from preaching by two black eyes, honestly earned by fighting'. However, More always saw her activities as supporting the work of the Church; she asked ministers for their cooperation and received much encouragement from dedicated members of the clergy. In her *Tales for the Common People* she takes care to portray the village minister as a source of helpful sanctity, keeping her more critical opinions in reserve for trusted friends.

Mendip Annals (1859) gives detailed descriptions in letters and journals by the sisters of how the schools developed over many years. There were heroic ventures into industrial villages, into the world of colliers and the fiery hell of the Nailsea glass-works. There were failures, but in most of the villages their moral influence became pervasive. A letter from More to Mr Bowdler outlines her teaching policy:

> ... my plan for instructing the poor is very limited and strict. They learn of week-days such coarse works as may fit them for servants. I allow of no writing. My object has not been to teach dogmas and opinions, but to form the lower class to habits of industry and virtue. I know no way of teaching morals but by infusing principles of Christianity, nor of teaching Christianity without a thorough knowledge of Scripture.[12]

She says that for many years she has given away annually near two hundred Bibles, Common Prayer Books and Testaments. 'To teach the poor to *read*, without providing them with safe books has always appeared to me a dangerous measure'. These were probably distributed as prizes at the annual feasts. The second part of *The History of Hester Wilmot* shows how important the Sunday School feast became to villagers; a new dress would be saved for all year. One such great outdoor feast, recorded in the Annals of 1793, was planned for the children of nine parishes. There were village bands, fine nosegays for the girls and white rods for the boys to carry. The children sang hymns and psalms, before sitting down in circles of fifteen to enjoy their beef and pudding. On one of these occasions four thousand spectators came.

More also records establishing a club for women (subscription three halfpence a week) to help them order their lives; they could claim three shillings a week if sick and seven shillings and sixpence for childbirth. She contributed regularly to the fund. Instead of random charity this was constructive help, much appreciated by the villagers. In the tale of *Betty Brown* she gives financial advice to a poor city girl on how to escape from the money-lender's credit trap by self-denial and planned saving. There were other ways in which good behaviour was rewarded. Brides who could produce a certificate of virtue signed by the vicar were entitled to five shillings, a Bible, and a pair of white stockings of the Mores' own knitting.[13]

When she began writing the Cheap Repository Tracts, she kept Sunday Schools in mind. Not only were they central to her theme of conversion in the tales but, as they had spread across the country, they were to become one of the main sources of readers. Stories about the schools, read in the schools, they often extend this reflexive intensity. The Shepherd appears to have pasted a cutting from Part One of his own tale – "The Shepherd's Hymn" – on the wall of his clean hovel, together with other Cheap Repository Tracts. By the end of the tale, he has been promoted to the post of Sunday School teacher. More brings many commercial advertising strategies to the promotion of her material; her authorial voice confides in the reader; she likes to establish narrative continuity, setting promising hooks at the end of tales to draw customers into monthly purchases, tempting them to leave corrupting chapbooks in the pedlar's basket in exchange for more nutritious reading.

The Cheap Repository stressed the importance of destroying this element of popular culture before religious regeneration could take place. Similar arguments about immorality and violence in film and television are heard today, but protesters seldom control the means of production and distribution; More and her friends arranged a mass-marketing system which helped them change national attitudes. Objections were certainly heard; they were seen by some as kill-joy puritans. In *The History of Hester Wilmot* the father asks his newly-literate daughter to read the book of songs he has brought back from the inn. She refuses, having glanced at them. From her Sunday School training she recognizes that they would damage her immortal soul. He reacts angrily; she was a merry girl until conversion chilled her into religious sobriety.

The ballads to which More objected did include many which would still be regarded as improper; young women give graphic accounts of their fall from virtue or their frustration at not being seduced. A few lines are given in the notes to the tales to illustrate the wording and tone of these songs.[14] 'Sinful Sally', in this edition, is an artful substitute for such impropriety; it tempts the reader into a narrative of sensual degeneration but invites shivers of fear rather than pleasure as the fallen woman slides towards the flames of hell.

Sally's words "Pleasure now – Damnation after' must have seemed to many Evangelicals a useful motto. More was regarded by some members of the movement as doctrinally unsound for trying to combine fiction with fact, entertainment with instruction. She was constantly aware of the judgement of 'the strict' upon her efforts, finding a degree of narrowness in them which was at this time alien to her nature, though her beliefs hardened in later life.

Marianne Thornton, a family friend, recounts her childhood memories of More, stressing the lighter side of her character. Even though religion informed every aspect of household life – the two cats were called 'Passive Obedience' and 'Non-resistance' – there was room for innocent enjoyment. She remembered a pastoral idyll at Barley Wood, 'that paradise of my childhood.' The sisters' house was so full of 'intellect and piety and active benevolence' and they lived in 'such uninterrupted harmony with each other ... that ... one felt oneself in a brighter and happier world'. More retold Bible stories dramatically, enthralling the young. Marianne Thornton travelled with the sisters to one of the Sunday Schools, leaving an account which corrects any impression of theological severity. Hannah or Patty gave eloquent addresses to the whole school 'in the most familiar homely language, full of anecdotes of the people round them ... and full of practical piety'.[15] But these women might be seen by alarmed traditionalists as preaching to a congregation instead of maternally teaching children to recite the Catechism; they were encroaching on a profession which would not be open to them in the Established Church for another two hundred years, although Methodist women, as shown in Eliot's *Adam Bede* (1859), were allowed to preach. As a supporter of patriarchal authority, More would never consciously commit the impropriety of seeking such a position, but there are similar inconsistencies in her life, such as disapproving of the theatre while continuing to reprint her plays, which suggest unresolved mental conflict.

'Vile trash' or tracts: reforming popular culture

As shown in the comments above on *The History of Hester Wilmot* and 'Sinful Sally', More was determined to destroy the corrupting influence of the penny chapbooks and ballads hawked round the villages by pedlars. She realized their effect on the minds of the poor after making a collection of popular material – her 'sans-culotte library' – to find out how far dangerously radical political views were represented; their immorality was what struck her more forcibly. Her research into these ephemeral writings was unusual at a time when the significance of popular culture was recognized by few, though the few included Romantic poets like Wordsworth and Coleridge, whose research led them to different moral conclusions. More's contemporaries, asked to explain her reputation as a writer, would probably have discussed her longer works on religion or education. Today, her treatise *Strictures on the Modern System of Education* might be put forward as an example of her best work by students of the history of women's writing. The short tales in this book come from a genre which has been valued less highly, perhaps because of its simplicity and popularity, though critics and historians have recently given more serious attention to the seemingly insignificant reading matter of children and the poor in a specific cultural context.

One of the most informative studies of More's tracts in the context of popular culture is an article by Susan Pedersen: 'Hannah More meets Simple Simon ...' (1986), though its view of More's experiment has been challenged by some critics. She refers to the extensive Harvard collection of eighteenth-century popular chapbooks, making comparisons with the Cheap Repository versions: the authentic texts, she says, are subversive, anti-authoritative, giving the poor unaccustomed power and good fortune:

> What unites all chapbook literature ... is the subordination of any message or moral to the dictates of amusement. It is, essentially, escapist literature ... Yet if they were not consciously radical, chapbooks nevertheless constituted a formidable bulwark against the ideological dominance of either the pious or the powerful ... Chapbooks presented a fictional world where the sexual and social order was fluid and changeable; the evangelicals countered by calling for strict domestic hierarchies and the grateful acceptance of one's social place.[16]

For Pedersen, More is not merely revising the content of this popular fiction but is attacking 'the very existence of a popular culture autonomous from dominant society'. Instead of a division between the elite and the popular, she is proposing a single Christian culture in which division is made between the godly and ungodly. Pedersen identifies two successful outcomes of the plan: the tracts 'contributed to the process by which domesticity, temperance, thrift and piety emerged as the criteria of working class respectability' and they recruited the upper class to the role of 'moral arbiter of popular culture'.

To understand the way in which this social transformation was achieved requires some knowledge of the careful planning of the Repository project and the plausibility of the substitute chapbooks. As this is not a facsimile edition, the original rough appearance of the tracts cannot be conveyed, though I have tried to suggest something of their character by using early texts, by not ironing out their minor irregularities, and by reproducing, with their narrative woodcuts, many of the title-pages which also served as covers. Details of the administration and promotion of the Cheap Repository scheme from 1795 to 1798 should be examined.

The description of More's plan, as set out and signed by Henry Thornton Esq., M.P., Treasurer to the Repository, is given below. More uses some of the wording in her later editions, so it may be jointly composed. The statement, which is followed by a list of subscribers, is bound in at the end of the annual volume of tracts published in 1795. A revised version appears as the 'Advertisement' in More's 1799 three-volume 'new edition'. In almost every account of the success of the scheme the figure of 'two million copies sold in one year' is quoted, but the Treasurer is more exact: 'two million have been *printed*'. The distinction may refer to the fact that most of the copies were freely distributed by benevolent societies who paid wholesale prices; it is hard to imagine customers who had previously bought 'vicious little books and ballads' from hawkers putting down 'The Maid's Lament for Want of a Dil-Doul' and picking up 'Patient Joe' instead. This is an abridged version:

> This Institution was opened in March, 1795. Its object is to furnish the People at large with useful Reading, at so low a price as to be within reach of the poorest purchaser. Most of the Tracts are made entertaining, with a view to supplant the corrupt and vicious little books and ballads which have been hung out at windows in the most alluring forms, or hawked through Town and Country, and have been found so highly mischievous to the Community, as to require every attention to counteract them.
>
> The Sale of the Repository Tracts has been exceedingly great, about two million having been printed within the year, besides great numbers in Ireland. The success of the Plan has been much extended, not only by the zeal of individuals, but also by the active co-operation of those very respectable Societies which have been formed in various towns for this purpose. These Societies have not only exerted their influence by circulating the Tracts in their own families, in their schools, and

among their dependants, but also by encouraging Booksellers to supply themselves with them; by inspecting Retailers and Hawkers; giving them a few in the first instance, and directing them in the purchase; also by recommending the Tracts to the occupier of a stall at a fair; and by sending them to hospitals, workhouses, and prisons. The Tracts have also been liberally distributed among soldiers and sailors through the influence of their Commanders.–All that seems wanting, is a little further attention of individuals to supplant the vicious Tracts of the Hawkers by substituting these, which is now doing with success in many instances since these are made so cheap.

The Conductors of the Cheap Repository have resolved to publish the future Tracts on two different sorts of paper; the one of a superior kind for Gentry, who wish to have them bound up together in a better form then could hitherto be done; the other of a kind very inferior, but so much cheaper as to remove an objection made by Shopkeepers and Hawkers, that they do not yield a profit equal to that which they gain by their ordinary books and ballads. The price of the inferior Edition of penny Tracts will be to Gentry 10d. for the Quire containing 24 Tracts; and the others proportionally cheap. The usual further allowance will be made to Shopkeepers and Hawkers.

Two different Editions of the Ballads will be also printed, one in the form of a little book for binding, the other in a very cheap manner in sheets.

The tracts of the last year may be had bound up in one volume, and many of the ballads which came out in sheets are now printed together in a penny book and bound up with them. The price of this 1ˢᵗ. Volume is 3s.6d. half bound and lettered.

As the Tracts have been found useful and acceptable in Boarding Schools, those also as well as private Families on sending an Order may be supplied with them every Month, in the same manner as with a Magazine. They will be sent periodically to Societies, Booksellers, and Individuals …

At the end of the passage quoted he notes that no more subscriptions are needed; this refers to the annual sums which were solicited from the gentry before the project began in order to fund it; clearly it is now self-financing. The list of those subscribers which follows is interesting; ten guineas were sent by the Bishop of London from The Society for Carrying into Effect his Majesty's Proclamation against Vice and Immorality. Other subscribers included the Archbishop of Canterbury (five guineas), the Bishop of Durham, several Duchesses and other members of the aristocracy. William Wilberforce, Sir Joseph Banks, the Treasurers of the Manchester Sunday School Society, etc, down through the other ranks to the family of S.Wegg. Hannah More knew many of the bishops and aristocrats personally, and had obviously applied moral pressure. Her friend Horace Walpole cajoled others into contributing.

In 1799 an 'Advertisement' appears at the front of the Rivington edition. Though unsigned, it appears to be by More, affirming that 'near two million' tracts were sold; she repeats some of the information in the 1795 report, but now seems to be directing the material towards a middle-class market. There are three volumes of tracts, available separately: shorter Stories and Ballads, longer Tales and some Poetry, and Sunday Readings. She recommends the volume of shorter pieces as 'well-suited to the use of Boarding Schools, as well as private families'; it contains several of the livelier tales in this edition, such as *Betty Brown*, *Black Giles* and *Tawney Rachel*. At nearly five hundred pages in length it would have been good value for money.

In her *Works* of 1801 she regroups the Tracts for the third time, and she makes some changes in later editions. She is indecisive about their rank and status and appropriate readership: 'Tales' and 'Stories' are socially mobile, some finding themselves in different volumes in 1818 and 1830. The *Shepherd,* theologically padded, becomes an 'Allegory' by 1830, joined by *The Two Shoemakers*, formerly classed as a Tale in six parts. In vol. 4 there is another 'Advertisement':

> These Stories, which were first published, among a great number of others, in the Cheap Repository, under the signature Z, are here presented to the reader, much enlarged and improved. Such of them as are comprised in this volume [i.e. the *Stories*] being adapted to persons in a superior station to those which are contained in the Fifth Volume [i.e. the *Tales*], it was thought better to separate and class them accordingly. A brief account of the institution here referred to will be given in the subsequent volume.

This account, which confusingly forms a third 'Advertisement', is more explicitly political than moral in tone: she uses the term 'common people' here, but shows greater sensitivity in 1818 when the term is changed to 'the mass of the people':

> To improve the habits and raise the principles of the common people, at a time when their dangers and temptations, moral and political were multiplied beyond the example of any former period, was the motive which impelled the Author of these volumes to devise and prosecute the institution of the Cheap Repository. This plan was established with an humble wish, not only to counteract vice and profligacy on the one hand, but error, discontent, and false religion on the other. And as an

appetite for reading had, from a variety of causes, been increasing among the inferior ranks in this country, it was judged expedient, at this critical period, to supply such wholesome aliment as might give a new direction to their task, and abate their relish for those corrupt and inflammatory [1818 version: 'impious'] publications which the consequences of the French Revolution have been so fatally pouring in on us ...

She repeats the boast of 'two million sold in the first year', which is the truth, even though it does give the impression of mass retail rather than wholesale trade.

Her letters record the difficulties she endured while working on the project. John Marshall, the official Printer to the Repository in London, proved unreliable; she wrote angrily in 1796 about his 'neglect, and other faults'.[17] By 8 September 1797, she writes to Zachary Macaulay that the bound volumes are selling well, but she has 'often been driven to the necessity of furnishing the three monthly pieces myself'. She complains again that 'Mr M [Marshall] has never belied my first opinion of him, selfish, tricking, and disobliging from first to last. You know I never had a good opinion of him, and it has been gradually growing worse and worse'. When she eventually dismissed him as Printer he proved her judgement correct by producing about forty spurious tracts with the Cheap Repository imprint; these add to the bibliographical complexity of this series.

In the same letter she writes, 'I had lately a large order from Philadelphia for tracts, by a Mr Cobbett'; this was William Cobbett, who intended to try them out in America.[18] He wrote again from London in 1800 to thank her for sending him copies of the collected tracts, telling her of the 'uncommon success' of the Cheap Repository in America, but his political sympathies were changing. On the back of his letter she noted 'This flatterer, on coming to England, joined Mr Bere's party, and became my mortal enemy'. The Victorian editor of her letters adds: 'Who would have expected that this man would become, in course of time *the* Mr Cobbett of Radical notoriety?'.[19]

Sales of the Tracts were certainly helped by the woodcuts. At a time when it was common for chapbook and ballad printers to use old blocks which might be loosely relevant to the subject, such as pairs of lovers in city or country settings, these cuts are designed to illustrate More's stories. Mrs Sponge is pocketing Betty's coins. Tawney Rachel has a basket full of dubious ballads. The winding mechanism for Patient Joe's pit is clearly shown; so is the flour mill attacked by rioters. The Missionary Man has caught Yamba in an arm-lock, saving her from suicidal despair. In some copies the name of the engraver Lee can be seen. According to the standard work issued a few years after More's death – Chatto's *A Treatise on Wood Engraving, Historical and Practical* (London, 1839) – J. Lee was one of the best wood-engravers in London in 1796; he died in 1804. Chatto describes his work for the Cheap Repository:

> Those cuts, though coarsely executed, as might be expected, considering the work for which they were intended, frequently display considerable merit in the design; and in this respect several of them are scarcely inferior to the cuts drawn and engraved by John Bewick in Dr Trusler's Progress of Man and Society.

Although these illustrations are usually referred to as woodcuts, or cuts, even by Chatto, he explains technical differences between cutting and engraving the blocks. Wood is much better than copper or steel for running off large impressions cheaply; the illustration can be printed with the letterpress, and 'at least one hundred thousand good impressions can be obtained from a wood-cut if properly engraved and carefully printed'.[20] So if two million copies were printed in one year, the blocks would need to be frequently recut or redesigned by Lee and other craftsmen, especially as the tracts were produced in London and Bath. This helps to account for the many variant versions, with the help of which Spinney and other bibliographers have tried to put unsigned and undated tracts in their proper sequence. Booksellers' catalogues distinguish between the April 1795 issue of a highwayman's execution tract, with two figures at the prison window and no body on the gallows, and the June version with three figures in prison and a swinging corpse.[21] In his Bristol collection relating to the *Bibliotheca Somersetensis* (1902) Emanuel Green bound up four or five versions of the tracts at a time, allowing detailed collation of imprints, texts and illustrations.[22]

Critical response to More's work: adulation, neglect, reassessment

In 1814, at the height of her fame as a writer on matters of religion, More had attracted tributes from such eminent men as Coleridge, as shown in his letter to Joseph Cottle:

> P.S. It is no small gratification to me that I have seen and conversed with Mrs H. More – She is indisputably the *first* literary female, I ever met with – In part, no doubt, because she is a Christian.[23]

His daughter Sara, writing to Miss Trevenen in 1834, the year after

More's death, values her less highly. She recalls arguing with a young chaplain 'who affirmed that Mrs. Hannah More was the greatest female writer of her age. "Whom," he asked, "did I think superior?" I mentioned a score of authoresses whose names my opponent had never even heard of before'. Among those she lists as superior are Baillie, de Staël, Burney, Edgeworth, and Austen. Although she agrees with the judgement of the *Spectator* that More's fame owed more to circumstance and the popular turn of her mind than to original genius, she adds:

> I am far from thinking her an *ordinary* woman. She must have had great energy of character and a sprightly versatile mind which did not originate much, but which readily caught the spirit of the day, and reflected all the phases of opinion in the pious and well-disposed portion of society, in a clear and lively manner. To read Mrs. More's new book was a sort of good work, which made the reader feel satisfied with him or herself when performed; and it is agreeable to have one's very own opinions presented to one in handsome language, and placed in a highly respectable point of view. [24]

The words 'reflected' and 'one's very own opinions' show no awareness of the way in which the Tracts and *Strictures* constructed those opinions for many young women who grew up to be eminent Victorians. George Eliot's letters record a complete reversal of her early regard for More. In a letter to Maria Lewis, 18 August 1838, Eliot writes: 'I have highly enjoyed Hannah More's letters; the contemplation of so blessed a character as hers is very salutary'.[25]

Ten years later she denounces More's views in the strongest terms:

> I am glad you detest Mrs. Hannah More's letters. I like neither her letters, nor her books, nor her character. She was that most disagreeable of all monsters, a blue-stocking – a monster that can only exist in a miserably false state of society, in which a woman with but a smattering of learning or philosophy is classed along with singing mice and card-playing pigs.[26]

Some later Victorians, who rejected either the Evangelical social constraints of their youth or the sanctimonious tone of much religious writing, blamed More's work as the source of both. By the end of the century memories of the little chapbooks had faded; to many her work suggested tedious morality in double columns. Augustine Birrell's reaction was extreme: he would no longer give shelf-space to the nineteen volumes of her *Collected Works*. As no one could be expected to buy the books of a 'stone-dead author', he buried them in his garden, and stamped them down.[27] This image of a man stamping on the body of a woman's work serves as a reminder of earlier patriarchal silencing of the outspoken female.

In spite of the work of biographers, her reputation declined through most of the twentieth century, in step with the decay in formal religious practice. Although she was routinely mentioned in historical and literary surveys, her work was seldom given close analysis except in terms of repressive piety and anti-Jacobinism. Some critics acknowledged her power, though discrediting it: E.P. Thompson questioned the value of her charitable labours, asserting that:

> ... the sensibility of the Victorian middle class was nurtured in the 1790s by frightened gentry who had seen miners, potters and cutlers reading The Rights of Man, and its foster-parents were William Wilberforce and Hannah More. It was in these counter-revolutionary decades that the humanitarian tradition became warped beyond recognition.[28]

He refers to the work of Blake, her contemporary, and his protest against 'the oppressors of Albion': 'They compel the poor to live upon a crust of bread by soft mild arts/ ... The praise of Jehovah is chaunted from lips of hunger and thirst'. There is something worth considering here; other Romantic poets resist her construction of charity. Wordsworth's poems 'The Old Cumberland Beggar', 'Michael', and 'The Leech-Gatherer' should be read in comparison with the *Shepherd of Salisbury Plain* for their different vision of pastoral dignity and independence in a state of poverty. The opposition between the two writers results partly from More's suspicion of nature and natural modes of being; she finds ignorance and vice in the 'humble and rustic life', which Wordworth idealizes as the best terrain for the growth of the spirit. Elizabeth Kowaleski-Wallace, in her study of patriarchal complicity and women writers, shows how More rejects the idea of natural maternal benevolence, believing that 'the return to nature is a return to the scene of primal aggression'. This 'savage principle' is the cause of her rejection of revolutionary arguments which are based on the rule of nature.[29]

Mitzi Myers, in an earlier article, had advanced the contrary claim that More's thinking is maternal:

> She dreaded being branded 'pert and political' and her woman's imagination bypassed democratic talk of the poor's rights for a maternal thinking oriented to needs and duties, to family feeling and domestic responsibilities ... [She channels] fledgling literacy towards a new social morality, teaching audiences to make the most of what they had and socializing them in bourgeois strategies for gaining ground in the world and bourgeois notions of family life.

Myers shows how More develops the emerging female ideology, nurturing and reformative, into a national mission; she sets women the standard of 'domestic heroism', and she is 'among the first to try her hand at interclass communication between England's "two nations"'.[30]

Olivia Smith discusses More's ability to communicate, relating her style to its political context:

> Because Hannah More did not believe in widely current notions of vulgarity, she had exceptional freedom as a writer. Her Cheap Repository Tracts contrast sharply with both conservative and radical literature in the simplicity of the language, the portrayal of the poor as individuals, the use of credible dialogue ...[31]

However, Gary Kelly, also examining the politics of language, questions More's mission:

> The converted poor are shown to be diminished and docile versions of the fully human middle-class Evangelicals who, in their turn, are divinely legitimized social leaders, teachers, counsellors. Not only did the Cheap Repository Tracts set out to expropriate popular culture, they represented a vision, a fantasy of social order inspired, reconstructed and presided over by the Evangelicals themselves.[32]

In a recent article on the Internet, Julia Saunders warns modern critics not to bring to a reading of More 'our own cultural assumptions, which tend to be secular, liberal and – until very recently – masculine', saying that we are otherwise likely to patronize More just as we accuse her of patronizing the lower classes. Pointing out that More's work was favourably received by radical publications of the day, like the *Analytical Review,* which published articles by Wollstonecraft, she argues that More's tracts were 'innovative in ways that went beyond definitions of gender' in their attempt to communicate across perceived class divisions, and should not be seen as conservative:

> The misreading of the tracts as ultra-conservative works is in part due to their didactic nature. Didacticism is deeply unfashionable. The history of children's literature is usually desribed as a flight from moralising works into the wonderful realms of fantasy ... More was joined by an acknowledged radical, Mary Wollstonecraft, in writing in a tradition of moral tales that had been exploited during the eighteenth century by progressives as well as conservatives.

Saunders asserts that 'once the moral tale is accepted as a potentially progressive genre', the first conclusion to be drawn is that More 'wrote on a radical new assumption: the lower classes were an audience worth addressing'.[33]

Contradictions and inconsistencies in More's work which provoke these opposing critical judgements should be given close attention. Modern readings of these apparently simple texts probe at the fissures which mark division between the creative mind and the dominant ideology. Critics find her work to be patriarchal and maternal, repressive and enabling, conservative and radical. She has been accused in the past of arrogance and spiritual vanity. An enemy in the Blagdon controversy called her Pope Joan; she was also accused of threatening order in Chuch and State by religious innovations which might take the country back to the Puritanism and civil discord of the seventeenth-century English Revolution. But other critics might attack her for a failure of courage, for keeping too closely to a narrow and orthodox reading of scripture, refusing licence to the questionings of the reason and the imagination. A shadow falls on the reader of her work, who may think of Blake's 'mind-forg'd manacles' and his determination to create his own system or to be enslaved by another man's. Her denial of the pleasures of the world is not balanced by any evidence of spiritual or metaphysical joy; even the promise of heaven is subordinate to the threat of hell. In the Notes which follow the Tales in this edition, I have analysed some of More's strategies, showing how her conversion narratives reward class deference, conformity and self-restraint. She attacks the Other in all its forms as the dangerous spirit of sedition, banishing from her ideal society not only villains like the trickster and money-lender but also the independent poor at the edge of the community who assert their right to question its values or choose alternative ways of surviving.

Her severe charity had constructive force within the community, though some of her fundamentalist readings of scripture were unduly restrictive and oppressive. As her enemy 'Rev. Sir Archibald Mac Sarcasm' (Rev. William Shaw) wrote in a pamphlet attacking her mission 'to puritanize the people':

> She is an enemy to toleration. Her christianity, though not popish, is more illiberal, and would persecute us hotly, if she had the power. He who loves not his brother, cannot love God. [Bath, 1802]

However, she must be given credit for achieving real power over the minds of her contemporaries from a position of social and political weakness shared by all her sex. She encouraged the poor to earn a sense of self-esteem and respect in the community by the application of Christian principles to daily life; in particular, she helped to transform women's perception of their social role, urging them to take on the responsibilities of moral authority within the family, which became the model for constructive reform rather than violent revolution in the nation. The contradictions in her work should perhaps be regarded as evidence of opposing energies — those Contraries, without which there is, in Blake's view, no progression.

Acknowledgements

I should like to thank my colleagues in the English Division at Nottingham Trent University for allowing me leave to work on this edition. I am particularly grateful to Dr Sharon Ouditt for moral support, and to Roberta Davari-Zanjani for typing the text. The staff at Bristol Central Library, especially Miss D. Dyer, were very helpful in making their special collections available to me. I must also thank the staff at the Bodleian, the British Library and The Nottingham Trent University Library.

Clare MacDonald Shaw, September 2001

Notes for Introduction

1. Jennifer Mori, *Britain in the Age of the French Revolution 1785-1820*, Harlow: Longman, 2000, p.124.
2. M.G. Jones, *Hannah More*, Cambridge, 1952, p.226.
3. Arthur Roberts, ed., *Mendip Annals, or, A Narrative of the Charitable Labours of Hannah and Martha More in their Neighbourhood. Being the Journal of Martha More, edited with Additional Matter*, second edition, London, Nisbet, 1859.
4. Hannah More, *Village Politics. Addressed to all the mechanics, journeymen, and day labourers in Great Britain. By Will Chip, a country carpenter*, third edition, F. and C. Rivington, 1792. Facsimile reprint of 1793 edition, London and New York: Woodstock, 1995.
5. Letter from H. More to Mr. Wilberforce, George Hotel, Cheddar, 1789, in R. Brimley Johnson ed., *The Letters of Hannah More*, John Lane/ The Bodley Head, 1925, p.165.
6. [Hannah More], *Questions and Answers for the Mendip and Sunday Schools*, Bath, J. Binns, 1795.
7. Letter from Jane Austen to Cassandra, 24 Jan. 1809, in R.W. Chapman ed., *Jane Austen: Letters to her Sister*, Oxford, second edition, [1952] 1979, p.254: 'I do not like the Evangelicals–of course I shall be delighted, when I read it, like other people, but till I do I dislike it'.
8. Letter from Jane Austen to Cassandra, 31 May 1811, Chapman, p.287.
9. David Masson, ed., *The Collected Writings of Thomas De Quincey, Vol.II: Autobiography and Literary Reminiscences*, Edinburgh: A.& C. Black, 1889, p.451.
10. Letter from Hannah More to William Wilberforce, 1825, in William Roberts, ed., *Memoirs of the Life and Correspondence of Mrs. Hannah More*, vol. IV, London, Seeley and Burnside, 1834, p.237: 'I think Miss Frowd says that I saw eighty persons last week'.
11. Letter from H. More to Mr. Wilberforce, George Hotel, Cheddar, 1789 in R. Brimley Johnson ed., *The Letters of Hannah More*, John Lane/ The Bodley Head, 1925, pp.163-5.
12. Letter from Hannah More to Mr Bowdler, A. Roberts, ed., *Mendip Annals*, p.6.
13. Martha More, *Journal*, A. Roberts, ed., *Mendip Annals*, p.66.
14. For collections of ballads which include examples from the late eighteenth century see V. de Sola Pinto and A. Rodway, ed., *The Common Muse*, Harmondsworth: Penguin, [1957] 1965, and John Holloway and Joan Black, ed., *Later English Broadside Ballads*, London:

Routledge & Kegan Paul, 1975 [containing ballads from the Madden Collection, Cambridge University Library]. See also the Douce collection, Bodleian Library, Oxford.

15. Marianne Thornton, 'Recollections', in E.M. Forster, *Marianne Thornton 1797-1887: A Domestic Biography*, London: Edward Arnold, 1956, pp.46-47.

16. Susan Pedersen, 'Hannah More meets Simple Simon: Tracts, Chapbooks, and Popular Culture in Later Eighteenth-Century England', *The Journal of British Studies*, Vol. 25, Chicago, Chicago University Press, 1986, pp.64-113.

17. Letter from Hannah More to Zachary Macaulay, Bath, Jan. 30, 1796, A. Roberts, ed., *Letters*, p.10.

18. Letter from H. More to Zachary Macaulay, Sept. 8, 1797, A. Roberts, ed., *Letters*, pp.16-17.

19. Letter from William Cobbett to Hannah More, Pall Mall, October 20, 1800, A. Roberts, ed., *Letters*, p.17.

20. W. Chatto, *A Treatise on Wood Engraving, Historical and Practical, with upward of three hundred illustrations engraved on wood by John Jackson*, London: Charles Knight and Co., 1839, pp.628.

21. Jarndyce, Catalogue CXXX, *Chapbooks, Tracts & Street Literature*, London, 1999.

22. The *Bibliotheca Somersetensis* holdings in Bristol Central Reference Library include Emanuel V. Green's extensive collection of Cheap Repository Tracts and other related works.

23. Letter from S.T.C. Coleridge to Joseph Cottle, Friday, 27 May 1814, in H.J. Jackson, ed., *Coleridge: Selected Letters*, Oxford, Clarendon Press, 1987, p.180.

24. Letter from Sara Coleridge to Miss Trevenen from Hampstead, August 1834, in *Memoir and Letters*, ed. by her daughter, fourth edition, abridged, London, H.S. King, 1875, p.52.

25. Letter from George Eliot to Maria Lewis, 18 Aug. 1838, in Gordon S. Haight, ed., *The George Eliot Letters*, Vol. 1: 1836-1851, London and New Haven: Oxford University Press, 1954, p.7.

26. Letter from George Eliot to John Sibree, Jr., Foleshill, 11 February 1848, in Gordon S. Haight, ed., *The George Eliot Letters*, vol. 1, p.245.

27. Augustine Birrell , 'Hannah More Once More', in *In the Name of the Bodleian and Other Essays*, second edition, London, Elliot Stock, 1906, p.118.

28. E.P. Thompson, *The Making of the English Working Class*, London, Gollancz, 1963.

29. Elizabeth Kowaleski-Wallace, *Their Father's Daughters: Hannah More, Maria Edgeworth, and Patriarchal Complicity*, New York, Oxford University Press, 1991, pp.40-43.

30. Mitzi Myers, 'Hannah More's Tracts for the Times: Social Fiction and Female Ideology' in Mary Anne Schofield and Cecilia Macheski, eds., *Fetter'd or Free: British Women Novelists, 1670-1815*, Athens, Ohio and London, Ohio University Press, 1986, pp.264-284.

31. Olivia Smith, *The Politics of Language, 1791-1819*, Oxford, Oxford University Press. 1984, p.92.

32. Gary Kelly, 'Revolution, Reaction, and the Expropriation of Popular Culture: Hannah More's *Cheap Repository*', in *Man and Nature/ L'Homme et la Nature*, Edmonton, Alberta, 1987, pp.154-155.

33. Julia Saunders, 'Putting the Reader Right': Reassessing Hannah More's *Cheap Repository Tracts*': *Romanticism on the Net* 16, Nov. 1999. <http//users.ox.ac.uk/~scat 0385/more.html>

BIBLIOGRAPHY

There is no complete modern edition of the *Cheap Repository Tracts*, but some examples of More's tales can be found in facsimile editions published by Garland (New York, 1977) and Woodstock (Oxford and New York, 1995), and in selections of her work. Robert Hole's edition of the *Selected Writings of Hannah More* (London, 1996) provides a good collection of extracts from More's extensive writings, including some from her major work *Strictures on the Modern System of Female Education* (1799), as well as examples of the Tracts; his Introduction gives a detailed account of the cultural background to her work.

Primary Sources:

Collections of tracts and manuscript letters, etc. in the British Library, the Bodleian Library, Oxford, and Bristol Central Library.

Cheap Repository Tracts

a) Separate undated issues of *Cheap Repository Tracts* in chapbook form by More (sometimes signed 'Z') and others, published by J. Marshall (London), S. Hazard (Bath), and other printers in the period 1795 - 8; there were also some early broadside versions of ballads. There are, however, many spurious tracts published by Marshall after More dismissed him as official Printer for the series. Other printers and sellers listed in this early period include R. White, J. Elder (Edinburgh) and William Watson (Dublin).

b) Annual collections of tracts published in 1795, 1796, and 1797 – each probably issued in the following year. These are obviously bound up; the pagination is not continuous.

c) A three-volume revised edition of *Cheap Repository Tracts* (divided into Shorter and Longer Tracts and Sunday Reading) sold by F. and C. Rivington, J. Evans, J. Hatchard, and S. Hazard (London and Bath), 1798; 'A New Edition', 1799. This division of the Tracts proved popular; reprints and different versions appeared under various imprints for several decades, e.g. in 1800, 1803, 1806, 1807, 1810, 1812, 1815, 1825, 1827, 1830, 1837; this means that the tales were still on sale at the beginning of the Victorian period.

d) Separate Tracts from the series were reprinted by various publishers for many years after the closing of the Cheap Repository project in 1798. More had granted the official printing rights to J. Evans and

Hatchard in November 1797. After the Repository closed in 1798, the right to publish reprints was sold (according to Weiss) to Evans, Hatchard and Rivington. In this edition the reproduced title-page of *Tawny Rachel* is taken from an edition of c.1810 with the Howard and Evans imprint.

e) Revised and 'improved' versions of a selection of More's Tracts, including some of the ballads and tales, appeared in the Cadell and Davies edition of her *Collected Works* published during her lifetime (London, 1801, 1818, 1830); other editions appeared in 1834 and later. The tracts are now divided into *Ballads, Stories for the Middle Ranks of Society* (section title: *Stories for Persons of the Middle Ranks*), and *Tales for the Common People*. The grouping of tales differs in the 1830 edition.

f) First two-volume edition (London, 1818) of More's revised tracts, issued by T. Cadell and W. Davies separately from the *Works* of the same year, with the titles *Stories for the Middle Ranks of Society* (Vol. I) and *Tales for the Common People* (Vol. II).

g) Versions of the two-volume *Stories* and *Tales* appeared later from other publishers, e.g. Thomas Tegg in the 1830s. It seems that these smaller books were widely used in schools and exported to outposts of empire.

h) New, revised, and reprinted Tracts by More appeared in *Cheap Repository Tracts for the Present Times* (London: Rivington, 1819). Rivington had published her *Village Politics* in 1792, two years before the founding of the Repository project; a revised version, entitled *The Village Disputants* is printed in this edition. The tracts were issued separately and distributed at this time of political unrest (1817-19) in a revival of the original system but I have not seen any in chapbook form.

Letters, journals, memoirs, polemics.

a) Published in her lifetime: writings by her critics and defenders in The Blagdon Controversy, with reference to More's Sunday Schools and to her Tracts, etc.

Elton, Rev. Sir Abraham. *A Letter to the Rev. Thomas Bere …Occasioned by his late unwarrantable attack on Mrs. Hannah More*, London: Cadell and Davies, 1801.

[Macaulay, Zachary]. 'Mrs. H. More's Schools; or, The Blagdon Controversy', in *Christian Observer* I, 1802, pp.180-185.

Mac Sarcasm, Rev. Sir Archibald [William Shaw]. *The Life of Hannah More, with a Critical Review of her Writings*, London: T. Hurst, 1802.

Spencer, Edward. *Truths, respecting Mrs. Hannah More's Meeting-Houses, and the Conduct of her Followers; Addressed to the Curate of Blagdon*, Bath: Meyler, 1802.

_____. *Candid Observations on Mrs Hannah More's Schools: in which is considered their Supposed Connection with Methodism*, Bath: S. Hazard, 1802.

b) Memoirs and letters published after her death:

Roberts, Arthur, ed. *Letters of Hannah More to Zachary Macaulay*, London: Nisbet, 1860.

Roberts, Arthur, ed. *Mendip Annals: or a Narrative of the Charitable Labours of Hannah and Martha More ... Being the Journal of Martha More*, London: Nisbet, Second edition, 1859.

Roberts, William, ed., *Memoirs of the Life and Correspondence of Mrs. Hannah More*, (4 vols.) London: Seeley and Burnside, 1834. According to More's friend, Marianne Thornton, the text of the letters is not always reliable.

Taylor, Thomas, *Memoir of Mrs Hannah More, With Notices of her Works, and Sketches of her Contemporaries*, Rickerby, 1838.

Thompson, Henry. *The Life of Hannah More, with Notices of her Sisters*, London: T. Cadell, 1838.

c) Modern editions:

There is no complete modern edition of More's letters, but a selection appears in R. Brimley Johnson, ed., *The Letters of Hannah More*, London, 1925, and in the edition of her work by R. Hole listed above.

Bibliographical Articles

Spinney, G.H. 'Cheap Repository Tracts: Hazard and Marshall Editions', in *The Library* 20, 1940, pp.295-340. This is the standard bibliographical article, essential for reference to the Tracts of the period 1795-8, although there are some issues and reprints which are not listed.

Weiss, Harry B. 'Hannah More's Cheap Repository Tracts in America', *Bulletin of the New York Public Library* 50, 1946, pp.539-641. Weiss makes reference to Spinney's work before examining the early publication of the Tracts in Philadelphia and other cities.

FURTHER READING

The books and articles in this limited selection refer to More's Tracts or to their specific social, religious, political and literary context. There are many other works by feminist critics and historians, not included here for reasons of space, which would be listed in a full bibliography of More's writing in this period.

Altick, Richard D. *The English Common Reader*, Chicago: Chicago University Press, 1957.

Armstrong, Nancy. 'The Rise of the Domestic Woman' in *The Ideology of Conduct and the History of Sexuality*, ed. N. Armstrong and L. Tennenhouse, New York and London: Metheun, 1987.

Balfour, Clara Lucas. *A Sketch of Mrs. Hannah More and her Sisters*, London: W. & F. G. Cash, 1854.

Birrell, Augustine. 'Hannah More', in *Men, Women, & Books*, [1894], *Papers and Essays*, London: Duckworth, 1912.

Bradley, Ian. *The Call to Seriousness; The Evangelical Impact on the Victorians*, London: Cape, 1976.

Collingwood, Jeremy & Margaret. *Hannah More*, Oxford: Lion, 1990.

Darton, F.J. Harvey. *Children's Books in England*, 3rd ed., Cambridge: Cambridge University Press, 1982.

Demers, Patricia. *The World of Hannah More*, Lexington: The University Press of Kentucky, 1996.

De Quincey, Thomas. *The Collected Writings of Thomas De Quincey*, new and enlarged edition, Vol.2: *Autobiography and Literary Reminiscences*, ed. David Masson, Edinburgh: A. and C. Black, 1889.

Ferguson, Moira. *Subject to Others: British Women Writers and Colonial Slavery, 1670-1834*, London: Routledge, 1992.

Forster, E.M. *Marianne Thornton: A Domestic Biography*, London: Edward Arnold, 1956.

Gaull, Marilyn. *English Romanticism: The Human Context*, New York & London: Norton, 1988.

Harland, Marion [M.V. Terhune]. *Hannah More*, New York: Putnam, 1900.

Hobsbawm, E.J. *The Age of Revolution, 1789-1848*, London: Weidenfeld and Nicholson, 1962.

Hopkins, Mary Alden. *Hannah More and Her Circle*, New York: Longmans, Green, 1947.

Jay, Elizabeth. *The Religion of the Heart: Anglican Evangelicalism and the Nineteenth-Century Novel*, Oxford: Clarendon, 1979.

Jones, Chris. *Radical Sensibility: Literature and Ideas in the 1790s*, London & New York: Routledge, 1993.

Jones, M. G. *Hannah More*, Cambridge: Cambridge University Press, 1952.

Kelly, Gary. *English Fiction of the Romantic Period, 1789-1830*, London: Longman, 1989.

Kelly, Gary. 'Revolution, Reaction, and the Expropriation of Popular Culture: Hannah More's *Cheap Repository*', in *Man and Nature* 6, 1987, pp.147-159.

Kowaleski-Wallace, Elizabeth. *Their Father's Daughters: Hannah More, Maria Edgeworth, and Patriarchal Complicity*, New York: Oxford University Press, 1991.

Laqueur, Thomas Walter. *Religion and Respectability: Sunday Schools and Working Class Culture, 1780-1850*, New Haven: Yale University Press, 1976.

Meakin, Annette. *Hannah More*, London: John Murray, 1911.

Mellor, Anne K. 'English Women Writers and the French Revolution', in *Rebel Daughters: Women and the French Revolution*, ed. S. E. Melzer and L.W. Rabine, New York: Oxford University Press, 1992.

Mori, Jennifer. *Britain in the Age of the French Revolution*, Harlow: Longman, 2000.

Myers, Mitzi. 'Hannah More's Tracts for the Times: Social Fiction and Female Ideology', in *Fetter'd or Free? British Women Novelists, 1670-1815*, ed. Mary Anne Schofield and Cecilia Macheski, Athens: Ohio University Press, 1986.

Myers, Mitzi. 'Reform or Ruin: "A Revolution in Female Manners"', *Studies in Eighteenth-Century Culture* 2, 1982, pp.199-216.

Myers, Mitzi. "' A Peculiar Protection": Hannah More and the Cultural Politics of the Blagdon Controversy' in *History, Gender and Eighteenth-Century Literature*, ed. Beth Fowkes Tobin, Athens: University of Georgia Press, 1994.

Myers, Sylvia Harcstark. *The Bluestocking Circle: Women, Friendship, and the Life of the Mind in Eighteenth-Century England*, Oxford: Clarendon, 1990.

Pedersen, Susan. 'Hannah More Meets Simple Simon: Tracts, Chapbooks, and Popular Culture in Late Eighteenth-Century England', *Journal of British Studies* 25, 1986, pp.84-113.

Poovey, Mary. *The Proper Lady and the Woman Writer: Ideology as Style in the Works of Mary Wollstonecraft, Mary Shelley, and Jane Austen*, Chicago: University of Chicago Press, 1984.

Prochaska, Frank K. *Women and Philanthropy in Nineteenth-Century England*,

Oxford: Clarendon, 1980.

Rogers, Katharine M. *Feminism in Eighteenth-Century England*, Urbana: University of Illinois Press, 1982.

Sangster, Paul. *Pity My Simplicity: The Evangelical Revival and the Religious Education of Children, 1738-1800*, London: Epworth, 1963.

Shiach, Morag. *Discourse on Popular Culture: Class, Gender and History in Cultural Analysis, 1730 to the Present*, Cambridge: Polity Press, 1989.

Smith, Olivia. *The Politics of Language, 1791-1819*, Oxford: Oxford University Press, 1984.

Tabor, Margaret E. *Pioneer Women*, London: Sheldon Press, 1927.

Thompson, E. P. *The Making of the English Working Class*, London: Gollancz, 1963.

Tobin, Beth Fowkes. *Superintending the Poor: Charitable Ladies and Paternal Landlords in British Fiction, 1770-1860*, New Haven: Yale University Press, 1993.

Todd, Janet. *The Sign of Angellica: Women, Writing, and Fiction, 1660-1800*, London: Virago, 1989.

Trimmer, Sarah. *The Family Magazine; or, A Repository of Religious Instruction and Rational Amusement*, London: J. Marshall, 1788-1789.

Wollstonecraft, Mary. *Vindication of the Rights of Woman: With Strictures on Political and Moral Subjects,* [1792], ed. with intro. by Miriam Brody, Harmondsworth: Penguin, 1983.

Yearsley, Ann. *Poems on Various Subjects by a Milkwoman of Clifton near Bristol. Being Her Second Work*, London: Robinson, 1791.

Yonge, Charlotte. *Hannah More*, London, 1888.

Note on Money, 1790-1800

Hannah More makes very frequent reference to money. Accordingly I have calculated the approximate value of the pound in 1790 against the pound in 2000. The official Bank of England ten-year figures for this period give the 1790 pound a value of £53.28 against the pound of August 2000. By 1800 the value has dropped to £29.91. To calculate the modern equivalent of coins and sums of money mentioned in the Tracts I have divided these values to give an estimate of £41 for the pound of 1795. However, this assumes a steady inflation during the decade; More's texts of 1795-6 show that the economy is unstable as a result of shortages in the hard winter of 1795, the effects of war, and continuing fears of revolution or invasion. The true value of money during the Cheap Repository period might be closer to the figure for 1800 given above.

Estimate for the rise in value of a 1795 pound sterling:
£1 = £41 at August 2000;
a crown (5 shillings) = £10.25;
a half-crown = £5.12;
a shilling= £2.05;
a sixpence (6d.) = £1;
a penny (1d.) =approx. 17 pence;
a halfpenny(1/2d.) = approx. 8 pence
The title-pages reproduced in this edition show the retail and wholesale costs of the Tracts, e.g. 4s. 6d per 100. In *The Way to Plenty, or Tom White Part II,* More notes that 'A poor man gets seven or eight shillings a week' (between £14.30 and £16.40 in 2000). Though the tales and ballads were affordable, many were distributed free by the local gentry or clergy.

Note on Texts

The texts of the tales and ballads are taken, with a few exceptions noted below, from the early Hazard and Marshall chapbook or broadside editions issued by the Cheap Repository from 1795-1797, including those bound up in annual collections, which retained their separate pagination although issued with a new title-page. For the text of *Tawney Rachel* I have used the 1799 selection, an anthology selected by More for publication by Rivington. Both parts of *The History of Hester Wilmot* are taken from the 1818 two-volume edition, which reprints the early prose tracts, with revisions, under the title *Stories for the Middle Ranks of Society* and *Tales for the Common People.* This appears to be bound up from the sheets of More's *Collected Works,* published by T. Cadell and W. Davies in the same year. For practical reasons I have sometimes chosen sharper woodcuts from later editions to illustrate this book, noting these departures in the footnotes.

In this edition there is unfortunately no space for the long tale of *The Two Shoemakers: In Six Parts.* More transferred this tale, with *The Shepherd of Salisbury Plain,* to the volume of *Stories for the Middle Ranks of Society* in 1830. Also omitted from this edition are two Allegories which were included in *Tales for the Common People.*

More's epigraph for the volume of *Tales* in 1801 is given below:

> Religion is for the man in humble life, and to raise his nature, and
> to put him in mind of a state in which the privileges of opulence
> will cease, when he will be equal by nature, and may be more than
> equal by virtue.
>
> BURKE on the French Revolution

TALES FOR THE COMMON PEOPLE

HANNAH MORE

CHEAP REPOSITORY.

THE HISTORY
OF
TOM WHITE,
THE
POSTILION.

PART I.

Sold by J. MARSHALL,
(PRINTER to the CHEAP REPOSITORY for Moral and
Religious Tracts,) No. 17, Queen-street, Cheapside,
and No. 4, Aldermary Church-Yard, Bow-Lane,
and R. WHITE, Piccadilly, London.
By S. HAZARD, at Bath; and by all Bookfellers,
Newfmen and Hawkers, in Town and Country.

Great Allowance will be made to Shopkeepers and Hawkers

PRICE ONE PENNY.

Or 4s. 6d. per 100.—2s. 6d. for 50 —1s. 6d. for 2 ç.

[Entered at Stationers Hall.]

THE HISTORY OF TOM WHITE THE POSTILION

or

The History of Tom White the Postboy[1]

PART I

TOM WHITE was one of the best drivers of a Post-chaise on the Bath Road. Tom was the son of an honest labourer at a little village in Wiltshire: he was an active industrious boy, and as soon as he was big enough he left his father, who was burthened with a numerous family, and went to live with Farmer Hodges, a sober worthy man in the same village. He drove the waggon all the week; and on Sundays, though he was now grown up, the farmer required him to attend the Sunday school,[2] carried on under the inspection of Dr. Shepherd, the worthy Vicar, and always made him read his Bible in the evening after he had served his beasts; and would have turned him out of his service if he had ever gone to the ale-house for his own pleasure.

Tom by carrying some waggon-loads of faggots, to the Bear inn at Devizes, soon made many acquaintances in the stable-yard. He compared his own Carter's frock, and shoes thick set with nails, with the smart red jacket and tight boots of the post-boys, and grew ashamed of his own homely dress; he was resolved to drive a chaise, to get money, and to see the world. Foolish fellow! he never considered, that, though it is true, a waggoner works hard all day, yet he gets a quiet evening, and undisturbed rest at night. However, as there must be chaise-boys as well as plough-boys, there was no great harm in the change. The evil company to which it exposed him, was the chief mischief. He left Farmer Hodges, though not without sorrow at quitting so kind a master, and got himself hired at the Black Bear.

Notwithstanding the temptations to which he was now exposed, Tom's good education stood by him for some time. At first he was frightened to hear the oaths and wicked words which are too often uttered in a stable-yard. However, though he thought it wrong, he had not the courage to reprove it, and the next step to being easy at seeing others sin, is to sin ourselves. By degrees he began to think it manly, and a mark of spirit in others to swear; though the force of good habits was so strong that at first when he swore himself it was with fear and in a low voice. But he was soon laughed out of his sheepishness, as they called it; and though he never became so profane and blasphemous as some of his companions, (for he never swore in cool blood or in mirth, as so many do,) yet he would too often use a dreadful bad word when he was in a passion with his horses. And here I cannot but drop a hint on the folly, as well as wickedness of being in a great rage with poor beasts, who, not having the gift of reason, cannot be moved like human creatures, with all the wicked words that are said to them; but who, unhappily, having the gift of feeling, suffer as much as human creatures can do, at the cruel and unnecessary beatings given them.[3] He had been bred up to think that drunkenness was a great sin, for he never saw Farmer Hodges drunk in his life; and where a farmer is so sober, his men are less likely to drink, or if they do, the master can reprove them with the better grace.

Tom was not naturally fond of drink, yet for the sake of being thought merry company, and a hearty fellow, he often drank more than he ought. As he had been used to go to church twice on a Sunday while he lived with the farmer, who seldom used his horses on that day except to carry his wife to church behind him, Tom felt a little uneasy when he was sent the very first Sunday a long journey with a great family; for I cannot conceal the truth, that too many gentlefolks will travel when there is no necessity for it on a Sunday, and when Monday would answer the end just as well. This is a great grief to all good and sober people, both rich and poor.[4] However, he kept his thoughts to himself, though he could not now and then help thinking how quietly things were going on at the farmer's, whose waggoner on a Sunday led as easy a life as if he had been a gentleman. But he soon lost all thoughts of this kind, and did not know Sunday from Monday. Tom went on prosperously, as it is called, for three or four years, got plenty of money, but saved not a shilling. As soon as his horses were once in the stable, whoever would might see them fed for Tom – He had other fish to fry. – Fives, cards, cudgel-playing, laying wagers, and keeping loose company, each of which he at first disliked, and then practised, ran away with all his money, and all his spare time; and though he was generally in the way as soon as the horses were ready, (because if there was no driving there was no pay,) yet he did not care whether the carriage was clean, if the horses looked well, if the harness was whole, or the horses well shod. The certainty that the gains of to-morrow would make up for the extravagance of to-day made him quite thoughtless and happy, for he was young, active, and healthy, and never foresaw that a rainy day might come, when he would want what he now squandered.

One day being a little flustered with liquor as he was driving his return chaise through Brentford, he saw just before him another empty carriage, driven by one of his acquaintance: he whipped up his horses, resolving to outstrip the other, and swearing dreadfully that he would be at the Red Lion first – for a pint – done, said the other – a wager. Both cut and spurred the poor beasts with the usual fury, as if their credit had been really at stake, or their lives had depended on this foolish contest. Tom's chaise had now got up to that of his rival, and they drove along-side of each other with great fury and many imprecations. But in a narrow part, Tom's chaise being in the middle, with his antagonist on one side, and a cart driving against him on the other, the horses reared, the carriages got entangled, Tom roared out a great oath to the other to stop, which he either could not, or would not do, but returned an horrid imprecation that he would win the wager if he was alive. Tom's horses took fright and he was thrown to the ground with great violence. As soon as he could be got from under the wheels, he was taken up senseless; his leg was broke in two places, and his body much bruised. Some people, whom the noise had brought together, put him in the Post-chaise, in which the waggoner kindly assisted, but the other driver seemed careless and indifferent, and drove off, observing with a brutal coolness, "I am sorry I have lost my pint: I should have beat him hollow, had it not been for this *little accident.*" Some gentlemen who came out of the inn, after reprimanding this savage, inquired who he was, wrote to inform his master, and got him discharged: resolving that neither they nor any of their friends would ever employ him, and he was long out of place.[5] Tom was taken to one of those excellent hospitals with which London abounds. His agonies were dreadful, his leg was set, and a high fever came on. As soon as he was left alone to reflect on his condition, his first thought was that he should die, and his horror was inconceivable:– "Alas!" said he, "what will become of my poor soul? I am cut off in the very commission of three great sins: – I was drunk, I was in a horrible passion, and I had oaths and blasphemies in my mouth." – He tried to pray, but he could not, his mind was all distraction, and he thought he was so very wicked that God would not forgive him; "because," says he, "I have sinned against light and knowledge and a sober education, and good examples and I deserve nothing but punishment." At length he grew light-headed, and there was little hope of his life. Whenever he came to his senses for a few minutes, he cried out,

"O! that my old companions could now see me, surely they would take warning by my sad fate, and repent before it is too late."

By the blessing of God on the skill of the surgeon, and the care of the nurses, he, however, grew better in a few days. And here let me stop to remark what a mercy it is that we live in a Christian country, where the poor, when sick, or lame, or wounded, are taken as much care of as any gentry; nay, in some respects more, because in hospitals and infirmaries there are more doctors and surgeons to attend, than most private gentlefolks can afford to have at their own houses, whereas *there never was an hospital in the whole heathen world.* Blessed be God for this, among the thousand other excellent fruits of THE CHRISTIAN RELIGION! [6]

It was eight weeks before Tom could be taken out of bed. This was a happy affliction; this long sickness and solitude gave him time to reflect on his past life. He began seriously to hate those darling sins which had brought him to the brink of ruin. He could now pray heartily; he confessed and lamented his iniquities with many tears, and began to hope that the mercies of God, through the merits of a Redeemer, might yet be extended to him on his sincere repentance. He resolved never more to return to the same evil courses, but he did not trust in his own strength, he prayed that God would give him grace for the future, as well as pardon for the past. He remembered, and he was humbled at the thought, that he used to have short fits of repentance, and to form resolutions of amendment in his wild and thoughtless days, and often when he had a bad headache after a drinking bout, or had lost his money at all-fours,[7] he vowed never to drink or play again. But as soon as his head was well, and his pockets recruited, he forgot all his resolutions. And how should it be otherwise? for he trusted in his own strength; he never prayed to God to strengthen him, nor ever avoided the next temptation.[8]

The case was now different. Tom began to find that *his strength was perfect weakness*[9] and that he could do nothing without the Divine assistance, for which he prayed heartily and constantly. He sent home for his Bible and Prayer-book, which he had not opened for two years, and which had been given him when he left the Sunday School. He spent the chief part of his time in reading them, and derived great comfort, as well as great knowledge from this employment of his time. The study of the Bible filled his heart with gratitude to God who had not cut him off in the midst of his sins, but had given him space for repentance; and the agonies he had lately suffered with his broken leg increased his thankfulness, that he had escaped the more dreadful pain of eternal misery. And here let me remark what encouragement this is for rich people to give away Bibles and good books, and not to lose all hope, though for a time, they see little or no good effect from it. According to all appearance, Tom's books were never likely to do him any good, and yet his generous benefactor, who had cast his bread upon the waters, found it after many days, for this Bible, which had lain untouched for years, was at last made the means of his reformation. God will work in his own good time.[10]

As soon as he got well, and was discharged from the hospital, Tom began to think he must return to get his bread. At first he had some scruples about going back to his old employ: but, says he, sensibly enough, gentlefolks must travel, travellers must have chaises, and chaises must have drivers: 'tis a very honest calling, and I don't know that goodness belongs to one sort of business more than another; and he who can be good in a state of great temptation, provided the calling be lawful, and the temptations are not of his own seeking, and he be diligent in prayer, may be better than another man for aught I know: and *all that belongs to us is, to do our duty in that state of life in which it shall please God to call us.* Tom had rubbed up his catechism[11] at the hospital, and 'tis a pity that people don't look at their catechism sometimes when they are grown up; for it is full as good for men and women as it is for children; nay, better, for though the answers contained in it are intended for children to *repeat,* yet the duties enjoined in it are intended for men and women to put in *practice.*

Tom now felt grieved that he was obliged to drive on Sundays. But people who are in earnest, and have their hearts in a thing, can find helps in all cases. As soon as he had set down his company at their stage, and had seen his horses fed, says Tom, "A man who takes care of his horses will generally think it right to let them rest an hour or two at least. In every town it is a chance but there may be a church open during part of that time. If the prayers should be over, I'll try hard for the Sermon; and if I dare not stay to the Sermon, it is a chance but I may catch the prayers; it is worth trying for, however; and as I used to think nothing of making a push, for the sake of getting an hour to gamble, I need not grudge to take a little pains extraordinary to serve God." By this watchfulness he soon got to know the hours of service at all the towns on the road he travelled, and while the horses fed, Tom went to church; and it became a favourite proverb with him, that *prayers and provender hinder no man's journey.*[12]

At first his companions wanted to laugh and make sport of this – but when they saw that no lad on the road was up so early or worked so hard as Tom; when they saw no chaise so neat, no glasses so bright, nor harness so tight, no driver so diligent, so clean, or so civil, they found he was no subject to make sport at. Tom indeed was very careful in looking after the linch-pins,[13] in never giving his horses too much water when they were hot; nor, whatever was his haste, would he ever gallop them up hill, strike them across the head, or when tired, cut and slash them in driving on the stones, as soon as he got into a town, as some foolish fellows do. What helped to cure Tom of these bad practices was that remark he met with in the Bible, that *a good man is merciful to his beast.* He was much moved one day on reading the Prophet Jonah, to observe what compassion the great God of heaven and earth had for poor beasts: for one of the reasons there given why the Almighty was unwilling to destroy the great city of Nineveh was, *because there was much cattle in it.* After this, Tom never could bear to see a wanton stroke inflicted.[14]

Tom soon grew rich for one in his station; for every gentleman on the road would be driven by no other lad if *careful Tom* was to be had. Being diligent, he *got* a great deal of money; being frugal, he *spent* but little; and having no vices, he *wasted* none. He soon found out that there was some meaning in that text which says, that *Godliness hath the promise of the life that now is, as well as of that which is to come*:[15] for the same principles which make a man sober and honest, have also a natural tendency to make him healthy and rich; while a drunkard and a spendthrift can hardly escape being sick and a beggar in the end. Vice is the parent of misery here as well as hereafter.

After a few years Tom begged a holiday, and made a visit to his native village; his good character had got thither before him. He found his father was dead; but during his long illness Tom had supplied him with money, and, by allowing him a trifle every week, had had the honest satisfaction of keeping him from the parish.[16] Farmer Hodges was still living; but, being grown old and infirm, he was desirous to retire from business. He retained a great regard for his old servant, Tom; and finding he was worth money, and knowing he knew something of country business, he offered to let him a small farm at an easy rate, and promised his assistance in the management for the first year, with the loan of a small sum of money, that he might set out with a pretty stock. Tom thanked him with tears in his eyes, went back and took a handsome leave of his master, who made him a present of a horse and cart, in acknowledgement of his long and faithful services: for, says he, "I have saved many horses by Tom's care and attention, and I could well afford to do the same by every servant who did the same by me; and should be a richer man at the end of every year by the same generosity, provided I could meet with just and faithful servants who deserved the same rewards."

Tom was soon settled in his new farm, and in less than a year had got every thing neat and decent about him. Farmer Hodges's long experience and friendly advice, joined to his own industry and hard labour, soon brought the farm to great perfection. The regularity, sobriety, peaceableness and piety of his daily life, his constant attendance at Church twice every Sunday, and his decent and devout behaviour when there, soon recommended him to the notice of Dr. Shepherd, who was still living, a pattern of zeal, activity, and benevolence to all parish priests. The doctor soon began to hold up Tom, or, as we must now properly term him, Mr. Thomas White, to the imitation of the whole parish; and the frequent and condescending conversation of this worthy clergyman contributed no less than his preaching to the improvement of his new parishioner.[17]

Farmer White soon found out that a dairy could not well be carried on without a mistress, and began to think seriously of marrying; he prayed to God to direct him in so important a business. He knew that a tawdry, vain, dressy girl was not likely to make good cheese and butter, and that a worldly and ungodly woman would make a sad wife and mistress of a family.[18] He soon heard of a young woman of excellent character, who had been bred up by the vicar's lady, and still lived in the family as upper maid. She was prudent, sober, industrious, and religious. Her neat, modest, and plain appearance at church (for she was seldom seen any where else out of her master's family) was an example to all persons in her station, and never failed to recommend her to strangers, even before they had an opportunity of knowing the goodness of her character. It was her character, however, which recommended her to Farmer White. He knew that *favour is deceitful, and beauty is vain, but a woman that feareth the Lord, she shall be praised*[19] – "aye, and not only praised, but chosen too," says Farmer White, as he took down his hat from the nail on which it hung, in order to go and wait on Dr. Shepherd, to break his mind and ask his consent; for he thought it would be a very unhandsome return for all the favours he was receiving from his Minister, to decoy away his faithful servant from her place without his consent.

This worthy gentleman, though sorry to lose so valuable a member of his little family, did not scruple a moment about parting with her, when he found it would be so greatly to her advantage. Tom was agreeably surprised to hear she had saved fifty pounds[20] by her frugality. The Doctor married them himself, Farmer Hodges being present.

In the afternoon, Dr. Shepherd condescended to call on Farmer and Mrs. White, to give a few words of advice on the new duties they had entered into; a common custom with him on those occasions. He often took an opportunity to drop, in the most kind and tender way, a hint on the great indecency of making marriages, christenings, and, above all, funerals, days of riot and excess, as is too often the case in country villages. The expectation that the vicar might possibly drop in, in his walks, on these festivities, sometimes restrained excessive drinking, and improper conversation, even among those who were not restrained by higher motives, as Farmer and Mrs. White were.

What the Dr. said was always in such a cheerful, good-humoured way, that it was sure to increase the pleasure of the day, instead of damping it. "Well, Farmer," said he, "and you my faithful Sarah, any other friend might recommend peace and agreement to you on your marriage; but I, on the contrary, recommend cares and strifes."[21] The company stared – but Sarah, who knew that her old master was a facetious gentleman, and always had some good meaning behind, looked serious. "Cares and strifes, Sir!" said the farmer, "what do you mean?" – "I mean," said he, "for the first, that your cares shall be who shall please God most, and your strifes, who shall serve him best, and do your duty most faithfully. Thus, all your cares and strifes being employed to the highest purposes, all petty cares and worldly strifes shall be at an end.

"Always remember, both of you, that you have still a better friend than each other." – The company stared again, and thought no woman could have so good a friend as her husband. "As you have chosen each other from the best motives," continued the Doctor, "you have every reasonable ground to hope for happiness; but as this world is a soil in which troubles and misfortunes will spring up; troubles from which you cannot save one another[22] – then remember, 'tis the best wisdom to go to that friend who is always near, always willing, and always able to help you; and that friend is God."

"Sir," said Farmer White, "I humbly thank you for all your kind instructions, of which I shall now stand more in need than ever, as I shall have more duties to fulfil. I hope the remembrance of my past offences will keep me humble, and the sense of my remaining sin will keep me watchful. I set out in the world, Sir, with what is called a good natural disposition, but I soon found, to my cost, that without God's grace, that will carry a man but a little way. A good temper is a good thing; but nothing but the fear of God can enable one to bear up against temptation, evil company, and evil passions. The misfortune of breaking my leg, as I then thought it, has proved the greatest blessing of my life. It showed me my own weakness, the value of the Bible, and the goodness of God. How many of my brother drivers have I seen since that time, cut off in the prime of life by drinking, or by some sudden accident, while I have not only been spared, but blessed and prospered. O, Sir! it would be the joy of my heart, if some of my old comrades, good natured, civil fellows (whom I can't help loving) could see, as I have done, the danger of evil courses before it is too late. Though they not hearken to you, Sir, or any other Minister, they may believe *me*, because I have been one of them: and I can speak from experience, of the great difference there is, even as to worldly comfort, between a life of sobriety and a life of sin. I could tell them, Sir, not as a thing I have read in a book, but as a truth I feel in my own heart, that to fear God, and keep his commandments, will not only "bring a man peace at the last," but will make him happy *now*. And I will venture to say, Sir, that all the stocks, pillories, prisons, and gibbets in the land, though so very needful to keep bad men in order, yet will never restrain a good man from committing evil, half so much as that single text, "*How shall I do this great wickedness, and sin against God?*"[23] Dr. Shepherd condescended to approve of what the farmer had said, kindly shook him by the hand, and took leave.

Thomas White had always been fond of singing, but he had for many years despised that vile trash which is too often sung in stable yards.[24] One Sunday evening he heard his mistress at the Bear read some verses out of a fine book called the Spectator. He was so struck with the picture it contained of the great mercies of God, of which he had himself partaken so largely, that he took the liberty to ask her for these verses, and she being a very good-natured woman, made her daughter write out for the postilion the following.

HYMN ON DIVINE PROVIDENCE[25]

[Addison's hymn, 'When all thy mercies, O my God', is printed here to end the tale, including these appropriate lines:]

When in the Slipp'ry paths of YOUTH
With hectic steps I ran
Thine arms unseen, convey'd me safe,
And led me up to MAN ...

CHEAP REPOSITORY.

THE
WAY TO PLENTY;
OR, THE
SECOND PART of TOM WHITE.

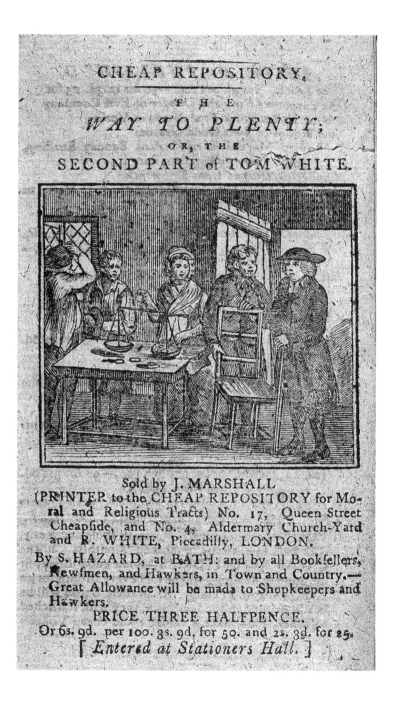

Sold by J. MARSHALL
(PRINTER to the CHEAP REPOSITORY for Moral and Religious Tracts) No. 17, Queen Street Cheapside, and No. 4, Aldermary Church-Yard and R. WHITE, Piccadilly, LONDON.

By S. HAZARD, at BATH: and by all Booksellers, Newsmen, and Hawkers, in Town and Country.— Great Allowance will be made to Shopkeepers and Hawkers.

PRICE THREE HALFPENCE.

Or 6s. 9d. per 100. 3s. 9d. for 50. and 2s. 3d. for 25.

[*Entered at Stationers Hall.*]

THE WAY TO PLENTY

or, the Second Part of Tom White

Written in 1795, the Year of Scarcity.[1]

TOM WHITE, as we have shown in the first part of this history, from an idle post-boy was become a respectable farmer. GOD had blessed his industry and he had prospered in the world. He was sober and temperate, and, as was the natural consequence, he was active and healthy. He was industrious and frugal, and he became prosperous in his circumstances. This is in the ordinary course of Providence. But it is not a certain and necessary rule. *GOD maketh his sun to shine on the just and the unjust.*[2] A man who uses every honest means of thrift and industry, will, in most cases, find success attend his labours. But still the *race is not always to the swift, nor the battle to the strong.*[3] GOD is sometimes pleased for wise ends to disappoint all the worldly hopes of the most upright man. His corn may be smitten by a blight. His barns may be consumed by fire. His cattle may be carried off by distemper.[4] And to these, and other misfortunes, he is as liable as the spendthrift or the knave. Success is the *common* reward of industry, but if it were its *constant* reward, the industrious would be tempted to look no further than the present state. They would lose one strong ground of their faith. It would set aside the Scripture scheme. This world would then be looked on as a state of reward, instead of a state of trial, and we should forget to look to a day of final retribution.

Farmer White never took it into his head that because he paid his debts, worked early and late, and ate the bread of carefulness,[5] he was therefore to come into no *misfortune like other folk,* but was to be free from the common trials and troubles of life. He knew that prosperity was far from being a sure mark of GOD's favour, and had read in good books, and especially in the Bible, of the great poverty and afflictions of the best of men. Though he was no great scholar, he had sense enough to observe, that a time of public prosperity was not always a time of public virtue; and he thought that what was true of a whole nation might be true of one man. So the more he prospered the more he prayed that prosperity might not corrupt his heart. And when he saw lately signs of public distress coming on, he was not half so much frightened as some others were, because he thought it might do us good in the long run; and he was in hopes that a little poverty might bring on a little penitence. The great grace he laboured after was that of a cheerful submission. He used to say, that if the Lord's prayer had only contained those four little words, THY WILL BE DONE, it would be worth more than the biggest book in the world without them.

Dr. Shepherd, the worthy vicar (with whom the farmer's wife had formerly lived as housekeeper) was very fond of taking a walk with him about his grounds, and he used to say, that he learnt as much from the farmer as the farmer did from him. If the Doctor happened to observe, "I am afraid these long rains will spoil this fine piece of oats," the farmer would answer, "but then, sir, think how good it is for the grass." If the doctor feared the wheat would be but indifferent, the farmer was sure the rye would turn out well. When grass faded, he did not doubt but turnips would be plenty. Even for floods and inundations he would find out some way to justify Providence. "'Tis better," said he, "to have our lands a little overflowed, than that the springs should be dried up, and our cattle faint for lack of water." When the drought came, he thanked GOD that the season would be healthy; and high winds, which frightened others, he said served to clear the air. Whoever, or whatever was wrong, he was always sure that PROVIDENCE was in the right. And he used to say, that a man with ever so small an income, if he had but frugality and temperance, and cast off all vain desires was richer than a lord who was tormented by vanity and covetousness. When he saw others in the wrong, he did not however abuse them for it, but took care to avoid the same fault. He had sense and spirit enough to break through many old but very bad customs of his neighbours. "If a thing is wrong in itself" (said he one day to Farmer Hodges) "a whole parish doing it can't make it right. And as to its being an old custom, why, if it be a good one, I like it the better for being old, because it has had the stamp of ages, and the sanction of experience on its worth. But if it be old as well as bad, that is another reason for my trying to put an end to it, that we may not mislead our children as our fathers have misled us."

THE ROOF-RAISING

Some years after he was settled, he built a large new barn. All the workmen were looking forward to the usual holiday of roof-raising. On this occasion it was a custom to give a dinner to the workmen, with so much liquor after it that they got so drunk, that they not only lost the remaining half day's work, but they were not always able to work the following day.

Mrs. White provided a plentiful dinner for roof-raising, and gave each man his mug of beer. After a hearty meal they began to grow clamorous for more drink. The farmer said, "My lads, I don't grudge you a few gallons of ale merely for the sake of saving my liquor, though that is some consideration, but I never will, knowingly, help any man to make a beast of himself. I am resolved to break through a bad custom. You are now well refreshed. If you will go cheerfully to your work, you will have half a day's pay to take on Saturday night more than you would, if this afternoon were wasted in drunkenness. For this your families will be the better: whereas, were I to give you more liquor, when you have already had enough, I should help to rob them of their bread. But I wish to shew you that I have your good at heart full as much as my own profit. If you will now go to work, I will give you all another mug at night when you leave off. Thus your time will be saved, your families helped, and my ale will not go to make reasonable creatures worse than brute beasts."

Here he stopped. "You are in the right on't, Master," said Tom the thatcher; "You are a hearty man, Farmer," said John Plane, the carpenter. – "Come along, boys," said Tom Brick the mason; so they all went merrily to work, fortified with a good dinner. There was only one drunken surly fellow that refused; this was Dick Guzzle the Smith. Dick never works above two or three days in the week, and spends the others at the Red Lion. He swore, that if the farmer did not let him have as much liquor as he liked at Roof-Raising he would not strike another stroke, but would leave the job unfinished, and he might get hands where he could. Farmer White took him at his word, and paid him off directly: glad enough to get rid of such a sot, whom he had only employed from pity to a large and almost starving family. When the men came for their mug in the evening, the farmer brought out the remains of the cold gammon; they made a hearty supper, and thanked him for having broke through a foolish custom, which was afterwards much left off in that parish, though Dick would not come into it, and lost most of his work.

Farmer White's labourers were often complaining, that things were so dear that they could not buy a bit of meat. He knew it was partly true, but not entirely; for it was before these very hard times. One morning he stept out to see how an outhouse which he was thatching went on. He was surprised to find the work at a stand. He walked over to the thatcher's house. "Tom," said he, "I desire that piece of work may be finished directly. If a shower comes my grain will be spoiled." "Indeed, Master, I shan't work to-day, nor to-morrow neither," said Tom. "You forget that 'tis Easter Monday, and to-morrow is Easter Tuesday. And so on Wednesday I shall thatch away, master. But 'tis hard if a poor man, who works all the seasons round, may not enjoy these few holidays which come but once a year."

"Tom," said the farmer, "when these days were first put into our Prayer-book, the good men who did it little thought that the time would come when *holyday* should mean *drunken-day*. How much dost think now I shall pay thee for this piece of thatch?" "Why you know, master you have let it to me by the great.⁶ I think between this and to-morrow night as the weather is so fine, I could clear about four shillings after I have paid my boy. But thatching does not come often, and other work is not so profitable." "Very well, Tom; and how much now do you think you may spend in these two holidays?" – "Why, master, if the ale is pleasant and the company merry, I do not expect to get off for less than three shillings." "Tom, can you do pounds, shillings, and pence?" "I can make a little score, master, behind the kitchen door with a bit of chalk, which is as much as I want." "Well Tom, add the four shillings you would have earned to the three you intend to spend, what does that make?" "Let me see! three and four make seven. Seven shillings, master." – "Tom, you often tell me the times are so bad that you can never buy a bit of meat. Now here is the cost of two joints at once; to say nothing of the sin of wasting time and getting drunk." "I never once thought of that," said Tom. "Now Tom," said the farmer, "If I were you, I would step over to Butcher Jobbins's, buy a shoulder of mutton, which being left from Saturday's market you will get a little cheaper. This I would make my wife bake in a deep dish full of potatoes. I would then go to work, and when the dinner was ready I would go and enjoy it with my wife and children; you need not give the mutton to the brats; the potatoes will have all the gravy, and be very savoury for them." "Aye, but I've got no beer, master: the times are so hard that a poor man can't afford to brew a drop of drink now as we used to do."

"Times are bad, and malt is very dear, Tom, and yet both don't prevent your throwing away seven shillings⁷ in keeping holiday. Now send for a quart of ale, as it is to be a feast; and you will even then be four shillings richer than if you had gone to the publick-house. I would put by these four shillings, till I could add a couple to them: with this I would get a bushel of malt, and my wife should brew it, and you may take a pint at home of a night, which will do you more good than a gallon at the Red

Lion." "I have a great mind to take your advice, master; but I shall be
made such fun of at the Lion, they will so laugh at me if I don't go."
"Let those laugh that win, Tom." "But, master, I have got a friend to
meet me there." "Then ask your friend to come and eat a bit of your
cold mutton at night, and here is six-pence for another pot, if you will
promise to brew a small cask of your own." "Thank you, master, and so
I will; and I won't go to the Lion. Come boy, bring the helm, and fetch
the ladder." And so Tom was upon the roof in a twinkling. The barn was
thatched, the mutton bought, the beer brewed, the friend invited, and the
holiday enjoyed.[8]

THE SHEEP-SHEARING

Dr. Shepherd happened to say to Farmer White one day, that there was
nothing he disliked more than the manner in which sheep-shearing and
harvest-home were kept by some in his parish. "What!" said the good
doctor, "just when we are blest with a prosperous gathering in of these
natural riches of our land, the fleece of our flocks; when our barns are
crowned with plenty, and we have reaped the fruits of the earth in due
season;[9] is that very time to be set apart for ribaldry, and riot, and
drunkenness? Do we thank God for his mercies, by making ourselves
unworthy and unfit to enjoy them?

"I thank you for the hint, sir," said the farmer. "I am resolved to
rejoice though, and others shall rejoice with me; and we will have a merry
night on't."

So Mrs. White dressed a very plentiful supper of meat and pudding,
and spread out two tables. The farmer sat at the head of one, consisting
of some of his neighbours, and all his work-people. At the other sat his
wife, with two long benches on each side of her. At these sat all the old
and infirm poor, especially those who lived in the workhouse, and had no
day of festivity to look forward to in the whole year but this. On the
grass, in the little court, sat the children of his labourers, and of the other
poor, whose employment it had been to gather flowers, and dress and
adorn the horns of the ram; for the farmer did not wish to put an end
to any old custom, if it was innocent.[10] His own children stood by the
table, and he gave them plenty of pudding, which they carried to the
children of the poor, with a little draught of cider to every one.

This feast, though orderly and decent, was yet hearty and cheerful. Dr.
Shepherd dropped in with a good deal of company he had at his house,
and they were much pleased. When the Doctor saw how the aged and

the infirm poor were enjoying themselves, he was much moved: he shook the farmer by the hand, and said, "But thou, when thou makest a feast, call the blind, and the lame, and the halt: they cannot recompense thee; but thou shalt be recompensed at the resurrection of the just."[11]

"Sir," said the farmer, "'tis no great matter of expense. I kill a sheep of my own; potatoes are as plenty as blackberries, with people who have a little forethought. I save much more cider in the course of a year by never allowing any carousing in my kitchen, or drunkenness in my fields, than would supply many such feasts as these, so that I shall be never the poorer at Christmas. It is cheaper to make people happy, sir, than to make them drunk." The Doctor and the ladies condescended to walk from one table to the other, and heard many merry stories, but not one profane word, or one indecent song; so that he was not forced to the painful necessity either of reproving them or leaving them in anger. When all was over, they sung the sixty-fifth psalm,[12] and the ladies all joined in it; and when they got home to the vicarage to tea, they declared they liked it better than any concert.

THE HARD WINTER [13]

In the famous cold winter of the present year, 1795, it was edifying to see how patiently Farmer White bore that long and severe frost. Many of his sheep were frozen to death, but he thanked GOD that he had still many left. He continued to find in-door work, that his men might not be out of employ. Mrs. White was so considerate, that just at that time she lessened the number of her hogs, that she might have more whey and skim milk to assist poor families. Nay, I have known her live on boiled meat for a long while together, in a sickly season, because the pot-liquor made such a supply of broth for the sick poor. As the spring came on, and things grew worse, she never had a cake, or a pudding in her house; though she used to have plenty of these good things, and will again I hope, when the present scarcity is over; though she says she never will use such white flour again, even if it should come down to five shillings a bushel.

All the parish now began to murmur. Farmer Jones was sure the frost had killed the wheat. Farmer Wilson said the rye would never come up. Brown, the maltster, insisted the barley was dead at the root. Butcher Jobbins said beef would be a shilling a pound. All declared there would not be a hop to brew with. The orchards were all blighted; there would not be apples enough to make a pye; and as to hay, there would be none to be had for love nor money. "I'll tell you what," said Farmer White, "the season is dreadful. The crops are unpromising just now; but 'tis too early to judge. Don't let us make things worse than they are. We ought to comfort the poor, and you are driving them to despair. Don't you know how much GOD was displeased with the murmurs of his chosen people? And yet, when they were tired of manna, he sent them quails,[14] but all did not do. Nothing satisfies grumblers. We have a promise on our side, that there shall be seed-time and harvest-time to the end.[15] Let us, then, hope for a good day, but provide against an evil one. Let us rather prevent the evil before it is come upon us, than sink under it when it comes. Grumbling can't help us. Activity can. Let us set about planting potatoes in every nook and corner, in case the corn *should* fail; which however I don't believe. Let us mend our management before we are driven to it by actual want. And if we allow our honest labourers to plant a few potatoes for their families in the head lands[16] of our ploughed fields, or other waste bits of ground, it will do us no harm, and be a great help to them."

The farmer had many temptations to send his corn, at an extravagant price, to *a certain sea-port town*;[17] but as he knew that it was intended to export it against law, he would not be tempted to encourage unlawful gain; so he threshed out a small mow at a time, and sold it to the neighbouring poor far below the market-price. He served his own workmen first. This was the same to them as if he had raised their wages, and even better, as it was a benefit of which their families were sure to partake. If the poor in the next parish were more distressed than his own, he sold to them at the same rate. "For," said he, "there is no distinction of parishes in heaven, and though charity begins at home, yet it ought not to end there."[18]

He had been used, in good times, now and then to catch a hare or a partridge, as he was qualified.[19] But he now resolved to give up that pleasure. So he parted from a couple of spaniels he had; for he said he could not bear that his dogs should be eating the meat, or the milk, which so many men, women, and children wanted.

THE WHITE LOAF

One day, it was about the middle of last July, when things seemed to be at the dearest, and the Rulers of the land had agreed to set the example of eating nothing but coarse bread, Dr. Shepherd read, before sermon in the church, their public declaration, which the magistrates of the county sent him, and had also signed themselves. Mrs. White of course was at church, and commended it mightily. Next morning the Doctor took a walk over to the farmer's, in order to settle further plans for the relief of the parish. He was much surprised to meet Mrs. White's little maid Sally with a very small white loaf, which she had been buying at a shop. He said nothing to the girl, as he never thought it right to expose the faults of a mistress to her servant; but walked on, resolving to give Mrs. White a severe lecture for the first time in his life. He soon changed his mind, for on going into the kitchen, the first person he saw was Tom the thatcher, who had had a sad fall from a ladder: his arm, which was slipped out of his sleeve, was swelled in a frightful manner. Mrs. White was standing at the dresser making the little white loaf into a poultice, which she laid upon the swelling in a large clean old linen cloth.

"I ask your pardon, my good Sarah," said the Doctor: "I ought not, however appearances were against you, to have suspected that so humble and prudent a woman as you are, would be led either to indulge any daintiness of your own, or to fly in the face of your betters, by eating white bread while they are eating brown. Whenever I come here I see it is not needful to be rich in order to be charitable. A bountiful rich man would have sent Tom to a surgeon, who would have done no more for him than you have done; for in those inflammations the most skilful surgeon could only apply a poultice. Your kindness in dressing the wound yourself, will, I doubt not, perform the cure at the expense of that three-penny loaf and a little hog's lard. And I will take care that Tom shall have a good supply of Rice from the Subscription."[20] "And he shan't want for skim milk," said Mrs. White; "and was he the best lord in the land, in the state he is in, a dish of good rice milk would be better for him than the richest meat."

THE PARISH MEETING

On the tenth of August the vestry[21] held another meeting, to consult on the best method of further assisting the poor. The abundant crops now cheered every heart. Farmer White had a mind to be a little jocular with his desponding neighbours. "Well, Neighbour Jones," said he "all the wheat was killed, I suppose. The barley all dead at the root." Farmer Jones looked sheepish, and said to be sure the crops had turned out better than he thought. "Then," said Dr. Shepherd, "let us learn to trust Providence another time."

Among other things they agreed to subscribe for a large quantity of rice, which was to be sold out to the poor at a very low price, and Mrs. White was so kind as to undertake the trouble of selling it. After their day's work was over, all who wished to buy at these reduced rates were ordered to come to the farm on the Tuesday evening. Dr. Shepherd dropped in at the same time, and when Mrs. White had done weighing her rice, the Doctor spoke as follows:

"My honest friends, it has pleased GOD to visit this land with a scarcity, to which we have been but little accustomed. There are some idle, evil minded people who are on the watch for public distresses, not that they may humble themselves under the mighty hand of GOD (which is the true use to be made of all troubles) but that they may benefit themselves by disturbing the public peace. These people, by riot and drunkenness, double the evil which they pretend to cure. Riot will compleat our misfortunes, while peace, industry, and good management, will go near to cure them. Bread to be sure is uncommonly dear. Among the various ways of making it cheaper, one is to reduce the quality of it, another to lesson the quantity we consume. If we cannot get enough of coarse wheaten bread, let us make it of other grain. Or let us mix one half of potatoes, and one half of wheat. This last is what I eat in my own family: it is pleasant and wholesome. Our blessed Saviour ate barley bread, you know, as we are told in the last month's Sunday Reading of the Cheap Repository,[22] which I hope you have all heard; as I desired the master of the Sunday-school to read it just after evening service, when I know many of the parents are apt to call in at the school. This is a good custom, and one of those little books shall be often read at that time.

"My good women, I truly feel for you at this time of scarcity; and I am going to shew my good will, as much by my advice as my subscription. It is my duty, as your friend and minister, to tell you, that one half of your present hardships is owing to BAD MANAGEMENT.[23] I often meet your children without shoes and stockings, with great luncheons of the very whitest bread, and that three times a day. Half that quantity, and still less if it were coarse, put into a dish of good onion or leek porridge, would make them an excellent breakfast. Many too of the very poorest of you eat your bread hot from the oven; this makes the difference of one loaf in five; I assure you, 'tis what I cannot afford to do. Come, Mrs. White, you must assist me a little. I am not very knowing in these matters myself; but I know that the rich would be twice as charitable, if the poor made a better use of their bounty. Mrs. White, do give these poor women a little advice how to make their pittance go further than it now does. When you lived with me you were famous for making us nice cheap dishes, and I dare say you are not less notable now you manage for yourself."

"Indeed neighbours," said Mrs. White, "what the good doctor says is very true. A halfpenny worth of oatmeal or groats, with a leek or onion, out of your own garden, which costs nothing, a bit of salt, and a little coarse bread, will breakfast your whole family. It is a great mistake at any time to think a bit of meat is so ruinous, and a great loaf of bread so cheap. A poor man gets seven or eight shillings a week:[24] If he is careful he brings it home. I dare not say how much of this goes for tea in the afternoon, now sugar and butter are so dear, because I should have you all upon me; but I will say, that too much of this little goes even for bread, from a notion that it is the hardest fare. This at all times, but particularly just now, is bad management. Dry pease, to be sure, have been very dear lately; but now they are plenty enough. I am certain then, that if a shilling or two of the seven or eight was laid out for a bit of coarse beef, a sheep's head, or any such thing, it would be well bestowed. I would throw a couple of pounds of this into the pot, with two or three handfuls of grey pease, an onion, and a little pepper. Then I would throw in cabbage or turnip, and carrot; or any garden stuff that was most plenty: let it stew two or three hours, and it will make a dish fit for his Majesty. The working man should have the meat; the children don't want it, the soup will be thick and substantial, and requires no bread."

RICE MILK

"You who can get skim milk, as all our workmen can, have a great advantage. A quart of this, and a quarter of a pound of the rice you have just bought, a little bit of all spice, and brown sugar, will make a dainty and cheap dish."

"Bless your heart!" muttered Amy Grumble, who looked as dirty as a cinder-wench, with her face and fingers all daubed with snuff; "rice milk, indeed! it is very nice to be sure for those who can dress it, but we have not a bit of coal; rice is of no use to us without firing;" "And yet" said the Doctor, "I see your tea-kettle boiling twice every day as I pass by the poor-house, and fresh butter at eleven-pence a pound on your shelf." – "Oh dear sir," cried Amy, "a few sticks serve to boil the tea-kettle." – "And a few more," said the Doctor, "will boil the rice milk, and give twice the nourishment at a quarter of the expence."

RICE PUDDING

"Pray, Sarah," said the doctor, "how did you use to make that pudding my children were so fond of? And I remember when it was cold, we used to have it in the parlour for supper." "Nothing more easy," said Mrs. White: "I put half a pound of rice, two quarts of skim milk, and two ounces of brown sugar." "Well," said the Doctor, "and how many will this dine?" – "Seven or eight, sir." – "Very well, and what will it cost?" – "Why, sir, it did not cost you so much, because we baked it at home, [25] and I used our own milk; but it will not cost above seven-pence to those who pay for both. Here, too, bread is saved."

"Pray, Sarah, let me put in a word," said Farmer White: "I advise my men to raise each a large bed of parsnips. They are very nourishing, and very profitable. Sixpennyworth of seed, well sowed, and trod in, will produce more meals than four sacks. Parsnips are very good the second day warmed in the frying-pan, and a little rasher of pork or bacon will give them a nice flavour."

Dr. Shepherd now said, "as a proof the nourishing quality of parsnips, I was reading in a history book this very day, that the American Indians make a great part of their bread of parsnips, though Indian corn is so famous: it will make a little variety too."

A CHEAP STEW

"I remember," said Mrs. White, "a cheap dish, so nice that it makes my mouth water. I peel some raw potatoes, slice them thin, put the slices into a deep frying-pan, or pot, with a little water, an onion, and a bit of pepper. Then I get a bone or two of a breast of mutton, or a little strip of salt pork, and put into it. Cover it down close, keep in the steam, and let it stew for an hour."

"You really get me an appetite, Mrs. White, by your dainty receipts," said the Doctor. "I am resolved to have this dish at my own table." "I could tell you another very good dish, and still cheaper," answered she. "Come, let us have it," cried the Doctor. "I shall write all down as soon as I get home, and I will favour any body with a copy of these receipts who will call at my house." "And I will do more, sir," said Mrs. White, "for I will put any of these women in the way how to dress it, the first time, if they are at a loss. But this is my dish.

"Take two or three pickled herrings, put them into a stone jar, fill it up with potatoes, and a little water, and let it bake in the oven till it is done. I would give one hint more," added she; "I have taken to use nothing but potato starch; and though I say it, that should not say it, nobody's linen in a common way looks better than ours."

The Doctor now said, "I am sorry for one hardship which many poor people labour under, I mean the difficulty of getting a little milk.[26] I wish all farmers' wives were as considerate as you are, Mrs. White. A little milk is a great comfort to the poor, especially when their children are sick; and I have known it answer to the seller as well as to the buyer, to keep a cow or two on purpose to sell it out by the quart.

"Sir," said Farmer White, "I beg leave to say a word to the men, if you please, for all your advice goes to the women. If you will drink less Gin you may get more meat. If you abstain from the alehouse, you may many of you get a little one-way beer[27] at home." – "Aye, that we can, Farmer," said poor Tom the thatcher, who was now got well. "Easter Monday for that – I say no more. – A word to the wise." The Farmer smiled, and went on: – "The number of public houses in many a parish brings on more hunger and rags than all the taxes in it, heavy as they are. All the other evils put together hardly make up the sum of that one. We are now raising a fresh subscription for you. This will be our rule of giving. We will not give to Sots, Gamblers, and Sabbath-breakers. Those who do not set their young children to work on week-days, and send them to school on Sundays, deserve little favour. No man should keep a dog till he has more food than his family wants. If he feeds them at home they rob his children. If he starves them, they rob his neighbours. We have heard in a neighbouring city, that some people carried back the subscription loaves, because they were too coarse; but we hope better things of you." Here Betty Plane begged, with all humility, to put in a word. "Certainly," said the doctor, "we will listen to all modest complaints, and try to redress them."[28] "You are pleased to say, sir," said she, "that we might find much comfort from buying coarse bits of beef. And so we might, but you do not know, sir, that we can seldom get them, even when we had the money, and times were so bad." "How so, Betty?" – "Sir, when we go to Butcher Jobbins for a bit of shin, or any other lean piece, his answer is, 'You can't have it to-day. The cook at the great house has bespoke it for gravy, or the Doctor's maid (begging your pardon, sir,) has just ordered it for soup.' Now, sir, if such kind gentlefolks were aware that this gravy and soup, not only consume a great deal of meat (which, to be sure, those have a right to do who can pay for it) but that it takes away those coarse pieces which the poor would buy, if they bought at all, they would not do it. For indeed the rich have been very kind, and I don't know what we should have done without them."

"I thank you for the hint, Betty," said the Doctor, "and I assure you

I will have no more gravy soup. My garden will supply me with soups that are both wholesomer and better. And I will answer for my lady at the great house, that she will do the same. I hope this will become a general rule, and then we shall expect that butchers will favour you in the prices of the coarse pieces, if *we* who are rich buy nothing but the prime. In our gifts we shall prefer, as the farmer has told you, those who keep steadily to their work. Such as come to the vestry for a loaf, and do not come to church for the sermon, we shall mark; and prefer those who come constantly whether there are any gifts or not. But there is one rule from which we never will depart. Those who have been seen aiding or abetting any RIOT,[29] any attack on butchers, bakers, wheat mows, mills, or millers, we will not relieve. With the quiet, contented, hard-working man, I will share my last morsel of bread. I shall only add, though it has pleased GOD to send us this visitation as a punishment, yet we may convert this short trial into a lasting blessing, if we all turn over a new leaf. Prosperity had made most of us careless. The thoughtless profusion of some of the rich could only be exceeded by the idleness and bad management of some of the poor. Let us now at last adopt that good old maxim, EVERY ONE MEND ONE. And may GOD add his blessing!"

The people now cheerfully departed with their rice, resolving, as many of them as could get milk, to put one of Mrs. White's receipts in practice that very night; and a rare supper they had. I hope to give a good account how this parish improved in ease and comfort, by their improvement in frugality and good management

THE END

Z.

CHEAP REPOSITORY.

THE
Shepherd of Salisbury-Plain.
PART I.

Sold by **J. MARSHALL**
(PRINTER to the CHEAP REPOSITORY for Moral and Religious Tracts) No. 17, Queen Street Cheapside, and No. 4, Aldermary Church-Yard and R. WHITE, Piccadilly, LONDON.

By S. HAZARD, at BATH: and by all Booksellers, Newsmen, and Hawkers, in Town and Country.—Great Allowance will be made to Shopkeepers and Hawkers.

PRICE ONE HALFPENNY.
Or 4s. 6d. per 100.—2s. 6d. for 50.—1s. 6d. for 25.
[*Entered at Stationers Hall.*]

THE SHEPHERD OF SALISBURY PLAIN.

PART ONE

MR. JOHNSON, a very worthy charitable Gentleman, was travelling sometime ago across one of those vast Plains which are well known in Wiltshire.[1] It was a fine summer's evening, and he rode slowly that he might have leisure to admire God in the works of his creation: for this Gentleman was of opinion, that a walk or a ride, was as proper a time as any to think about good things, for which reason, on such occasions, he seldom thought so much about his money, or his trade, or public news, as at other times, that he might with more ease and satisfaction enjoy the pious thoughts which the visible works of the great Maker of heaven and earth are intended to raise in the mind.[2]

His attention was all of a sudden called off by the barking of a Shepherd's dog, and looking up he spied one of those little huts which are here and there to be seen on these great Downs; and near it was the Shepherd himself busily employed with his dog in collecting together his vast flock of sheep. As he drew nearer, he perceived him to be a clean, well-looking, poor man, near fifty years of age. His coat, though at first it had probably been of one dark colour, had been in a long course of years so often patched with different sorts of cloth, that it was now become hard to say which had been the original colour. But this, while it gave a plain proof of the Shepherd's poverty, equally proved the exceeding neatness, industry, and good management of his wife. His stockings no less proved her good housewifery, for they were entirely covered with darns of different coloured worsted, but had not a hole in them; and his shirt, though nearly as coarse as the sails of a ship, was as white as the drifted snow, and neatly mended where time had either made a rent or worn it thin. This is a rule of judging, by which one shall seldom be deceived. If I meet with a labourer, hedging, ditching, or mending the highways, with his stockings and shirt tight and whole, however mean and bad his other garments are, I have seldom failed, on visiting his cottage, to find that also clean and well ordered, and his wife notable[3] and worthy of encouragement. Whereas a poor woman, who will be lying a-bed, or gossipping with her neighbours when she ought to be fitting out her husband in a cleanly manner, will seldom be found to be very good in other respects.

This was not the case with our Shepherd: and Mr. Johnson was not more struck with the decency of his mean and frugal dress, than with his open honest countenance, which bore strong marks of health, cheerfulness, and spirit.

Mr. Johnson, who was on a journey, and somewhat fearful from the appearance of the sky, that rain was at no great distance, accosted the Shepherd with asking what sort of weather he thought it would be on the morrow. – "It will be such weather as pleases me," answered the Shepherd. Though the answer was delivered in the mildest and civilest tone that could be imagined, the Gentleman thought the words themselves rather rude and surly, and asked him how that could be, "Because," replied the shepherd, "it will be such weather as shall please God, and whatever pleases Him always pleases me."

Mr. Johnson, who delighted in good men and good things, was very well satisfied with his reply. For he justly thought that though a hypocrite may easily contrive to appear better than he really is to a stranger; – and that no one should be too soon trusted, merely for having a few good words in his mouth; yet as he knew that "out of the abundance of the heart the mouth speaketh⁴ he always accustomed himself to judge favourably of those who had a serious deportment and solid manner of speaking. "It looks as if it proceeded from a good habit," said he; "and though I may now and then be deceived by it, yet it has not often happened to me to be so. Whereas, if a man accosts me with an idle, dissolute, vulgar, indecent, or profane expression, I have never been deceived in him, but have generally, on inquiry, found his character to be as bad as his language gave me room to expect."

He entered into conversation with the Shepherd in the following manner. "Yours is a troublesome life, honest friend," said he.⁵ "To be sure, Sir." replied the Shepherd. 'tis not a very lazy life; but 'tis not near so toilsome as that which my GREAT MASTER led for my sake, and he had every state and condition of life at his choice, and *chose* a hard one – while I only submit to the lot that is appointed me." – "You are exposed to great cold and heat, said the Gentleman." "True, Sir," said the Shepherd; "but then I am not exposed to great temptations; and so throwing one thing against another, God is pleased to contrive to make things more equal than we poor, ignorant, short-sighted creatures, are apt to think. David was happier when he kept his father's sheep on such a plain as this, and singing some of his own Psalms, perhaps, than ever he was when he became king of Israel and Judah. And I dare say we should never have had some of the most beautiful texts in all those fine Psalms, if he had not been a Shepherd, which enabled him to make so many fine comparisons and similitudes, as one may say, from a country life, flocks of sheep, hills and vallies, and fountains of water."[6]

"You think, then," said the Gentleman, "that a laborious life is a happy one." "I do, Sir, and more so especially, as it exposes a man to fewer sins. If King Saul had continued a poor laborious man to the end of his days, he might have lived happy and honest, and died a natural death in his bed at last, which you know, Sir, was more than he did.[7] But I speak with reverence, for it was divine Providence over ruled all that, you know, Sir, and I do not presume to make comparisons. Besides, Sir, my employment has been particularly honoured – Moses was a shepherd in the plains of Midian.[8] It was to "Shepherds keeping their flocks by night," that the angels appeared in Bethlehem, to tell the best news, the gladdest tidings, that ever were revealed to poor sinful men: often and often has the thought warmed my poor heart in the coldest night, and filled me with more joy and thankfulness than the best supper could have done."

Here the Shepherd stopped, for he began to feel that he had made too free, and had talked too long. But Mr. Johnson was so well pleased with what he said, and with the cheerful contented manner in which he said it, that he desired him to go on freely, for that it was a pleasure to him to meet with a plain man, who, without any kind of learning but what he had got from the Bible, was able to talk so well on a subject in which all men, high and low, rich and poor, are equally concerned.

"Indeed I am afraid I make too bold, Sir; for it better becomes me to listen to such a Gentleman as you seem to be, than to talk in my poor way; but as I was saying, Sir, I wonder all working men do not derive as great joy and delight as I do from thinking how God has honoured poverty! Oh! Sir, what great, or rich, or mighty men have had such honour put on them, or their condition, as Shepherds, Tent-makers, Fishermen, and Carpenters have had."[9] "My honest friend." said the gentleman," I perceive you are well acquainted with scripture." "Yes, Sir, pretty well, blessed be God! through his mercy I learnt to read when I was a little boy; though reading was not so common when I was a child, as I am told, through the goodness of Providence, and the generosity of the rich, it is likely to become now a-days. I believe there is no day for the last thirty years that I have not peeped at my Bible. If we can't find time to read a chapter, I defy any man to say he can't find time to read a verse; and a single text,

Sir, well followed and put in practice every day, would make no bad figure at the year's end; three hundred and sixty-five texts, without the loss of a moment's time, would make a pretty stock, a little golden treasury, as one may say, from new-year's day to new-year's day, and if children were brought up to it, they would look for their text naturally as they do for their breakfast. No labouring man, 'tis true, has so much leisure as a Shepherd, for while the flock is feeding, I am obliged to be still, and at such times I can now and then tap a shoe[10] for my children or myself, which is a great saving to us, and while I am doing that I repeat a bit of a chapter, which makes the time pass pleasantly in this wild solitary place. I can say the best part of the Bible by heart,[11] I believe I should not say the best part, for every part is good, but I mean the greatest part. I have led but a lonely life, and have often had but little to eat, but my Bible has been meat, drink, and company to me, as I may say, and when want and trouble have come upon me, I don't know what I should have done, indeed, Sir, if I had not had the promises of this book for my stay and support."

"You have had great difficulties, then?" said Mr. Johnson. "Why, as to that, sir, not more than neighbours fare; I have but little cause to complain, and much to be thankful; but I have had some little struggles, as I will leave you to judge. I have a wife and eight children,[12] whom I bred up in that little cottage which you see under the hill about half a mile off." "What, that with the smoke coming out of the chimney?" said the Gentleman. "O, no, Sir," replied the shepherd, smiling, "we have seldom smoke in the evening, for we have little to cook, and firing is very dear in these parts. 'Tis that cottage which you see on the left hand of the church, near that little tuft of hawthorns." "What, that hovel with only one room above and below, with scarcely any chimney, how is it possible you can live there with such a family!" "O! it is very possible and very certain too," cried the Shepherd. "How many better men have been worse lodged! How many good christians have perished in prisons and dungeons, in comparison of which my cottage is a palace! The house is very well, Sir and if the rain did not sometimes beat down upon us through the thatch when we are a-bed, I should not desire a better; for I have health, peace, and liberty, and no man maketh me afraid."[13]

"Well, I will certainly call on you before it be long; but how can you contrive to lodge so many children?" "We do the best we can, sir. My poor wife is a very sickly woman, or we should always have done tolerably well. There are no gentry in the parish, so that she has not met with any great assistance in her sickness. The good curate of the parish, who lives in that pretty parsonage in the valley, is very willing, but not very able to assist us on these trying occasions, for he has little enough for himself, and a large family into the bargain. Yet he does what he can, and more than many richer men do, and more than he can well afford. Besides that, his prayers and good advice we are always sure of, and we are truly thankful for that; for a man must give, you know, Sir, according to what he hath, and not according to what he hath not."[14]

"Are you in any distress at present?" said Mr. Johnson. "No, Sir, thank God," replied the Shepherd. "I get my shilling a day, and most of my children will soon be able to earn something; for we have only three under five years old."[15] "Only!" said the Gentleman; "that is a heavy burden." – "Not at all; God fits the back to it. Though my wife is not able to do any out of door work, yet she breeds up our children to such habits of industry, that our little maids before they are six years old, can first get a halfpenny, and then a penny a day by knitting. The boys who are too little to do hard work get a trifle by keeping the birds off the corn; for this the farmers will give them a penny or two pence, and now and then a bit of bread and cheese into the bargain. When the season of crow-keeping is over, then they glean or pick stones; any thing is better than idleness, Sir; and if they did not get a farthing by it, I would make them do it just the same, for the sake of giving them early habits of labour.

"So you see, Sir, I am not so badly off as many are; nay, if it were not that it costs me so much in 'pothecary's stuff for my poor wife, I should reckon myself well off. Nay, I do reckon myself well off, for blessed be God, he has granted her life to my prayers, and I would work myself to a 'natomy,[16] and live on one meal a day to add any comfort to her valuable life; indeed, I have often done the last, and thought it no great matter neither."

While they were in this part of the discourse, a fine plump cherry-cheek little girl ran up out of breath, with a smile on her young happy face, and, without taking any notice of the gentleman, cried out with great joy, – "Look here, father; only see how much I have got to-day!" Mr. Johnson was much struck with her simplicity, but puzzled to know what was the occasion of this great joy. On looking at her, he perceived a small quantity of coarse wool, some of which had found its way through the holes of her clean but scanty and ragged woollen apron. The father said, "this has been a successful day, indeed, Molly; but don't you see the gentleman?" Molly now made a curtsey down to the very ground; while Mr. Johnson inquired into the cause of the mutual satisfaction which both father and daughter had expressed at the unusual good fortune of the day.

"Sir," said the Shepherd, "poverty is a great sharpener of the wits. My wife and I cannot endure to see our children (poor as they are) without shoes and stockings, not only on account of the pinching cold which cramps their poor little limbs, but because it degrades and debases them; and poor people who have but little regard to appearances will seldom be found to have any great regard for honesty and goodness; I don't say this is always the case; but I am sure it is so too often. Now shoes and stockings being very dear we could never afford to get them without a little contrivance. I must show you how I manage about the shoes when you condescend to call at our cottage, Sir: as to stockings, this is one way we take to help to get them. My young ones who are too little to do much work, sometimes wander at off hours over the hills for the chance of finding what little wool the sheep may drop when they rub themselves, as they are apt to do, against the bushes.[17] These scattered bits of wool the children pick out of the brambles, which I see have torn sad holes in Molly's apron to-day: they carry this wool home, and when they have got a pretty parcel together their mother cards it; for she can sit and card in the chimney-corner when she is not able to wash, or work about house. The biggest girl then spins it: it does very well for us without dyeing, for poor people must not stand for the colour of their stockings. After this our little boys knit it for themselves, while they are employed in keeping cows in the fields, and after they get home at night. As for the knitting which the girls and their mother do, that is chiefly for sale, which helps to pay our rent." [18]

Mr. Johnson lifted up his eyes in silent astonishment at the shifts which honest poverty can make rather than beg or steal; and was surprised to think how many ways of subsisting there are, which those who live at their ease little suspect. He secretly resolved to be more attentive to his own petty expenses than he had hitherto been; and to be more watchful that nothing was wasted in his family.

But to return to the Shepherd. Mr. Johnson told him, that, as he must needs be at his friend's house, who lived many miles off that night, he could not as he wished to do, make a visit to his cottage at present. "But I will certainly do it," said he, "on my return; for I long to see your wife and her nice little family, and to be an eye-witness of her neatness and good management." The poor man's tears started into his eyes on hearing the commendation bestowed on his wife; and wiping them off with the sleeve of his coat, for he was not worth a handkerchief in the world, he said – "O, Sir, you just now, I am afraid, called me an humble man, but indeed I am a very proud one." – "Proud!" exclaimed Mr. Johnson, "I hope not – pride is a great sin;[19] and as the poor are liable to it as well as the rich, so good a man as you seem to be ought to guard against it."

"Sir," said he, "you are right, but I am not proud of myself, God knows, I have nothing to be proud of. I am a poor sinner, but indeed, sir, I am proud of my wife: she is not only the most tidy, notable woman on the plain, but she is the kindest wife and mother, and the most contented, thankful Christian that I know. Last year I thought I should have lost her in a violent fit of the rheumatism, caught by going to work too soon after her lying-in,[20] I fear; for 'tis but a bleak coldish place, as you may see, Sir, in winter; and sometimes the snow lies so long under the hill, that I can hardly make myself a path to get out and buy a few necessaries in the next village; and we are afraid to send out the children, for fear they should be lost when the snow is deep. So, as I was saying, the poor soul was very bad indeed, and for several weeks lost the use of all her limbs except her hands: a merciful providence spared her the use of these; so that, when she could not turn in her bed, she could contrive to patch a rag or two for her family. She was always saying, had it not been for the great goodness of God, she might have had her hands lame, as well as her feet;[21] or the palsy instead of the rheumatism, and then she could have done nothing: but nobody had so many mercies as she had.

"I will not tell you what we suffered during that bitter weather, sir; but my wife's faith and patience, during that trying time, were as good a lesson to me as any Sermon I could hear, and yet Mr. Jenkins gave us very comfortable ones, too, that helped to keep up my spirits.[22] One Sunday afternoon, when she was at the worst, as I was coming out of Church, for I went one part of the day, and my eldest daughter the other, so my poor wife was never left alone; – As I was coming out of church, I say, Mr. Jenkins, the minister, called out to me, and asked me how my wife did, saying he had been kept from coming to see her by the deep fall of snow, and indeed from the parsonage-house to my hovel it was quite impassable. I gave him all the particulars he asked, and I am afraid a good many more, for my heart was quite full. He kindly gave me a shilling, and said he would certainly try to pick out his way and come and see her in a day or two.

"While he was talking to me, a plain farmer-looking Gentleman in boots, who stood by, listened to all I said, but seemed to take no notice. It was Mr. Jenkins's wife's father, who was come to pass the Christmas holidays at the parsonage-house. I had always heard him spoken of as a plain frugal man, who lived close himself, but was remarked to give away more than any of his show-away neighbours.

"Well, I went home with great spirits at this seasonable and unexpected supply; for we had tapped our last six-pence, and there was little work to be had on account of the weather. I told my wife I was not come back empty-handed. "No, I dare say not," says she, "you have been serving a Master who filleth the hungry with good things, though he sendeth the rich empty away."[23] "True, Mary," says I. "we seldom fail to get good spiritual food from Mr. Jenkins, but to-day he has kindly supplied our bodily wants." She was more thankful when I showed her the shilling, than, I dare say, some of your great people are when they get a hundred pounds."

Mr. Johnson's heart smote him[24] when he heard such a value set upon a shilling. Surely, said he to himself, I will never waste another; but he said nothing to the shepherd, who thus pursued his story.

"Next morning before I went out, I sent part of the money to buy a little ale and brown sugar to put into her water-gruel; which, you know, sir, made it nice and nourishing. I went out to cleave wood in a farm-yard, for there was no standing out on the plain, after such snow as had fallen in the night. I went with a lighter heart than usual, because I had left my poor wife a little better; and comfortably supplied for this day; and I now resolved more than ever to trust God for the supplies of the next. When I came back at night, my wife fell a crying as soon as she saw me. This, I own I thought but a bad return for the blessings she had so lately received, and so I told her. "O" said she, "it is too much, we are too rich; I am now frightened, not lest we should have no portion in this world, but for fear we should have our whole portion in it. Look here, John!" – So saying, she uncovered the bed whereon she lay, and shewed me two warm, thick, new blankets. I could not believe my own eyes, Sir, because when I went out in the morning I had left her with no other covering than our little old, thin, blue rug. I was still more amazed when she put half a crown into my hand, telling me she had had a visit from Mr. Jenkins and Mr. Jones, the latter of whom had bestowed all these good things upon us. Thus, Sir, have our lives been crowned with mercies. My wife got about again, and I do believe, under Providence, it was owing to these comforts; for the rheumatism, Sir, without blankets by night, and flannel by day, is but a baddish job, especially to people who have little or no fire. She will always be a weakly body; but thank God, her soul prospers and is in health. But I beg your pardon, Sir, for talking on at this rate." "Not at all, not at all," said Mr. Johnson; "I am much pleased with your story, you shall certainly see me in a few days. Good night." So saying, he slipped a crown into his hand and rode off. "Surely," said the shepherd, "*goodness and mercy have followed me all the days of my life*,"[25] as he gave the money to his wife when he got home at night.

As to Mr. Johnson, he found abundant matter for his thoughts during the rest of his journey. On the whole, he was more disposed to envy than to pity the Shepherd. "I have seldom seen," said he, "so happy a man. It is a sort of happiness which the world could not give, and which, I plainly see, it has not been able to take away. This must be the true spirit of Religion. I see more and more, that true goodness is not merely a thing of words and opinions, but a Living Principle brought into every common action of a man's life. What else could have supported this poor couple under every bitter trial of want and sickness? No, my honest shepherd, I do not pity, but I respect and even honour thee; and I will visit thy poor hovel on my return to Salisbury with as much pleasure as I am now going to the house of my friend."

If Mr. Johnson keeps his word in sending me the account of his visit to the Shepherd's cottage, I shall be very glad to entertain my readers with it, and shall conclude this first part with

THE SHEPHERD'S HYMN

The Lord my pasture shall prepare,
And feed me with a Shepherd's care;
His presence shall my wants supply,
And guard me with a watchful eye:
My noon-day walks he shall attend,
And all my midnight hours defend ... [26]

THE SHEPHERD OF SALISBURY PLAIN

PART TWO

I AM willing to hope that my readers will not be sorry to hear some farther particulars of their old acquaintance, *the Shepherd of Salisbury Plain.* They will call to mind, that, at the end of the first part, he was returning home full óf gratitude to the favours he had received from Mr. Johnson, whom we left pursuing his journey, after having promised to make a visit to the Shepherd's Cottage.

Mr. Johnson, after having passed some time with his friend, set out on his return to Salisbury, and on the Saturday evening reached a very small inn, a mile or two distant from the Shepherd's Village; for he never travelled on a Sunday.[1] He went the next morning to the Church nearest the house where he had passed the night; and after taking such refreshment as he could get at that house, he walked on to find out the Shepherd's cottage. His reason for visiting him on a Sunday was chiefly, because he supposed it to be the only day which the Shepherd's employment allowed him to pass at home with his family, and as Mr. Johnson had been struck with his talk, he thought it would be neither unpleasant nor unprofitable to observe how a Man who carried such an appearance of piety spent his Sunday; for though he was so low in the world, this Gentleman was not above entering very closely into his character, of which he thought he should be able to form a better judgment, by seeing whether his practice at home kept pace with his professions abroad: for it is not so much by observing how people talk, as how they live, that we ought to judge of their characters.

After a pleasant walk Mr. Johnson got within sight of the cottage, to which he was directed by the clump of hawthorns and the broken chimney. He wished to take the family by surprise; and walking gently up the house he stood awhile to listen. The door being half open, he saw the Shepherd (who looked so respectable in his Sunday Coat that he should hardly have known him), his Wife, and their numerous young family, drawing round their little table, which was covered with a clean though very coarse cloth. There stood on it a large dish of potatoes, a brown pitcher, and a piece of coarse loaf. The wife and children stood in silent attention, while the Shepherd, with uplifted hands and eyes, devoutly begged the blessing of heaven on their homely fare. Mr. Johnson could not help sighing to reflect, that he had sometimes seen better dinners eaten with less appearance of thankfulness.

The Shepherd and his wife then sat down with great seeming cheerfulness, but the children stood; and while the mother was helping them, little fresh-coloured Molly, who had picked the wool from the bushes with so much delight, cried out, "Father, I wish I was big enough to say grace, I am sure I should say it very heartily to day, for I was thinking what must *poor* people do who have no salt to their potatoes, and do but look, our dish is quite full." – "That is the true way of thinking, Molly," said the father; "in whatever concerns bodily wants, and bodily comforts, it is our duty to compare our own lot with the lot of those who are worse off, and this will keep us thankful. On the other hand, whenever we are tempted to set up our own wisdom or goodness, we must compare ourselves with those who are wiser and better, and that will keep us humble." Molly was now so hungry, and found the potatoes so good, that she had no time to make any more remarks; but was devouring her dinner very heartily, when the barking of the great dog drew her attention from her trencher[2] to the door, and spying the stranger, she cried out, "Look, father, see here, if yonder is not the good Gentleman!" Mr. Johnson, finding himself discovered, immediately walked in, and was heartily welcomed by the honest Shepherd, who told his wife that this was the Gentleman to whom they were so much obliged.

The good Woman began, as some very neat people are rather too apt to do, with making many apologies that her house was not cleaner, and that things were not in fitter order to receive such a Gentleman. Mr. Johnson, however, on looking round, could discover nothing but the most perfect neatness. The trenchers on which they were eating were almost as white as their linen; and notwithstanding the number and smallness of the children, there was not the least appearance of dirt or litter. The furniture was very simple and poor, hardly, indeed, amounting to bare necessaries. It consisted of four brown wooden chairs, which by constant rubbing were become as bright as a looking glass; an iron pot and kettle; a poor old grate, which scarcely held a handful of coals, and out of which the little fire that had been in it appeared to have been taken, as soon as it had answered the end for which it had been lighted – that of boiling their potatoes. Over the chimney stood an old fashioned broad bright candlestick, and a still brighter spit; it was pretty clear that this last was kept rather for ornament than use. An old carved elbow chair, and a chest of the same date which stood in the corner, were considered as the most valuable part of the Shepherd's goods, having been in his family for three generations.[3] But all these were lightly esteemed by him, in comparison of another possession, which added to the above made up the whole of what he had inherited from his father; and which last he would not have parted with, if no other could have been had, for a king's ransom: this was a large old Bible, which lay on the window seat, neatly covered with brown cloth, variously patched. This sacred book was most reverently preserved from dogs' ears, dirt, and every other injury, but such as time and much use had made it suffer in spite of care. On the clean white walls were pasted, a hymn on the Crucifixion of our Saviour, a print of the Prodigal Son, the Shepherd's Hymn, and a New History of a True Book.[4]

After the first salutations were over, Mr. Johnson said, that if they would go on quietly with their dinner he would sit down. Though a good deal ashamed, they thought it more respectful to obey the Gentleman, who having cast his eye on their slender provisions, gently rebuked the Shepherd for not having indulged himself, as it was Sunday, with a morsel of Bacon to relish his Potatoes. The Shepherd said nothing, but poor Mary coloured, and hung down her head, saying, "indeed, Sir, it is not my fault, I did beg my husband to allow himself a bit of meat to-day out of your honour's bounty; but he was too good to do it, and it is all for my sake." The shepherd seemed unwilling to come to an explanation, but Mr. Johnson desired Mary to go on. So she continued, – "you must know, Sir, that both of us, next to a sin, dread a debt, and, indeed, in some cases a debt is a sin; but with all our care and pains we have never been able quite to pay off the Doctor's bill, for that bad fit of the Rheumatism which I had last winter. Now when you were pleased to give my husband that kind present the other day, I heartily desired him to buy a bit of meat for Sunday, as I said before, that he might have a little refreshment for himself out of your kindness. "But," answered he, "Mary, it is never out of my mind long together that we still owe a few shillings to the Doctor, (and thank God it is all we did owe in the world). Now if I carry him this money directly it will not only show him our honesty and our good will, but it will be an encouragement to him to come to you another time in case you should be taken once more in such a bad fit; for I must own," added my poor husband, "that the thought of your being so terribly ill without any help is the only misfortune that I want courage to face."

Here the grateful woman's tears ran down so fast that she could not go on. She wiped them with the corner of her apron, and humbly begged pardon for making so free. "Indeed, Sir," said the Shepherd, "though my wife is full as unwilling to be in debt as myself, yet I could hardly prevail on her to consent to my paying this money just then, because she said it was hard I should not have a taste of the Gentleman's bounty myself. But for once, Sir, I would have my own way. For you must know, as I pass the best part of my time alone, tending my sheep, 'tis a great point with me, Sir, to get comfortable matter for my own thoughts; so that 'tis rather self interest in me to allow myself in no pleasures and no practices that won't bear thinking on over and over. For when one is a good deal alone you know, Sir, all one's bad deeds do so rush in upon one, as I may say, and so torment one, that there is no true comfort to be had but in keeping clear of wrong doings, and false pleasures; and that I suppose may be one reason why so many folks hate to stay a bit by themselves. – But as I was saying – when I came to think the matter over on the hill yonder, said I to myself, A good dinner is a good thing I grant, and yet it will be but cold comfort to me a week after, to be able to say – to be sure I had a nice shoulder of mutton last Sunday for dinner, thanks to the good Gentleman! but then I am in debt – I *had* a rare dinner, that's certain, but the pleasure of that has long been over, and the debt still remains. I have spent the crown,[5] and now if my poor wife should be taken in one of those fits again, die she must, unless God work a miracle to prevent it, for I can get no help for her. This thought settled all; and I set off directly and paid the crown to the Doctor with as much cheerfulness as I should have felt on sitting down to the fattest shoulder of mutton that ever was roasted. And if I was contented at the time, think how much more happy I have been at the remembrance! O, sir, there are no pleasures worth the name but such as bring no plague or penitence after them."

Mr. Johnson was satisfied with the Shepherd's reasons; and agreed, that though a good dinner was not to be despised, yet it was not worthy to be compared with *a contented Mind, which,* as the Bible truly says, *is a continual feast.*[6] "But come," said the good Gentleman, "what have we got in this brown mug?" – "As good water," said the Shepherd, "as any in the king's dominions. I have heard of countries beyond sea in which there is no wholesome water; nay, I have been myself in a great town not far off, where they are obliged to buy all the water they get, while a good Providence sends to my very door a spring as clear and fine as Jacob's well. When I am tempted to repine that I have often no other drink, I call to mind, that it was nothing better than a cup of cold water which the woman of Samaria drew for the greatest guest that ever visited this world."[7]

"Very well," replied Mr. Johnson; "but as your honesty has made you prefer a poor meal to being in debt, I will at least send and get something for you to drink. I saw a little public house just by the church, as I came along. Let that little rosy-faced fellow fetch a mug of beer."

So saying, he looked full at the Boy, who did not offer to stir; but cast an eye at his father to know what he was to do. "Sir," said the Shepherd, "I hope we shall not appear ungrateful, if we seem to refuse your favour: my little boy would, I am sure, fly to serve you on any other occasion. But, good sir, it is Sunday, and should any of my family be seen at a Public-house on a Sabbath-day, it would be a much greater grief to me than to drink water all my life. I am often talking against these doings to others, and if I should say one thing and do another, you can't think what an advantage it would give many of my neighbours over me, who would be glad enough to report that they had caught the Shepherd's Son at the Alehouse without explaining how it happened. Christians, you know, Sir, must be doubly watchful, or they will not only bring disgrace on themselves, but what is much worse, on that holy name by which they are called."

"Are you not a little too cautious, my honest friend?" said Mr. Johnson. – "I humbly ask your pardon, Sir," replied the Shepherd, "if I think that is impossible. In my poor notion I no more understand how a man can be too cautious, than how he can be too strong, or too healthy."

"You are right, indeed," said Mr. Johnson, "as a general principle, but this struck me as a very small thing." – "Sir," said the Shepherd, "I am afraid you will think me very bold, but you encourage me to speak out." – "'Tis what I wish," said the gentleman. – "Then sir," resumed the Shepherd, "I doubt if, where there is a temptation to do wrong, any thing can be called small; that is, in short, if there is any such thing as a small wilful sin. A poor man like me is seldom called out to do great things, so that it is not by a few great deeds his character can be judged by his neighbours, but by the little round of daily customs he allows himself in."[8]

While they were thus talking, the children who had stood very quietly behind, and had not stirred a foot, now began to scamper about all at once, and in a moment ran to the window-seat to pick up their little old hats. Mr. Johnson looked surprised at this disturbance; the Shepherd asked his pardon, telling him it was the sound of the Church Bell which had been the cause of their rudeness: for their Mother had brought them up with such a fear of being too late for Church, that it was but who could catch the first stroke of the bell, and be first ready. He had always taught them to think that nothing was more indecent than to get into Church after it was begun; for as the service opened with an exhortation to repentance, and a confession of sin, it looked very presumptuous not to be ready to join in it; it looked as if people did not feel themselves to be sinners. And though such as lived at a great distance might plead difference of clocks[9] as an excuse, yet those who lived within the sound of the bell could pretend neither ignorance nor mistake.

Mary and her children set forward. Mr. Johnson and the Shepherd followed, taking care to talk the whole way on such subjects as might fit them for the solemn duties of the place to which they were going. "I have often been sorry to observe," said Mr. Johnson, "that many who are reckoned decent, good kind of people, and who would on no account neglect going to church, yet seem to care but little in what frame or temper of mind they go thither. They will talk of their worldly concerns till they get within the door, and then take them up again the very minute the sermon is over, which makes me ready to fear they lay too much stress on the mere form of going to a place of worship. Now, for my part, I always find that it requires a little time to bring my mind into a state fit to do any *common* business well, much more this great and most necessary business of all." – "Yes, Sir," replied the Shepherd; "and then I think too how busy I should be in preparing my mind, if I was going into the presence of a great gentleman, or a Lord, or the King; and shall the King of Kings be treated with less respect? Besides, one likes to see people feel as if going to Church was a thing of choice and pleasure, as well as a duty, and that they were as desirous not to be the last here, as they would be if they were going to a feast or a fair."

After service, Mr. Jenkins the clergyman, who was well acquainted with the character of Mr. Johnson, and had a great respect for him, accosted him with much civility; expressing his concern that he could not enjoy just now so much of his conversation as he wished, as he was obliged to visit a sick person at a distance, but hoped to have a little talk with him before he left the Village. As they walked along together, Mr. Johnson made such enquiries about the Shepherd, as served to confirm him in the high opinion he entertained of his piety, good-sense, industry, and self-denial. They parted, the Clergyman promising to call in at the Cottage in his way home.

The Shepherd, who took it for granted that Mr. Johnson was gone to the Parsonage, walked home with his wife and children, and was beginning in his usual way to catechise[10] and instruct his family, when Mr. Johnson came in, and insisted that the Shepherd should go on with his instructions, just as if he were not there. This Gentleman, who was very desirous of being useful to his own Servants and workmen in the way of religious instruction, was sometimes sorry to find that though he took a good deal of pains, they did not now and then quite understand him for though his meaning was very good, his language was not always very plain; and though the *things* he said were not hard to be understood, yet the *words* were, especially to such as were very ignorant. And he now began to find out that if people were ever so wise and good, yet if they had not a simple, agreeable, and familiar way of expressing themselves, some of their plain hearers would not be much the better for them. For this reason he was not above listening to the plain, humble way in which this honest man taught his family; for though he knew that he himself had many advantages over the Shepherd, had more learning, and could teach him many things, yet he was not too proud to learn even of so poor a Man, in any point where he thought the shepherd might have the advantage of him.

This Gentleman was much pleased with the knowledge and piety which he discovered in the answers of the children, and desired the Shepherd to tell him how he contrived to keep up a sense of divine things in his own mind, and in that of his family, with so little leisure and so little reading. "O as to that, Sir," said the Shepherd, "we do not read much, except in one book, to be sure: but by hearty prayer for God's blessing on the use of that book, what little knowledge is needful seems to come of course, as it were. And my chief study has been to bring the fruits of the Sunday reading into the week's business, and to keep up the same sense of GOD in the heart, when the Bible is in the cupboard as when it is in the hand. In short, to apply what I read in the book to what I meet with in the Field."

"I don't quite understand you," said Mr. Johnson. "Sir," replied the Shepherd, "I have but a poor gift at conveying these things to others, though I have much comfort from them in my own mind; but I am sure that the most ignorant and hard working people, who are in earnest about their salvation, may help to keep up devout thoughts and good affections during the week, though they have hardly any time to look at a book. And it will help them to keep out bad thoughts too, which is no small matter. But then they must know the Bible; they must have read the word of God; that is a kind of stock in trade for a Christian to set up with; and it is this which makes me so diligent in teaching it to my children; and even in storing their memories with Psalms and Chapters. This is a great help to a poor hard-working Man, who will hardly meet with any thing in them but what he may turn to some good account. If one lives in the fear and the love of GOD, almost every thing one sees abroad will teach one to adore his power and goodness, and bring to mind some texts of Scripture, which shall fill the heart with thankfulness, and the mouth with praise. When I look upwards, *the Heavens declare the glory of God;* and shall I be silent and ungrateful? if I look round, and see the vallies standing thick with Corn, how can I help blessing that Power who *giveth me all things richly to enjoy?* I may learn gratitude from the beasts of the field; for the *Ox knoweth his owner, and the Ass his Master's Crib,* and shall a Christian not know, shall a Christian not consider, what great things GOD has done for him? I, who am a shepherd, endeavour to full my soul with a constant remembrance of that good Shepherd, who *feedeth me in green pastures, and maketh me to lie down beside the still waters, and whose rod and staff comfort me.*[11]

"You are happy," said Mr. Johnson, "in this retired life, by which you escape the corruptions of the world." – "Sir," said the Shepherd, "I do not escape the corruptions of my own evil nature. Even there on that wild solitary hill, I can find out that my heart is prone to evil thoughts. I suppose, sir, that different states have different temptations. You great folks that live in the world, perhaps, are exposed to some, of which such a poor man as I am know nothing. But to one who leads a lonely life like me, evil thoughts are a chief besetting Sin; and I can no more withstand these without the grace of God, than a rich Gentleman can withstand the snares of evil company, without the same grace. And I feel that I stand in need of God's help continually; and if he should give me up to my own evil heart I should be lost."

Mr. Johnson approved of the Shepherd's sincerity; for he had always observed, that where there was no humility, and no watchfulness against Sin, there was no religion, and he said that the Man who did not feel himself to be a sinner in his opinion, could not be a Christian.

Just as they were in this part of their discourse, Mr. Jenkins, the Clergyman, came in. After the usual salutations, he said, "Well, Shepherd, I wish you joy: I know you will be sorry to gain any advantage by the death of a neighbour; but old Wilson, my Clerk, was so infirm, and I trust so well prepared, that there is no reason to be sorry for his death. I have been to pray by him, but he died while I staied. I have always intended you should succeed to his place: 'tis no great matter, but every little is something."

"No great matter, Sir!" cried the Shepherd; "indeed, it is a great thing to me: it will more than pay my rent. Blessed be God for all his goodness;" Mary said nothing, but lifted up her eyes full of tears in silent gratitude.

"I am glad of this little circumstance," said Mr. Jenkins, "not only for your sake, but for the sake of the office itself. I so heartily reverence every religious institution, that I would never have even the *Amen* added to the excellent prayers of our Church by vain or profane lips; and if it depended on me, there should be no such thing in the land as an idle, drunken, or irreligious Parish Clerk.[12] Sorry I am to say, that this matter is not always sufficiently attended to, and that I know some of a very indifferent character."

Mr. Johnson now enquired of the Clergyman whether there were many children in the Parish. "More than you would expect," replied he, "from the seeming smallness of it, but there are some little Hamlets which you do not see." – "I think," returned Mr. Johnson, "I recollect that in the conversation I had with the Shepherd on the hill yonder, he told me you had no Sunday School." – "I am sorry to say we have none," said the Minister: "I do what I can to remedy this misfortune by public catechising; but having two or three Churches to serve, I cannot give so much time as I wish to private instruction; and having a large family of my own, and no assistance from others, I have never been able to establish a School."

"There is an excellent institution in London," said Mr. Johnson, "called the Sunday School Society,[13] which kindly gives books and other helps, on the application of such pious Ministers as stand in need of their aid, and which I am sure would have assisted you, but I think we shall be able to do something ourselves. – "Shepherd," continued he, "if I was a King, and had it in my power to make you a rich and a great Man with a word speaking, I would not do it. Those who are raised by some sudden stroke, much above the station in which divine Providence had placed them, seldom turn out very good or very happy. I have never had any great things in my power, but as far as I have been able, I have been always glad to assist the worthy. I have, however, never attempted or desired to set any poor Man much above his natural condition, but it is a pleasure to me to lend him such assistance as may make that condition more easy to himself, and put him in a way which shall call him to the performance of more duties than perhaps he could have performed without my help, and of performing them in a better manner. What rent do you pay for this cottage?"

"Fifty Shillings a Year, Sir."[14]

"It is in a sad tattered condition, is there not a better to be had in the Village?"

"That in which the poor Clerk lived," said the Clergyman, "is not only more tight and whole, but has two decent chambers, and a very large light kitchen." – That will be very convenient," replied Mr. Johnson, "pray what is the rent?" – "I think," said the shepherd, "poor neighbour Wilson gave somewhat about four pounds a year, or it might be guineas." – "Very well," said Mr. Johnson; "and what will the clerk's place be worth, think you?" – "About three pounds," was the answer.

"Now," continued Mr. Johnson, "my plan is, that the shepherd should take that house immediately; for as the poor Man is dead, there will be no need of waiting till quarter day, if I make up the difference." – "True, sir," said Mr. Jenkins; "and I am sure my wife's father, whom I expect to-morrow, will willingly assist a little towards buying some of the Clerk's old goods. And the sooner they remove the better, for poor Mary caught that bad rheumatism by sleeping under a leaky thatch." The Shepherd was too much moved to speak, and Mary could hardly sob out, "Oh, Sir! you are too good, indeed this house will do very well." – "It may do very well for you and your children, Mary," said Mr. Johnson, gravely; "but it will not do for a School: the kitchen is neither large nor light enough. Shepherd," continued he, "with your good Minister's leave, and kind assistance, I propose to set up in this parish a Sunday School, and to make you the Master. It will not at all interfere with your weekly calling; and it is the only lawful way in which you could turn the Sabbath into a day of some little profit to your family, by doing, as I hope, a great deal of good to the Souls of others. The rest of the week you will work as usual. The difference of rent between this house and the Clerk's I shall pay myself; for to put you into a better house at your own expense, would be no great act of kindness. – As for honest Mary, who is not fit for hard labour, or any out-of door work, I propose to endow a small weekly school, of which she shall be the mistress, and employ her notable turn to good account, by teaching ten or a dozen girls to knit, sew, spin, card, or any other useful way of getting their bread; for all this I shall only pay her the usual price, for I am not going to make you rich, but useful."[15]

"Not rich, Sir!" cried the Shepherd: "How can I ever be thankful enough for such blessings? And will my poor Mary have a dry thatch over her head? and shall I be able to send for the doctor when I am like to lose her? Indeed, my cup runs over with blessings; I hope God will give me humility." – Here he and Mary looked at each other and burst into tears. The Gentlemen saw their distress, and kindly walked out upon the little green before the door, that these honest people might give vent to their feelings. As soon as they were alone, they crept into one corner of the room where they thought they could not be seen, and fell on their knees, devoutly blessing and praising GOD for his mercies. Never were heartier prayers presented than this grateful couple offered up for their benefactors. The warmth of their gratitude could only be equalled by the earnestness with which they besought the blessing of GOD on the work in which they were going to engage.

The two Gentlemen now left this happy family, and walked to the Parsonage, where the evening was spent in a manner very edifying to Mr. Johnson, who the next day took all proper measures for putting the Shepherd in immediate possession of his now comfortable habitation. Mr. Jenkins's father-in-law, the worthy Gentleman who gave the Shepherd's Wife the blankets, in the first part of this history, arrived at the parsonage before Mr. Johnson left it, and assisted in fitting up the Clerk's Cottage.

Mr. Johnson took his leave, promising to call on the worthy minister and his new Clerk once a year, in his Summer's journey over the Plain, as long as it should please God to spare his life. We hope he will never fail to give us an account of those visits which we shall be glad to lay before our before our readers, if they should contain instruction or amusement.[16]

Z

CHEAP REPOSITORY.

BETTY BROWN,

THE

St. GILES's ORANGE GIRL:

WITH

Some Account of Mrs. SPONGE, the Money-lender.

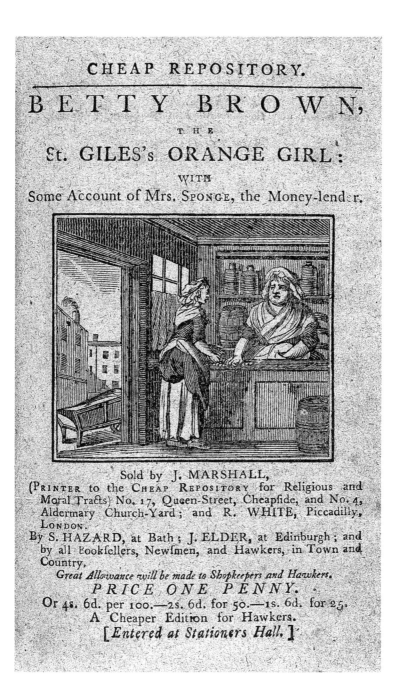

Sold by J. MARSHALL,
(PRINTER to the CHEAP REPOSITORY for Religious and
Moral Tracts) No. 17, Queen-Street, Cheapside, and No. 4,
Aldermary Church-Yard; and R. WHITE, Piccadilly,
LONDON.

By S. HAZARD, at Bath; J. ELDER, at Edinburgh; and
by all Bookfellers, Newfmen, and Hawkers, in Town and
Country.

Great Allowance will be made to Shopkeepers and Hawkers.

PRICE ONE PENNY.

Or 4s. 6d. per 100.—2s. 6d. for 50.—1s. 6d. for 25.
A Cheaper Edition for Hawkers.

[*Entered at Stationers Hall.*]

BETTY BROWN, THE ST. GILES'S ORANGE GIRL:

with Some Account of Mrs. Sponge,
the Money Lender.

BETTY BROWN, the Orange Girl, was born nobody knows where, and bred nobody knows how. No girl in all the streets of London could drive a barrow more nimbly, avoid pushing against passengers more dextrously, or cry her "Fine China Oranges" in a shriller voice. But then she could neither sew, nor spin, nor knit, nor wash, nor iron, nor read, nor spell. Betty had not been always in so good a situation as that in which we now describe her. She came into the world before so many good gentlemen and ladies began to concern themselves so kindly that the poor might have a little learning. There was no charitable Society then, as there is now, to pick up poor friendless children in the streets and put them into a good house, and give them meat, and drink, and lodging, and learning, and teach them to get their bread in an honest way, into the bargain. Whereas, this now is often the case in London; blessed be God for all his mercies.[1]

The longest thing that Betty can remember is, that she used to crawl up out of a night cellar, stroll about the streets, and pick cinders from the scavengers' carts. Among the ashes she sometimes found some ragged gauze and dirty ribbons; with these she used to dizen herself out, and join the merry bands on the first of May. This was not however quite fair, as she did not lawfully belong either to the female dancers who foot it gaily round the garland, or to the sooty tribe, who, on this happy holiday, forget their whole year's toil; she often, however, got a few scraps, by appearing to belong to both parties.[2]

Betty was not an idle girl; she always put herself in the way of doing something. She would run of errands for the footmen, or sweep the door for the maid of any house where she was known: she would run and fetch some porter, and never was once known either to sip a drop or steal the pot. Her quickness and fidelity in doing little jobs got her into favour with a lazy cook-maid, who was too apt to give away her master's cold meat and beer, not to those who were most in want, but to those who waited upon her, and did the little things for her which she ought to have done herself.

The cook, who found Betty a dextrous girl, soon employed her to sell ends of candles, pieces of meat and cheese, and lumps of butter, or any thing else she could crib from the house. These were all carried to her friend Mrs. Sponge, who kept a little shop and a kind of eating-house for poor working people, not far from the Seven Dials.[3] She also bought as well as sold many kinds of second hand things, and was not scrupulous to know whether what she bought was honestly come by, provided she could get it for a sixth part of what it was worth. But if the owner presumed to ask for it's real value, she had sudden qualms of conscience, suspected the things were stolen, and gave herself airs of honesty, which often took in poor silly people, and gave her a sort of half reputation among the needy and the ignorant, whose friend she pretended to be.

To this artful woman Betty carried the cook's pilferings, and as Mrs. Sponge would give no great price for these in money, the cook was willing to receive payment for her eatables in Mrs. Sponge's drinkables; for she dealt in all kinds of spirits. I shall only just remark here, that one receiver, like Mrs. Sponge, makes many pilferers, who are tempted to these petty thieveries, by knowing how easy it is to dispose of them at such iniquitous houses.

Betty was faithful to both her employers, which is extraordinary, considering the greatness of the temptation, and her utter ignorance of good and evil. One day, she ventured to ask Mrs. Sponge if she could not assist her to get into a more settled way of life. She told her, that when she rose in the morning she never knew where she should lie at night, nor was she ever sure of a meal before hand. Mrs. Sponge asked her what she thought herself fit for. Betty, with fear and trembling, said, there was one trade for which she thought herself qualified, but she had not the ambition to look so high. It was far above her humble views. This was, to have a barrow, and sell fruit, as several other of Mrs. Sponge's customers did, whom she had often looked at with envy.

Mrs. Sponge was an artful woman. Bad as she was, she was always aiming at something of a character; this was a great help to her trade. While she watched keenly to make every thing turn to her own profit, she had a false fawning way of seeming to do all she did out of pity and kindness to the distressed; and she seldom committed an extortion, but she tried to make the person she cheated believe themselves highly obliged to her kindness. By thus pretending to be their friend she gained their confidence, and she grew rich herself while they thought she was only shewing favour to them. Various were the arts she had of getting rich. The money she got by grinding the poor, she spent in the most luxurious living; and, while she would haggle with her hungry customers for a farthing, she would spend pounds on the most costly delicacies for herself.

Mrs. Sponge, laying aside that haughty look and voice, well known to such as had the misfortune to be in her debt, put on the hypocritical smile and soft tone which she always assumed, when she meant to *take in* her dependants. "Betty," said she, "I am resolved to stand your friend. These are sad times to be sure. Money is money now. Yet I am resolved to put you into a handsome way of living. You shall have a barrow, and well furnished, too." Betty could not have felt more joy or gratitude, if she had been told that she should have a coach. "O, madam" said Betty, "it is impossible. I have not a penny in the world towards helping me to set up." "I will take care of that," said Mrs. Sponge; "only you must do as I bid you. You must pay me interest for my money. And you will of course be glad also to pay so much every night for a nice hot supper which I get ready, quite out of kindness, for a number of poor working people. This will be a great comfort for such a friendless girl as you, for my victuals and drink are the best; and my company the merriest of any house in all St. Giles's." Betty thought all this only so many more favours, and, courtesying to the ground, said, "to be sure, Ma'am, and thank you a thousand times into the bargain."[4]

Mrs. Sponge knew what she was about. Betty was a lively girl, who had a knack at learning any thing; and so well looking through all her dirt and rags, that there was little doubt she would get custom. A barrow was soon provided, and five shillings put into Betty's hands. Mrs. Sponge kindly condescended to go to shew her how to buy the fruit, for it was a rule with this prudent gentlewoman, and one from which she never departed, that no one should cheat but herself.

Betty had never possessed such a sum before. She grudged to lay it out all at once, and was ready to fancy she could live upon the capital. The crown, however, was laid out to the best advantage. Betty was carefully taught in what manner to cry her Oranges; and received many useful lessons how to get off the bad with the good, and the stale with the fresh. Mrs. Sponge also lent her a few bad sixpences, for which she ordered her to bring home good ones at night. – Betty stared. Mrs. Sponge said, "Betty, those who would get money, must not be too nice about trifles. Keep one of these sixpences in your hand, and if an ignorant young customer gives you a good sixpence do you immediately slip it into your other hand,

and give him the bad one, declaring, that it is the very one you have just received, and that you have not another sixpence in the world. You must also learn how to treat different sorts of customers. To some you may put off with safety goods which would be quite unsaleable to others. Never offer bad fruit, Betty, to those who know better; never waste the good on those who may be put off with worse; put good Oranges at top, and the mouldy ones under."[5]

Poor Betty had not a nice conscience, for she had never learnt that grand, but simple rule of all moral obligation, "Never do that to another which you would not have another do to you". She set off with her barrow as proud and as happy as if she had been set up in the finest shop in Covent Garden. Betty had a sort of natural good-nature, which made her unwilling to impose, but she had no principle which told her it was a sin.[6] She had such good success, that, when night came she had not an Orange left. With a light heart, she drove her empty barrow to Mrs. Sponge's door. She went in with a merry face, and threw down on the Counter every farthing she had taken. "Betty," said Mrs. Sponge, "I have a right to it all, as it was got by my money. But I am too generous to take it. I will therefore only take sixpence for this day's use of my five shillings. This is a most reasonable interest, and I will lend you the same sum to trade with to-morrow, and so on; you only paying me sixpence for the use of it every night, which will be a great bargain to you. You must also pay me my price every night for your supper, and you shall have an excellent lodging above stairs; so you see every thing will now be provided for you in a genteel manner, through my generosity."[7]

Poor Betty's gratitude blinded her so completely that she forgot to calculate the vast proportion which this generous benefactress was to receive out of her little gains. She thought herself a happy creature, and went in to supper with a number of others of her own class. For this supper, and for more porter and gin than she ought to have drank, Betty was forced to pay so high, that it eat up all the profits of the day, which, added to the daily interest, made Mrs. Sponge a rich return for her five shillings.

Betty was reminded again of the gentility of her new situation, as she crept up to bed in one of Mrs. Sponge's garrets five stories high. This loft, to be sure, was small, and had no window, but what it wanted in light was made up in company, as it had three beds, and thrice as many lodgers. Those gentry had one night, in a drunken frolic, broke down the door, which happily had never been replaced; for, since that time, the lodgers had died much seldomer of infectious distempers.[8] For this lodging Betty paid twice as much to her good friend as she would have done to a stranger.

Thus she continued, with great industry and a thriving trade, as poor as on the first day, and not a bit nearer to saving money enough to buy her even a pair of shoes, though her feet were nearly on the ground.

One day, as Betty was driving her barrow through a street near Holborn, a lady from a window called out to her that she wanted some Oranges. While the servants went to fetch a plate, the lady entered into some talk with Betty, having been struck with her honest countenance and civil manner. She questioned her as to her way of life, and the profits of her trade – and Betty, who had never been so kindly treated before by so genteel a person, was very communicative. She told her little history as far as she knew it, and dwelt much on the generosity of Mrs. Sponge, in keeping her in her house, and trusting her with so large a capital as five shillings. At first it sounded like a very good-natured thing but the lady, whose husband was one of the Justices of the new Police,[9] happened to know more of Mrs. Sponge than was good, which led her to inquire still further. Betty owned, that to be sure it was not all clear profit, for that besides that the high price of the supper and bed ran away with all she got, she paid sixpence a day for the use of the five shillings. "And how long have you done this?" said the lady. "About a year, Madam."

The lady's eyes were at once opened. "My poor girl," said she, "do you know that you have already paid for that single five shillings the enormous sum of 7*l*. 10*s*.? I believe it is the most profitable five shillings Mrs. Sponge ever laid out." "O, no, Madam," said the girl, "that good gentlewoman does the same kindness to ten or twelve other poor friendless creatures like me." "Does she so?" said the lady; "then I never heard of a better trade than this woman carries on, under the mask of charity, at the expence of her poor deluded fellow-creatures."

"But, Madam," said Betty, who did not comprehend this lady's arithmetic, "what can I do? I now contrive to pick up a morsel of bread without begging or stealing. Mrs. Sponge has been very good to me; and I don't see how I can help myself."

"I will tell you," said the lady. "If you will follow my advice, you may not only maintain yourself honestly, but independently. Only oblige yourself to live hard for a little time, till you have saved five shillings out of your own earnings. Give up that expensive supper at night, drink only one pint of porter, and no gin at all. As soon as you have scraped together the five shillings, carry it back to your false friend; and if you are industrious, you will, at the end of the year, have saved 7*l*. 10*s*. If you can make a shift to live now, when you have this heavy interest to pay, judge how things will mend when your capital becomes your own.[10] You will put some cloaths on your back, and by leaving the use of spirits, and the company in which you drink them, your health, your morals, and your condition will mend."

The lady did not talk thus to save her money. She would gladly have given the girl the five shillings; but she thought it was beginning at the wrong end. She wanted to try her. Besides, she knew there was more pleasure as well as honour in possessing five shillings of one's own saving than of another's giving. Betty promised to obey. She owned she had got no good by the company or the liquor at Mrs. Sponge's. She promised that very night to begin saving the expence of the supper, and that she would not taste a drop of gin till she had the five shillings beforehand. The lady, who knew the power of good habits, was contented with this, thinking, that if the girl could abstain for a certain time, it would become easy to her.[11] In a very few weeks Betty had saved up the five shillings. She went to carry back this money with great gratitude to Mrs. Sponge. This kind friend began to abuse her most unmercifully. She called her many hard names not fit to repeat, for having forsaken the supper, by which she swore she got nothing at all; but as she had the charity to dress it for such beggarly wretches, she insisted they should pay for it, whether they eat it or not. She also brought in a heavy score for lodging, though Betty had paid for it every night, and had given notice of her intending to quit her. By all these false pretences, she got from her not only her own five shillings, but all the little capital with which Betty was going to set up for herself. All was not sufficient to answer her demands, she declared she would send her to prison; but while she went to call a Constable, Betty contrived to make off.

With a light pocket and a heavy heart, she went back to the lady; and with many tears told her sad story. The lady's husband, the Justice, condescended to listen to Betty's tale. He said Mrs. Sponge had long been upon his books as a receiver of stolen goods. Betty's evidence strengthened his bad opinion of her. "This petty system of usury," said the gentleman, "may be thought trifling, but it will no longer appear so, when you reflect, that if one of these female sharpers possesses a capital of seventy shillings, or 3*l*. 10*s*. with fourteen steady regular customers, she can realize a fixed income of 100 guineas a year. Add to this the influence such a loan gives her over these friendless creatures, by compelling them to eat at her house, or lodge, or buy liquors, or by taking their pawns, and you will see the extent of the evil. I pity these poor victims: You, Betty, shall point out some of them to me. I will endeavour to open their eyes on their own bad management. It is one of the greatest acts of kindness to the poor to mend their economy, and to give them right views of laying out their little money to advantage. These poor blinded creatures look no farther than to be able to pay this heavy interest every night, and to obtain the same loan on the same hard terms the next day. Thus are they kept in poverty and bondage all their lives; but I hope as many as hear of this will get on a better plan, and I shall be ready to help any who are willing to help themselves."[12] This worthy Magistrate went directly to Mrs. Sponge's with proper officers; and he soon got to the bottom of many iniquities. He not only made her refund poor Betty's money, but committed her to prison for receiving stolen goods, and various other offences, which may perhaps make the subject of another history.

Betty was now set up in trade to her heart's content. She had found the benefit of leaving off spirits, and she resolved to drink them no more. The first fruits of this resolution was, that in a fortnight she bought her a new pair of shoes, and as there was now no deductions for interest or for gin, her earnings became considerable. The lady made her a present of a gown and a hat, on the easy condition that she should go to church. She accepted the terms, at first rather as an act of obedience to the lady than from a sense of higher duty. But she soon began to go from a better motive. This constant attendance at church, joined to the instructions of the lady, opened a new world to Betty. She now heard for the first time that she was a sinner; that God had given a law which was holy, just, and good; that she had broken this law, had been a swearer, a sabbath-breaker, and had lived without God in the world. All this was sad news to Betty; she knew, indeed, that there were sinners, but she thought they were only to be found in the prisons, or at Botany Bay, or in those mournful carts which she had sometimes followed, with her barrow, with the unthinking crowd, to Tyburn.[13] She was deeply struck with the great truths revealed in the Scripture, which were quite new to her. She was desirous of improvement, and said, she would give up all the profits of her barrow, and go into the hardest service, rather than live in sin and ignorance.

"Betty," said the lady, "I am glad to see you so well disposed, and will do what I can for you. Your present way of life, to be sure, exposes you to much danger; but the trade is not unlawful in itself, and we may please God in any calling, provided it be not a dishonest one. In this great town there must be barrow women to sell fruit. Do you, then, instead of forsaking your business, set a good example to those in it, and shew them, that though a dangerous trade, it need not be a bad one. Till Providence points out some safer way of getting your bread, let your companions see, that it is possible to be good even in this. Your trade being carried on in the open street, and your fruit bought in an open shop, you are not so much obliged to keep sinful company as may be thought. Take a garret in an honest house, to which you may go home in safety at night. I will give you a bed and a few necessaries to furnish your room; and I will also give you a constant Sunday's dinner. A barrow woman, blessed be God and our good laws, is as much her own mistress on Sundays as a Duchess; and the Church and the Bible are as much open to her. You may soon learn all that such as you are expected to know. A barrow woman may pray as heartily morning and night, and serve God as acceptably all day, while she is carrying on her little trade, as if she had her whole time to spare.

To do this well, you must mind the following

RULES FOR RETAIL DEALERS:[14]

Resist every temptation to cheat.
Never impose bad goods on false pretences.
Never put off bad money for good.
Never use profane or uncivil language.
Never swear your goods cost so much, when you know it is false. By so doing you are guilty of two sins in one breath, a lie and an oath.

To break these rules, will be your chief temptation. God will mark how you behave under them, and will reward or punish you accordingly. These temptations will be as great to you as higher trials are to higher people; but you have the same God to look to for strength to resist them as they have. You must pray to him to give you this strength. You shall attend a Sunday School, where you will be taught these good things; and I will promote you as you shall be found to deserve."

Poor Betty here burst into tears of joy and gratitude, crying out, "What, shall such a poor friendless creature as I be treated so kindly and learn to read the word of God too? Oh, Madam, what a lucky chance brought me to your door" "Betty," said the lady, "what you have just said, shews the need you have of being better taught: there is no such thing as chance; and we offend God when we call that luck or chance which is brought about by his will and pleasure. None of the events of your life have happened by chance; but all have been under the direction of a good and kind Providence. He has permitted you to experience want and distress,[15] that you might acknowledge his hand in your present comfort and prosperity. Above all, you must bless his goodness in sending you to me, not only because I have been of use to you in your worldly affairs, but because he has enabled me to shew you the danger of your state from sin and ignorance, and to put you in a way to know his will and to keep his commandments."

How Betty, by industry and piety, rose in the world, till at length she came to keep that handsome Sausage-Shop near the Seven Dials, and was married to an honest Hackney-Coachman, may be told at some future time, in a Second Part.[16]

BLACK GILES the Poacher;

With some Account of a
Family who had rather live by their Wits than
their Work.

PART I.

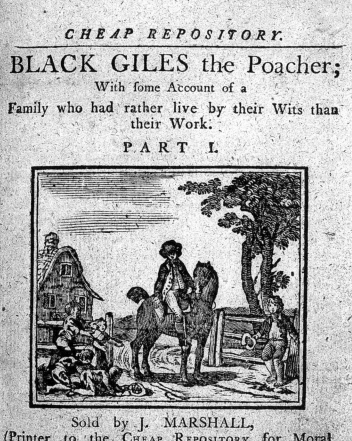

Sold by J. MARSHALL,
(Printer to the CHEAP REPOSITORY for Moral
and Religious Tracts) No. 17, Queen-Street,
Cheapside, and No. 4, Aldermary Church Yard;
and R. WHITE, Piccadilly, LONDON.
By S. HAZARD, at Bath, and by all Booksellers,
Newsmen, and Hawkers in Town and Country.
—Great Allowance will be made to Shopkeepers
and Hawkers.

PRICE ONE PENNY.

Or 4s. 6d. per 100.—2s. 6d. for 50.—1s. 6d. for 25.
A Cheaper Edition for Hawkers.

[*Entered at Stationers Hall.*]

BLACK GILES THE POACHER;

with Some Account of a Family who had rather live by their Wits than their Work.

PART I

POACHING GILES lived on the borders of one of those great moors in Somersetshire. Giles, to be sure, has been a sad fellow in his time; and it is none of his fault if his whole family do not end either at the gallows or at Botany Bay. He lives at that Mud Cottage with the broken windows, stuffed with dirty rags, just beyond the gate which divides the upper from the lower Moor. You may know the house at a good distance by the ragged tiles on the roof, and the loose stones which are ready to drop out from the chimney; though a short ladder, a hod of mortar, and half an hour's leisure time would have prevented all this, and made the little dwelling tight enough. But as Giles had never learnt any thing that was good, so he did not know the value of such useful sayings, as that *"a tile in time saves nine."*

Besides this, Giles fell into that common mistake, that a beggarly looking cottage, and filthy ragged children raised most compassion, and of course drew most charity. But as cunning as he was in other things, he was out in his reckoning here for it is neatness, housewifery, and a decent appearance, which draw the kindness of the rich and charitable, while they turn away disgusted from filth and laziness; not out of pride, but because they see that it is next to impossible to mend the condition of those who degrade themselves by dirt and sloth.

The common on which Giles's hovel stands is quite a deep marsh in a wet winter; but in summer it looks green and pretty enough. To be sure it would be rather convenient when one passes that way in a carriage if one of the children would run out and open the gate, as it would save the post boy from getting off, which is not very safe for the people within the chaise, but instead of any *one* of them running out as soon as they hear the wheels, which would be quite time enough, what does Giles do, but set all his ragged brats, with dirty faces, matted locks, and naked feet and legs, to lie all day upon a sand bank hard by the gate, waiting for the slender chance of what may be picked up from travellers. At the sound of a carriage, a whole covey of these little scare-crows start up, rush to the gate, and all at once thrust out their hats and aprons; and for fear this, together with the noise of their clamorous begging, should not sufficiently frighten the horses, they are very apt to let the gate slap full against you, before you are half way through, in their eager scuffle to snatch from each other the halfpence which you may have thrown out to them. I know two ladies who were one day very near being killed by these abominable tricks.

Thus five or six little idle creatures, who might be earning a trifle by knitting at home; who might be useful to the public by working in the field, and who might assist their families by learning to get their bread twenty honest ways, are suffered to lie about all day, in the hope of a few chance halfpence, which, after all, they are by no means sure of getting. Indeed, when the neighbouring gentlefolks found out that opening the gate was the family trade, they soon left off giving any thing. And I myself,[1] though I used to take out a penny ready to give, had there been only *one* to receive it, when I see a whole family established in so beggarly a trade, quietly put it back again in my pocket, and give nothing at all. And so few travellers pass that way, that some times, after the whole family have lost a day, their gains do not amount to two-pence.

As Giles had a far greater taste for living by his wits, than his work, he was at one time in hopes that his children might have got a pretty penny by tumbling[2] for the diversion of travellers, and he set about training them in that indecent practice; but, unluckily, the Moors being level, the carriages travelled faster than the children tumbled. He envied those parents who lived on the London road, over the Wiltshire Downs, which being very hilly, enables the tumbler to keep pace with the traveller, till he sometimes extorts from the light and unthinking a reward instead of a reproof. I beg leave, however, to put all gentlemen and ladies in mind that such tricks are a kind of apprenticeship to the trades of begging and thieving.

Giles, to be sure, as his children grew older, began to train them to such other employments as the idle habits they had learned at the gate very properly qualified them for. The right of Common,[3] which some of the poor Cottagers have in that part of the country, and which is doubtless a considerable advantage to many, was converted by Giles into the means of corrupting his whole family, for his children, as soon as they grew too big for the trade of begging at the gate, were promoted to the dignity of thieving on the Moor. Here he kept two or three asses, miserable beings, which, if they had the good fortune to escape an untimely death by starving, did not fail to meet with it by beating. Some of the biggest boys were sent out with these lean and galled animals to carry sand or coals about the neighbouring towns. Both sand and coals were often stolen before they got them to sell, or if not, they always took care to cheat in selling them. By long practice in this art they grew so dextrous, that they could give a pretty good guess how large a coal they could crib out of every bag before the buyer would be likely to miss it.

All their odd time was taken up under the pretence of watching their asses on the moor, or running after five or six half-starved geese: but the truth is, these boys were only watching for an opportunity to steal an odd goose of their neighbour's. They used also to pluck the quills or the down from these poor live creatures, or half milk a cow before the farmer's maid came with her pail. They all knew how to calculate to a minute what time to be down in a morning to let out their lank, hungry beasts, which they had turned over night into the farmer's field, to steal a little good pasture. They contrived to get there just time enough to escape being caught in replacing the stakes they had pulled out for the cattle to get over. For Giles was a prudent, long-headed fellow,[4] and, wherever he stole food for his colts, took care never to steal stakes from the hedges at the same time. He had sense enough to know that the gain did not make up for the danger; he knew that a loose faggot, pulled from a neighbour's pile of wood after the family were gone to bed, answered the end better, and was not half the trouble.

Among the many trades which Giles professed, he sometimes practised that of a rat catcher; but he was addicted to so many tricks that he never followed the same trade long. Whenever he was sent for to a farm-house, his custom was to kill a few of the old rats, always taking care to leave a little stock of young ones alive sufficient to keep up the breed; for, said he, "If I were to be such a fool as to clear a house or a barn at once, how would my trade be carried on?" And where any barn was overstocked, he used to borrow a few rats from thence just to people a neighbouring granary which had none; and he might have gone on till now, had he not unluckily been caught one evening emptying his cage of young rats under Parson Wilson's barn-door.[5]

This worthy Minister, Mr. Wilson, used to pity the neglected children of Giles as much as he blamed the wicked parents. He one day picked up Dick, who was far the best of Giles's bad boys. Dick was loitering about in a field behind the Parson's garden in search of a hen's nest, his mother having ordered him to bring home a few eggs that night by hook or by crook, as Giles was resolved to have some pancakes for supper, though he knew that eggs were a penny a-piece. Mr. Wilson had long been desirous of snatching some of this vagrant family from ruin, and his chief hopes were bent on Dick, as the least hackneyed in knavery. He had once given him a new pair of shoes, on his promising to go to school next Sunday; but no sooner had Rachel, the boy's mother, got the shoes into her clutches, than she pawned them for a bottle of gin,[6] and ordered the boy to keep out of the Parson's sight; and to be sure to play his marbles on Sundays for the future, at the other end of the parish and not near the church yard. Mr. Wilson, however, picked up the boy once more; for it was not his way to despair of any body. Dick was just going to take to his heels, as usual for fear the old story of the shoes should be brought forward; but finding he could not get off, what does he do but run into a little puddle of muddy water which lay between him and the Parson, that the sight of his naked feet might not bring on the dreaded subject. Now it happened that Mr. Wilson was planting a little field of beans, so he thought this a good opportunity to employ Dick; and he told him he had got some pretty easy work for him. Dick did as he was bid: he willingly went to work, and readily began to plant his beans with despatch and regularity, according to the directions given him.

While the boy was busily at work by himself, Giles happened to come by, having been skulking round the back way to look over the Parson's garden wall, to see if there was any thing worth climbing over for, on the ensuing night. He spied Dick, and began to scold him for working for the stingy old Parson; for Giles had a natural antipathy to whatever belonged to the Church.[7] "What has he promised thee a day?" said he, "little enough I dare say." "He is not to pay me by the day," said Dick; "but says he will give me so much when I have planted this peck, and so much for the next." "Oh, oh! that alters the case," said Giles. "One may, indeed, get a trifle by this sort of work.[8] Come, give me a handful of the beans: I will teach thee how to plant when thou art paid for planting by the peck. All we have to do in that case is to dispatch the work as fast as we can, and get rid of the beans with all speed; and as to the seed coming up or not, that is no business of ours; we are paid for planting, not for growing. At the rate thou goest on thou would'st not get six-pence to-night. Come along, bury away." So saying, he took his hatful of the seed, and where Dick had been ordered to set one bean, Giles buried a dozen, so the beans were soon out. But though the peck was emptied, the ground was unplanted. But cunning Giles knew this could not be found out till the time when the beans might be expected to come up; "and then Dick," said he, "the snails and the mice may go shares in the blame; or we can lay the fault on the rooks or the blackbirds." So saying, he sent the boy into the Parsonage to receive his pay, taking care to secure about a quarter of the peck of beans for his own colt; he put both bag and beans into his own pocket to carry home, bidding Dick tell Mr. Wilson that he had planted the beans and lost the bag.

In the mean time Giles's other boys were busy in emptying the ponds and trout-streams in the neighbouring manor. They would steal away the carp and tench when they were no bigger than gudgeons. By this untimely depredation they plundered the owner of his property, without enriching themselves. But the pleasure of mischief was reward enough. These, and a hundred other little thieveries they committed with such dexterity that old Tim Crib, whose son was transported last assizes for sheep stealing, used to be often reproaching his boys, that Giles's sons were worth a hundred of such blockheads as he had; for scarce a night past but Giles had some little comfortable thing for supper which his boys had pilfered in the day, while *his* undutiful dogs never stole any thing worth having. Giles, in the mean time, was busy in his way, but as busy as he was in laying nets, starting coveys, and training dogs, he always took care that his depredations should not be confined merely to game.

Giles's boys had never seen the inside of a church since they were christened, and the father thought he knew his own interest better than to force them to it; for church-time was the season of their harvest.[9] Then the hens' nests were searched, a stray duck was clapped under the smock frock, the tools which might have been left by chance in a farm-yard were picked up, and all the neighbouring pigeon-houses were thinned, so that Giles used to boast to Rachel his wife, that Sunday was to them the most profitable day in the week. With her it was certainly the most laborious day, as she always did her washing and ironing on the Sunday morning, it being, as she said, the only leisure day she had, for on the other days she went about the country telling fortunes, and selling dream books, and wicked songs.[10] Neither her husband's nor her children's cloaths were ever mended, and if Sunday, her idle day, had not come about once in every week, it is likely they would never have been washed neither. You might, however, see her as you were going to church smoothing her own rags on her best red cloak, which she always used for her ironing-cloth on Sundays, for her cloak when she travelled, and for her blanket at night; such a wretched manager was Rachel! Among her other articles of trade, one was to make and sell peppermint and other distilled waters.[11] These she had the cheap art of making without trouble, and without expence, for she made them without herbs and without a still. Her way was, to fill so many quart bottles with plain water, putting a spoonful of mint water in the mouth of each; these she corked down with rosin, carrying to each customer a phial of real distilled water to taste by way of sample. This was so good that her bottles were commonly bought up without being opened; but if any suspicion arose, and she was forced to uncork a bottle, by the few drops of distilled water lying at top, she even then escaped detection, and took care to get out of reach before the bottle was opened a second time. She was too prudent ever to go twice to the same house.

THE UPRIGHT MAGISTRATE[12]

There is hardly any petty mischief that is not connected with the life of a poacher. Mr. Wilson was aware of this, he was not only a pious clergyman, but an upright justice. He used to say that people who were truly conscientious, must be so in small things as well as in great ones, or they would destroy the effect of their own precepts, and their example would not be of general use. For this reason he never would accept of a hare or a partridge from any unqualified[13] person in his parish. He did not content himself with shuffling the thing off by asking no questions, and pretending to take it for granted in a general way that the game was fairly come at; but he used to say that by receiving the booty he connived at a crime; made himself a sharer in it, and if he gave a present to the man who brought it, he even tempted him to repeat the fault.

One day poor Jack Weston, an honest fellow in the neighbourhood, whom Mr. Wilson had kindly visited and relieved in a long sickness, from which he has but just recovered, was brought before him as he was sitting on the Justice's bench; Jack was accused of having knocked down a hare, and of all the birds in the air, who should the informer be but Black Giles the poacher? Mr. Wilson was grieved at the charge, he had a great regard for Jack, but he had still a greater regard for the law. The poor fellow pleaded guilty. He did not deny the fact, but said he did not consider it a crime, he did not think game was private property, and he owned he had a strong temptation for doing what he had done, which he hoped would plead in his excuse. The Justice desired to know what this temptation was. "Sir," said the poor fellow, "you know I was given over this spring in a bad fever. I had no friend in the world but you, Sir. Under God you saved my life by your charitable relief; and I trust also you may have helped to save my soul by your prayers and your good advice. I know I can never make you amends for all your goodness, but I thought it would be some comfort to my full heart if I could but once give you some little token of my gratitude. So I had trained a pair of nice turtle doves for Madam Wilson, but they were stolen from me, Sir, and I do suspect Black Giles stole them. Yesterday morning, Sir, as I was crawling out to my work, for I am still but very weak, a fine hare ran across my path. I did not stay to consider whether it was wrong to kill a hare, but I felt it was right to shew my gratitude; so, Sir, without a moment's thought I did knock down the hare, which I was going to carry to your Worship, because I knew Madam was fond of hare. I am truly sorry for my fault, and will submit to whatever punishment your Worship may please to inflict."

Mr. Wilson was much moved with this honest confession, and touched with the poor fellow's gratitude. What added to the effect of the story was the weak condition and pale sickly looks of the offender. But this worthy Justice never suffered his feelings to bias his integrity; he knew that he did not sit on that bench to indulge pity, but to administer justice. And while he was sorry for the offender, he would not justify the offence. "John," said he, "I am surprised that you could for a moment forget that I never accept any gift which causes the giver to break a law. On Sunday I teach you from the pulpit the laws of God, whose minister I am. At present I fill the chair of the magistrate, to enforce and execute the laws of the land. Between those and the others there is more connexion than you are aware. I thank you, John, for your affection to me, and I admire your gratitude; but I must not allow either affection or gratitude to be brought as a plea for a wrong action. It is not your business nor mine, John, to settle whether the game laws are good or bad. Till they are repealed we must obey them.[14] Many, I doubt not, break these laws through ignorance, and many, I am certain, who would not dare to steal a goose or a turkey, make no scruple of knocking down a hare or a partridge. You will hereafter think yourself happy that this your first attempt has proved unsuccessful, as I trust you are too honest a fellow ever to intend to turn poacher. With poaching, much moral evil is connected; a habit of nightly depredation; a custom of prowling in the dark for prey, produces in time a disrelish for honest labour. He whose first offence was committed without much thought or evil intention, if he happen to succeed a few times in carrying off his booty undiscovered, grows bolder and bolder; and when he fancies there is no shame attending it, he very soon gets to persuade himself that there is also no sin. While some people pretend a scruple about stealing a sheep, they partly live by plundering of warrens.[15] But remember that the warrener pays a high rent, and that therefore his rabbits are as much his property as his sheep. Do not then deceive yourselves with these false distinctions. All property is sacred,[16] and as the laws of the land are intended to fence in that property, he who brings up his children to break down any of these fences, brings them up to certain sin and ruin. He who begins with robbing orchards, rabbit warrens, and fish-ponds, will probably end with horse-stealing or highway robbery. Poaching is a regular apprenticeship to bolder crimes. He whom I may commit as a boy to sit in the stocks for killing a partridge, may be likely to end at the gallows for killing a man.

"Observe, you who now hear me, the strictness and impartiality of justice. I know Giles to be a worthless fellow, yet it is my duty to take his information; I know Jack Weston to be an honest youth, yet I must be obliged to make him pay the penalty. Giles is a bad man, but he can prove this fact; Jack is a worthy lad, but he has committed this fault. I am sorry for you, Jack; but do not let it grieve you that Giles has played worse tricks a hundred times, and yet got off, while you were detected in the very first offence; for that would be grieving because you are not so great a rogue as Giles. At this moment you think your good luck is very unequal; but all this will one day turn out in your favour. Giles is not the more a favourite of heaven because he has hitherto escaped Botany Bay or the Hulks;[17] nor is it any mark of God's displeasure against you, John, that you were found out in your very first attempt."

Here the good Justice left off speaking, and no one could contradict the truth of what he had said. Weston humbly submitted to his sentence, but he was very poor, and knew not where to raise the money to pay his fine. His character had always been so fair, that several farmers present kindly agreed to advance a trifle each, to prevent his being sent to prison, and he thankfully promised to work out the debt.[18] The Justice himself, though he could not soften the law, yet showed Weston so much kindness, that he was enabled, before the year was out, to get out of this difficulty. He began to think more seriously than he had ever yet done, and grew to abhor poaching, not merely from fear but from principle.

We shall soon see whether poaching Giles always got off so successfully. Here we have seen that prosperity is no sure sign of goodness. Next month we may, perhaps, see that the "triumphing of the wicked is short;" for I then promise to give the Second Part of the Poacher, together with the entertaining Story of the Widow Brown's Apple Tree.[19]

Z

BLACK GILES THE POACHER

PART TWO

History of Widow Brown's Apple Tree

I THINK my readers got so well acquainted last month with Black Giles the Poacher that they will not expect, this month, to hear any great good, either of Giles himself, his wife Rachel, or any of their family. I am sorry to expose their tricks, but it is their fault, not mine. If I pretend to speak about people at all, I must tell the truth. I am sure, if folks would but turn about and mend, it would be a thousand times pleasanter to me to write their histories; for it is no comfort to tell of any body's faults. If the world would but grow good, I should be glad enough to tell of it; but till it really becomes so, I must go on describing it as it is; otherwise, I should only mislead my readers, instead of instructing them.[1]

As to Giles and his boys, I am sure old Widow Brown has good reason to remember their dexterity. Poor Woman! she had a fine little bed of onions in her neat and well-kept garden; she was very fond of her onions, and many a rheumatism has she caught by kneeling down to weed them in a damp day, notwithstanding the little flannel cloak and the bit of an old mat which Madam Wilson gave her, because the old woman would needs weed in wet weather. Her onions she always carefully treasured up for her Winter's store; for an onion makes a little broth very relishing, and is, indeed, the only savoury thing poor people are used to get. She had also a small orchard, containing about a dozen apple trees, with which in a good year she has been known to make a couple of barrels of cider, which she sold to her landlord towards paying her rent, besides having a little keg which she was able to keep back for her own drinking. Well! would you believe it, Giles and his boys marked both onions and apples for their own; indeed, a man who stole so many rabbits from the warren, was likely enough to steal onions for sauce. One day, when the widow was abroad on a little business, Giles and his boys made a clear riddance of the onion bed; and when they had pulled up every single onion, they then turned a couple of pigs into the garden, who, allured by the smell, tore up the bed in such a manner, that the widow, when she came home, had not the least doubt but the pigs had been the thieves. To confirm this opinion, they took care to leave the little hatch half open at one end of the garden, and to break down a bit of a fence at the other end.

I wonder how anybody can find in his heart not to pity and respect poor old widows! There is something so forlorn and helpless in their condition, that methinks it is a call on every body, men, women, and children, to do them all the kind services that fall in their way. Surely their having no one to take their part, is an additional reason for kind-hearted people not to hurt and oppress them. But it was this very reason which led Giles to do this woman an hurt.[2]

It happened unluckily for this poor widow that her cottage stood quite alone. On several mornings together (for roguery gets up much earlier than industry) Giles and his boys stole regularly into her orchard, followed by their Jack-asses. She was so deaf that she could not hear the asses if they had brayed ever so loud, and to this Giles trusted; for he was very cautious in his rogueries; since he could not otherwise have contrived so long to keep out of prison; for though he was almost always suspected, he had seldom been taken up, and never convicted. The boys used to fill their bags, load their asses, and then march off; and if in their way to the town where the apples were to be sold, they chanced to pass by one of their neighbours who might be likely to suspect them, they then all at once began to scream out, "Buy my coal! – buy my sand!"

Besides the trees in her orchard, poor widow Brown had in her small garden one Apple-tree[3] particularly fine; it was a Redstreak, so tempting and so lovely, that Giles's family had watched it with longing eyes, till at last they resolved on a plan for carrying off all this fine fruit in their bags. But it was a nice point to manage. The Tree stood directly under her chamber-window, so that there was some danger that she might spy them at the work. They therefore determined to wait till the next Sunday morning, when they knew she would not fail to be at church. Sunday came, and during service Giles attended. It was a lone house, as I said before, and the rest of the parish were safe at church. In a trice the tree was cleared, the bags were filled, the asses were whipt, the thieves were off, the coast was clear, and all was safe and quiet by the time the sermon was over.

Unluckily, however, it happened, that this tree was so beautiful, and the fruit so fine, that the people, as they used to pass to and from church, were very apt to stop and admire Widow Brown's Redstreak; and some of the farmers rather envied her, that in that scarce season, when *they* hardly expected to make a pye out of a large orchard, she was likely to make cider from a single tree. I am afraid, indeed, if I must speak out, she herself rather set her heart too much upon this tree, and had felt as much pride in her tree as gratitude to a good Providence for it; but this failing of her's was no excuse for Giles. The covetousness of this thief had for once got the better of his caution; the tree was too completely stripped, though the youngest boy Dick did beg hard that his father would leave the poor old woman enough for a few dumplings, and when Giles ordered Dick in his turn to shake the tree, the boy did it so gently that hardly any apples fell, for which he got a good shake of the stick with which the old man was beating down the apples.

The neighbours on their return from church stopped as usual, but it was – not, alas! to admire the apples, for apples there were none left, but to lament the robbery, and console the widow: meantime the Redstreaks were safely lodged in Giles's hovel under a few bundles of new hay which he had contrived to pull from the farmers mow the night before, for the use of his jack asses. Such a stir, however, began to be made about the widow's apple tree, that Giles, who knew how much his character laid him open to suspicion, as soon as he saw the people safe in church again in the afternoon, ordered his boys to carry each a hatful of the apples and thrust them in at a little casement window which happened to be open in the house of Samuel Price, a very honest carpenter in that parish, who was at church with his whole family. Giles's plan, by this contrivance, was to lay the theft on Price's sons, in case the thing should come to be further enquired into. Here Dick put in a word, and begged and prayed his father not to force them to carry the apples to Price's. But all that he got by his begging was such a knock as had nearly laid him on the earth. "What, you cowardly rascal," said Giles, "you will go and peach, I suppose, and get your father sent to gaol."

Poor widow Brown, though her trouble had made her still weaker than she was, went to church again in the afternoon; indeed, she rightly thought that her being in trouble was a new reason why she ought to go. During the service she tried with all her might not to think of her Redstreaks, and whenever they would come into her head, she took up her prayer book directly, and so she forgot them a little, and, indeed she found herself much easier when she came out of the church than when she went in. Now it happened oddly enough, that on that Sunday, of all the Sundays in the year, she should call in to rest a little at Samuel Price's, to tell over again the lamentable story of the apples, and to consult with him how the thief might be brought to justice. But, O reader! guess if you can, for

I am sure I cannot tell you, what was her surprise when, on going into Samuel Price's kitchen she saw her own Redstreaks lying in the window! The apples were of a sort too remarkable for colour, shape, and size, to be mistaken. There was not such another tree in the parish. Widow Brown immediately screamed out, "'las-a-day! as sure as can be here are my Redstreaks; I could swear to them in any court." Samuel Price, who believed his sons to be as honest as himself, was shocked and troubled at the sight. He knew he had no Redstreaks of his own; he knew there were no apples in the window when he went to church. He did verily believe them to be the widow's. But how they came there he could not possibly guess. He called for Tom, the only one of his sons who now lived at home. Tom was at the Sunday school, which he had never once missed since Mr. Wilson the Minister had set up one in the parish. Was such a boy likely to do such a deed?

A crowd was by this time got about Price's door, among which was Giles and his boys, who had already taken care to spread the news that Tom Price was the thief. Most people were unwilling to believe it. His character was very good, but appearances were strongly against him. Mr. Wilson, who had staid to christen a child, now came in. He was much concerned that Tom Price, the best boy in his school, should stand accused of such a crime. He sent for the boy, examined, and cross examined him. No marks of guilt appeared. But still, though he pleaded *not guilty,* there lay the Redstreaks in his father's window. All the idle fellows in the place, who were most likely to have commited such a theft themselves, fell with vengeance on poor Tom. The wicked seldom give any quarter. "This is one of your sanctified ones!" cried they. "This was all the good that Sunday schools did! For their parts they never saw any good come by religion. Sunday was the only day for a little pastime, and if poor boys must be shut up with their godly books when they ought to be out taking a little pleasure, it was no wonder they made themselves amends by such tricks." Another said, he should like to see parson Wilson's righteous one well whipped. A third hoped he would be clapped in the stocks for a young hypocrite as he was; while old Giles, who thought to avoid suspicion by being more violent than the rest, declared, "that he hoped the young dog would be transported for life."

Mr. Wilson was too wise and too just to proceed against Tom without full proof. He declared the crime was a very heavy one, and he feared that heavy must be the punishment. Tom, who knew his own innocence, earnestly prayed to God that it might be made to appear as clear as the noon-day; and very fervent were his secret devotions on that night.

Black Giles passed his night in a very different manner. He set off as soon as it was dark, with his sons and their jack-asses laden with their stolen goods. As such a cry was raised about the apples he did not think it safe to keep them longer at home, but resolved to go and sell them at the next town; borrowing without leave a lame colt out of the moor to assist in carrying off his booty.

Giles and his eldest sons had rare sport all the way in thinking, that while they were enjoying the profit of their plunder, Tom Price would be whipped round the market place at least, if not sent beyond sea. But the younger boy, Dick, who had naturally a tender heart, though hardened by his long familiarity with sin, could not help crying when he thought that Tom Price might perhaps be transported for a crime which he himself had helped to commit. He had had no compunction about the robbery, for he had not been instructed in the great principles of truth and justice. Nor would he therefore, perhaps, have had much remorse about accusing an innocent boy. But, though utterly devoid of principle he had some remains of natural feeling and of gratitude. Tom Price had often given him a bit of his own bread and cheese; and once, when Dick was like to be drowned, Tom had jumped into the pond with his cloaths on, and saved his life when he was just sinking: the remembrance of all this made his heart heavy. He said nothing; as he trotted bare foot after the asses, he heard his father and brothers laugh at having outwitted the godly ones; and he grieved to think how poor Tom would suffer for his wickedness, yet fear kept him silent: they called him sulky dog and lashed the asses till they bled.

In the mean time Tom Price kept up his spirits as well as he could. He worked hard all day, and prayed heartily night and morning. "It is true," said he to himself, "I am not guilty of this sin; but let this accusation set me on examining myself, and truly repenting of all my other sins; for I find enough to repent of, though I thank God I did not steal those apples."

At length Sunday came. Tom went to school as usual. As soon as he walked in there was a deal of whispering and laughing among the worst of the boys; and he over heard them say, "Who would have thought it? This is master's favourite! This is Parson Wilson's sober Tommy! We shan't have Tommy thrown in our teeth again if we go to get a bird's nest, or gather a few nuts of a Sunday." "Your demure ones are always hypocrites," says another. "The still sow sucks all the milk," says a third.

Giles's family had always kept clear of the school. Dick, indeed, had sometimes wished to go, not that he had much sense of sin, or desire after goodness, but he thought if he could once read, he might rise in the world,

and not be forced to drive asses all his life. Through this whole Saturday
night he could not sleep. He longed to know what would be done to Tom.
He began to wish to go to school, but he had not courage; sin is very
cowardly; so on the Sunday morning he went and sat himself down under
the church wall. Mr. Wilson passed by. It was not his way to reject the
most wicked, till he had tried every means to bring them over, and even
then he pitied and prayed for them. He had, indeed, long left off talking
to Giles's sons; but, seeing Dick sitting by himself, he once more spoke
to him, desired him to leave off his vagabond life, and go with him into
the school. The boy hung down his head, but made no answer. He did
not however either rise up and run away, or look sulky as he used to do.
The Minister desired him once more. "Sir," said the boy, "I can't go; I am
so big I am ashamed to learn my letters." "The shame is not in beginning
to learn them, but in being contented never to know them." "But, Sir, I
am so ragged!" "God looks at the heart and not at the coat." "But, Sir, I
have no shoes and stockings." "So much the worse. I remember who gave
you both," (here Dick coloured). "It is bad to want shoes and stockings;
but still if you can drive your asses a dozen miles without them, you may
certainly walk to school without them." "But, Sir, the good boys will hate
me, and won't speak to me." "Good boys hate nobody, and as to not
speaking to you, to be sure they will not keep you company while you go
on in your present evil courses; but as soon as they see you wish to reform,
they will help you, and pity you, and teach you, and so come along." Here
Mr. Wilson took this dirty boy by the hand, and gently pulled him forward,
kindly talking to him all the way.[4]

How the whole school stared to see Dick Giles come in! No one however
dared to say what he thought. The business went on, and Dick slunk into
a corner, partly to hide his rags, and partly to hide his sin; for last Sunday's
transaction sat heavy at his heart, not because he had stolen the apples,
but because Tom Price had been accused. This I say made him slink behind.
Poor boy! he little thought there was ONE saw him who sees all things,
and from whose eye no hole nor corner can hide the sinner.[5]

It was the custom in that school for the master, who was a good and
wise man, to mark down in his pocket book all the events of the week,
that he might turn them to some account in his Sunday evening instructions
such as any useful story in the newspaper, any account of boys being
drowned as they were out in a pleasure-boat on Sundays; any sudden death
in the parish, or any other remarkable visitation of Providence, insomuch,
that many young people in the place, who did not belong to the school,
and many parents also, used to drop in for an hour on a Sunday evening,

when they were sure to hear something profitable.[6] The Minister greatly approved this practice, and often called in himself, which was a great support to the master, and encouragement to the people.

The master had taken a deep concern in the story of widow Brown's apple tree. He could not believe Tom Price was guilty, nor dared he pronounce him innocent; but he resolved to turn the instructions of the present evening to this subject. He began thus: "My dear boys, however light some of you may make of robbing an orchard, yet I have often told you there is no such thing as a *little* sin, if it be wilful or habitual. I wish now to explain it to you also that there is hardly such a thing as a single solitary sin. You know I teach you not merely to repeat the commandments as an exercise for your memory, but as a rule for your conduct. If you were to come here only to learn to read and spell on a Sunday, I should think that was not employing God's day for God's work; but I teach you to read, that you may by this means come so to understand the Bible and the Catechism, as to make every text in the one, and every question and answer in the other; to be so fixed in your hearts, that they may bring forth in you the fruits of good living."

Master. How many commandments are there? [7]

Boy. Ten.

Master. How many did that boy break who stole widow Brown's apples?

Boy. Only one, Master. The eighth.

Master. What is the eighth?

Boy. Thou shalt not steal.

Master. And you are very sure that this was the only one he broke? Now suppose I could prove to you that he probably broke not less than six out of those ten commandments, which the great Lord of heaven himself stooped down from his eternal glory to deliver to men; would you not, then, think it a terrible thing to steal, whether apples or guineas?

Boy. Yes, master.

Master. I will put the case. Some wicked boy has robbed widow Brown's orchard. (Here the eyes of every one were turned on poor Tom Price, except those of Dick Giles, who fixed his on the ground.) I accuse no one, continued the master, Tom Price is a good boy, and was not missing at the time of the robbery; these are two reasons why I presume that he is innocent; but whoever it was, you allow that by stealing these apples he broke the eighth commandment?

Boy. Yes master.

Master. On what day were these apples stolen?

Boy. On Sunday.

Master. What is the fourth commandment?

Boy. Thou shalt keep holy the Sabbath Day.

Master. Does that person keep holy the Sabbath Day who loiters in an orchard on Sunday, when he should be at church, and steals apples when he ought to be saying his prayers?

Boy. No, master.

Master. What command does he break?

Boy. The fourth.

Master. Suppose this boy had parents who had sent him to church, and that he had disobeyed them by not going, would that be keeping the fifth commandment?

Boy. No master; for the fifth commandment says, Thou shalt *honour* thy father and thy mother.

This was the only part in the case in which poor Dick Giles's heart did not smite him, for he knew he had disobeyed no father; for his father, alas! was, still wickeder than himself, and had brought him up to commit the sin. But what a wretched comfort was this! The master went on.

Master. Suppose this boy earnestly coveted this fruit, though it belonged to another person, would that be right?

Boy. No, master; for the tenth commandment says, *Thou shalt not covet.*

Master. Very well. Here are four of God's positive commands already broken. Now do you think thieves ever scruple to use wicked words?

Boy. I am afraid not, master.

Here Dick Giles was not so hardened but that he remembered how many curses had passed between him and his father while they were filling the bags, and he was afraid to look up. The master went on.

"I will now go one step further. If the thief, to all his other sins, has added that of accusing the innocent to save himself, if he should break the ninth commandment, by *bearing false witness against a harmless neighbour,* then six commandments are broken for an *Apple!* But if it be otherwise, if Tom Price should be found guilty, it is not his good character shall save him. I shall shed tears over him, but punish him I must." "No, that you shan't," roared out Dick Giles, who sprung from his hiding-place, fell on his knees, and burst out a crying, "Tom Price is as good a boy as ever lived: it was father and I stole the apples!"

It would have done your heart good to have seen the joy of the master, the modest blushes of Tom Price, and the satisfaction of every honest boy in the school. All shook hands with Tom, and even Dick got some portion of pity. I wish I had room to give my readers the moving exhortation which the master gave. But while Mr. Wilson left the guilty boy to the management of the master, he thought it became himself, as a Minister and a Magistrate, to go to the extent of the law in punishing the father. Early on the Monday morning he sent to apprehend Giles; in the mean time Mr. Wilson was sent for to a gardener's house two miles distant, to attend a man who was dying. This was a duty to which all others gave way in his mind. He set out directly, but what was his surprise on his arrival to see, on a little bed on the floor, poaching Giles lying in all the agonies of death. Jack Weston, the same poor young man against whom Giles had informed for killing a hare, was kneeling by him, offering him some broth, and talking to him in the kindest manner. Mr. Weston spoke as follows:

"At four this morning, as I was going out to mow, passing under the high wall of this garden, I heard a most dismal moaning. The nearer I came the more dismal it grew. At last, who should I see but poor Giles groaning, and struggling under a quantity of bricks and stones, but not able to stir. The day before he had marked a fine large net on this old wall, and resolved to steal it, for he thought it might do as well to catch partridges as to preserve cherries; so, Sir, standing on the very top of this wall, and tugging with all his might to loosen the net from the hooks which fastened it, down came Giles, net, wall, and all; for the wall was gone to decay.[8] It was very high indeed,; and poor Giles not only broke his thigh, but has got a terrible blow on his head and is bruised all over like a mummy. On seeing me, sir, poor Giles cried out, "oh Jack! I did try to ruin thee by lodging that information, and now thou wilt be revenged by letting me lie here and perish." God forbid, Giles" cried I "thou shalt see what sort of revenge a Christian takes." So, Sir, I sent off the gardener's boy to fetch a surgeon, while I scampered home and brought on my back this bit of a hammock, which is indeed my own bed, and put Giles upon it, we then lifted him up, bed and all, as tenderly as if he had been a gentlemen, and brought him in here. My wife has just brought him a drop of nice broth; and now, Sir, as I have done what I could for his poor perishing body, it was I who took the liberty to send to you to come to try to help his poor soul, for the Doctor says he can't live."

Mr. Wilson could not help saying to himself, "Such an action as this is worth a whole volume of comments on that precept of our blessed Master, "Love your enemies; do good to them that hate you.""[9] Giles's dying groans confirmed the sad account Weston had just given. The poor wretch could neither pray himself nor attend to the minister. He could only cry out, "Oh! sir, what will become of me? I don't know how to repent. Oh, my poor wicked children! Sir, I have bred them all up in sin and ignorance. Have mercy on them, sir; let me not meet them in the place of torment to which I am going. He languished a few days, and died in great misery.[10]

Except the Minister and Jack Weston, no one came to see poor Giles, besides Tommy Price, who had been so sadly wronged by him. Tom often brought him his own rice milk or apple dumpling; and Giles, ignorant and depraved as he was, often cried out, "That he thought now there must be some truth in religion, since it taught even a boy to *deny himself* and to *forgive an injury*." Mr. Wilson the next Sunday made a moving discourse on the danger of what are called petty offences. This, together with the awful death of Giles, produced such an effect that no Poacher has been able to shew his head in that parish ever since.

Z

Cheap Repository.

TAWNEY RACHEL;

OR, THE

FORTUNE TELLER:

with some Account of

DREAMS, OMENS, & CONJURORS.

Sold by HOWARD and EVANS,

(Printers to the CHEAP REPOSITORY for Moral and Religious
Tracts) No. 41 and 42 *Long-Lane, West-Smithfield,*
and J. HATCHARD, 190, *Piccadilly, London:* by
J. BINNS, *Bath:*—And by all Booksellers, Newsmen,
and Hawkers, in Town and Country.

** *Great allowance will be made to Shopkeepers and Hawkers.*

PRICE ONE-PENNY, or Six-Shillings *per* Hundred.

Entered at Stationers' Hall.

TAWNEY RACHEL; or, THE FORTUNE-TELLER:

with some account of DREAMS, OMENS,
& CONJURORS.

TAWNEY RACHEL was the wife of Poaching Giles. There seemed to be a conspiracy in Giles's whole family to maintain themselves by tricks and pilfering. Regular labour and honest industry did not suit their idle habits. They had a sort of genius at finding out every unlawful means to support a vagabond life.[1] Rachel travelled the country with a basket on her arm. She pretended to get her bread by selling laces, cabbage nets, ballads, and history books, and used to buy old rags and rabbit skins. Many honest people trade in these things, and I am sure I do not mean to say a word against honest people, let them trade in what they will. But Rachel only made this traffic a pretence for getting admittance into farmers' kitchens, in order to tell fortunes.

She was continually practising on the credulity of silly girls; and took advantage of their ignorance to cheat and deceive them. Many an innocent servant has she caused to be suspected of a robbery, while she herself, perhaps, was in league with the thief. Many a harmless maid has she brought to ruin by first contriving plots and events herself, and then pretending to foretell them. She had not, to be sure, the power of really foretelling things, because she had no power of seeing into futurity; but she had the art sometimes to bring them about according as she had foretold them. So she got that credit for her wisdom which really belonged to her wickedness[2]

Rachel was also a famous interpreter of dreams, and could distinguish exactly between the fate of any two persons who happened to have a mole on the right or the left cheek. She had a cunning way of getting herself off when any of her prophecies failed. When she explained a dream according to the natural appearance of things, and it did not come to pass, then she would get out of that scrape by saying, that "this sort of dreams went by contraries". Now of two very opposite things the chance always is that one of them may turn out to be true; so in either case she kept up the cheat.

Rachel, in one of her rambles, stopped at the house of Farmer Jenkins. She contrived to call when she knew the master of the house was from home, which, indeed, was her usual way. She knocked at the door; the maids being out hay-making, Mrs. Jenkins went to open it herself. Rachel asked her if she would please to let her light her pipe? This was a common pretence, when she could find no other way of getting into a house. While she was filling her pipe, she looked at Mrs. Jenkins and said, she could tell her some good fortune. The farmer's wife, who was a very inoffensive, but a weak and superstitious woman, was curious to know what she meant. Rachel then looked about very carefully, and shutting the door with a mysterious air, asked her if she was sure nobody would hear them. This appearance of mystery was at once delightful and terrifying to Mrs. Jenkins, who, with trembling agitation, bid the cunning woman speak out. "Then," said Rachel in a solemn whisper, "there is to my certain knowledge a pot of money hid under one of the stones in your cellar." "Indeed" said Mrs. Jenkins, "it is impossible, for now I think of it, I dreamt last night I was in prison for debt." – "Did you really?" said Rachel, "that is quite surprising. Did you dream this before twelve o'clock or after?" – "O it was this morning, just before I awoke." – "Then I am sure it is true, for morning dreams always go by contraries," cried Rachel. "How lucky it was you dreamt it so late!" – Mrs. Jenkins could hardly contain her joy, and asked how the money was to be come at. – "There is but one way," said Rachel: "I must go into the cellar. I know by my art under which stone it lies, but I must not tell." Then they both went down into the cellar, but Rachel refused to point at the stone unless Mrs. Jenkins would put five pieces of gold into a bason and do as she directed.[3] The simple woman, instead of turning her out of doors for a cheat, did as she was bid. She put the guineas into a bason which she gave into Rachel's hand. Rachel strewed some white powder over the gold, muttered some barbarous words, and pretended to perform the black art. She then told Mrs. Jenkins to put the bason quietly down within the cellar; telling her that if she offered to look into it, or even to speak a word, the charm would be broken. She also directed her to lock the cellar door, and on no pretence to open it in less than forty-eight hours. "If," added she, "you closely follow these directions, then, by the power of my art, you will find the bason conveyed to the very stone under which the money lies hid, and a fine treasure it will be" Mrs. Jenkins, who believed every word the woman said, did exactly as she was told, and Rachel took her leave with a handsome reward.

When farmer Jenkins came home he desired his wife to draw him a cup of cider; this she put off doing so long that he began to be displeased.

At last she begged he would drink a little beer instead. He insisted on knowing the reason, and when at last he grew angry she told him all that had passed; and owned that as the pot of gold happened to be in the cider cellar, she did not dare open the door, as she was sure it would break the charm. "And it would be a pity, you know," said she, "to lose a good fortune for the sake of a draught of cider." The farmer, who was not so easily imposed upon, suspected a trick. He demanded the key, and went and opened the cellar door: there he found the bason, and in it five round pieces of tin covered with powder. Mrs. Jenkins burst out a-crying; but the farmer thought of nothing but of getting a warrant to apprehend the cunning woman. Indeed she well proved her claim to that name, when she insisted that the cellar door might be kept locked till she had time to get out of the reach of all pursuit.

Poor Sally Evans! I am sure she rued the day that ever she listened to a fortune-teller! Sally was as harmless a girl as ever churned a pound of butter; but Sally was ignorant, and superstitious.[4] She delighted in dream-books, and had consulted all the cunning women in the country to tell her whether the two moles on her cheek denoted that she was to have two husbands, or only two children. If she picked up an old horse-shoe going to church she was sure that would be a lucky week. She never made a black-pudding without borrowing one of the parson's old wigs to hang in the chimney, firmly believing there were no other means to preserve them from bursting. She would never go to bed on Midsummer-eve without sticking up in her room the well-known plant called Midsummer-men,[5] as the bending of the leaves to the right or to the left would not fail to tell her whether Jacob, of whom we shall speak presently, was true or false. She would rather go five miles about than pass near a church-yard at night. Every seventh year she would not eat beans because they grew downward in the pod, instead of upward; she would rather have gone with her gown open than have taken a pin of an old woman, for fear of being bewitched. Poor Sally had so many unlucky days in her calendar, that a large portion of her time became of little use, because on these days she did not dare set about any new work. And she would have refused the best offer in the country if made to her on a Friday, which she thought so unlucky a day that she often said what a pity it was that there were any Friday in the week. Sally had twenty pounds[6] left her by her grandmother. She had long been courted by Jacob, a sober lad, with whom she lived fellow-servant at a creditable farmer's. Honest Jacob, like his namesake of old, thought it little to wait seven years to get this damsel to wife, because of the love he bore her;[7] for Sally had promised to marry him when he could match her twenty pounds with another of his own.

Now there was one Robert, a rambling, idle young gardener, who, instead of sitting down steadily in one place, used to roam about the country, and do odd jobs where he could get them. No one understood any thing about him, except that he was a down-looking fellow, who came nobody knew whence, and got his bread nobody knew how, and never had a penny in his pocket. Robert, who was now in the neighbourhood, happened to hear of Sally Evans and her twenty pounds. He immediately conceived a longing desire for the latter. So he went to his old friend Rachel, told her all he had heard of Sally, and promised if she could bring about a marriage between them, she should go shares in the money.

Rachel undertook the business. She set off to the farm-house, and fell to singing one of her most enticing songs just under the dairy window. Sally was so struck with the pretty tune, which was unhappily used, as is too often the case, to set off some very loose words[8] that she jumped up, dropped the skimming-dish into the cream, and ran out to buy the song. While she stooped down to rummage the basket for those songs which had the most tragical pictures, (for Sally had a tender heart, and delighted in whatever was mournful) Rachel looked stedfastly in her face, and told her she knew by her art that she was born to good fortune, but advised her not to throw herself away. "These two moles on your cheek," added she, "shew you are in some danger." – "Do they denote husbands or children?" cried Sally, starting up, and letting fall the song of the children in the wood; – "Husbands," muttered Rachel. – "Alas! poor Jacob!" said Sally, mournfully, "then he will die first, won't he?" – "Mum for that," quoth the fortune-teller; "I will say no more." Sally was impatient, but the more curiosity she discovered, the more mystery Rachel affected. At last she said, "If you will cross my hand with a piece of silver, I will tell your fortune. By the power of my art I can do this three ways; by cards, by the lines of your hand, or by turning a cup of tea-grounds; which will you have?" – "O, all! all!" cried Sally, looking up with reverence to this sun-burnt oracle of wisdom, who knew no less than three different ways of diving into the secrets of futurity. Alas! persons of better sense than Sally have been so taken in; the more is the pity! The poor girl said, she would run up stairs to her little box, where she kept her money tied up in a bit of an old glove, and would bring down a bright queen Ann's six-pence, very crooked. "I am sure," added she, "it is a lucky one, for it cured me of a very bad ague[9] last spring, by only laying it nine nights under my pillow without speaking a word. But then you must know what gave the

virtue to this six-pence was, that it had belonged to three young men of
the name of John; I am sure I had work enough to get it. But true it is,
it certainly cured me. It must be the six-pence, you know, for I am sure
I did nothing else for my ague, except, indeed, taking some bitter stuff
every three hours which the doctor called bark. To be sure I lost my ague
soon after I took it; but I am certain it was owing to the crooked sixpence,
and not to the bark. And so, good woman, you may come in if you will,
for there is not a soul in the house but me." This was the very thing
Rachel wanted to know, and very glad she was to learn it.

While Sally was above stairs untying her glove, Rachel slipped into the
parlour, took a small silver cup from the beaufet,[10] and clapped it into her
pocket. Sally ran down lamenting that she had lost her sixpence, which
she verily believed was owing to her having put it into a left glove, instead
of a right one. Rachel comforted her by saying, that if she gave her two
plain ones instead, the charm would work just as well. Simple Sally thought
herself happy to be let off so easily, never calculating that a smooth shilling
was worth two crooked six-pences. But this skill was a part of the black
art[11] in which Rachel excelled. She took the money, and began to examine
the lines of Sally's left hand. She bit her withered lip, shook her head,
and bade her poor dupe beware of a young man who had black hair.
"No, indeed," cried Sally all in a fright, "you mean black eyes, for our
Jacob has got brown hair, 'tis his eyes that are black." – "That is the very
thing I was going to say," muttered Rachel, – "I meant eyes though I said
hair, for I know his hair is as brown as a chesnut, and his eyes as black
as a sloe." – "So they are, sure enough," cried Sally: "how in the world
could you know that?" forgetting that she herself had just told her so.
And it is thus that these hags pick out of the credulous all which they
afterwards pretend to reveal to them. "O, I know a pretty deal more than
that," said Rachel, "but you must be aware of this man." – "Why so?"
cried Sally with great quickness. – "Because," answered Rachel, "you are
fated to marry a man worth a hundred of him, who has blue eyes, light
hair, and a stoop in the shoulders." – "No indeed, but I can't," said Sally:
"I have promised Jacob, and Jacob I will marry." – "You cannot, child,"
returned Rachel, in a solemn tone: "it is out of your power; you are *fated*
to marry the grey eyes and light hair." – "Nay, indeed," said Sally, sighing
deeply: "if I am fated, I must; I know there is no resisting one's fate."
This is a common cant with poor deluded girls, who are not aware that
they themselves make their fate by their folly, and then complain there is
no resisting it. – "What can I do?" said Sally. – "I will tell you that too,"
said Rachel. "You must take a walk next Sunday afternoon to the church-

yard, and the first man you meet in a blue coat, with a large posy of pinks and southernwood in his bosom,[12] sitting on the church-yard wall, about seven o'clock, he will be the man." "Provided," said Sally, much disturbed, "that he has grey eyes, and stoops." – "O, to be sure," said Rachel, "otherwise it is not the right man." – "But if I should mistake," said Sally; "for two men may happen to have a coat and eyes of the same colour?" – "To prevent that," replied Rachel, "if it is the right man, the two first letters of his name will be R.P. This man has got money beyond sea." – "O, I do not value his money," said Sally, with tears in her eyes, "for I love Jacob better than house or land; but if I am fated to marry another, I can't help it: you know there is no struggling against my fate."

Poor Sally thought of nothing, and dreamt of nothing all the week but the blue coat and the grey eyes. She made an hundred blunders at her work. She put her rennet into the butter-pan, instead of the cheese-tub. She gave the curd to the hogs, and put the whey into the vats.[13] She put her little knife out of her pocket for fear it should cut love, and would not stay in the kitchen, if there was not an even number of people, lest it should break the charm. She grew cold and mysterious in her behaviour to faithful Jacob, whom she truly loved. But the more she thought of the fortune-teller, the more she was convinced that brown hair and black eyes were not what she was fated to marry, and, therefore, though she trembled to think it, Jacob could not be the man.

On Sunday she was too uneasy to go to church; for poor Sally had never been taught that her being uneasy was only a fresh reason why she ought to go thither. She spent the whole afternoon in her little garret, dressing in all her best. First she put on her red ribbon, which she had bought at last Lammas fair;[14] then she recollected that red was an unlucky colour, and changed if for a blue ribbon, tied in a true lover's knot; but suddenly calling to mind that poor Jacob had bought this knot for her of a pedlar at the door, and that she had promised to wear it for his sake, her heart smote her, and she laid it by, sighing to think she was not fated to marry the man who had given it to her. When she had looked at herself twenty times in the glass (for one vain action always brings on another), she set off, trembling and quaking every step she went. She walked eagerly towards the church-yard, not daring to look to the right or left, for fear she should spy Jacob, who would have offered to walk with her, and so have spoilt all. As soon as she came within sight of the wall, she spied a man sitting upon it. Her heart beat violently. She looked again; but, alas! the stranger not only had on a black coat, but neither hair nor eyes answered the description. She now happened to cast her eyes on the church-clock, and found she was two hours before her time. This was some comfort. She walked away, and got rid of the two hours as well as she could, paying great attention as she went not to walk over any straws which lay across, and carefully looking to see if there were never an old horse-shoe in the way, that infallible symptom of good fortune. While the clock was striking seven, she returned to the church-yard, and, O! the wonderful power of fortune-tellers! there she saw him! there sat the very man! his hair as light as flax, his eyes as blue as butter-milk, and his shoulders as round as a tub.[15] Every tittle agreed, to the very nosegay in his waistcoat button-hole. At first, indeed, she thought it had been sweetbriar, and, glad to catch at a straw, whispered to herself, "It is not he, and I shall marry Jacob still;" but on looking again, she saw it was southernwood plain enough, and that of course all was over. The man accosted her with some very nonsensical, but too acceptable, compliments. Sally was naturally a modest girl, and but for Rachel's wicked arts would not have had courage to talk with a strange man; but how could she resist her fate, you know? After a little discourse, she asked him, with a trembling heart, what might be his name? "Robert Price at your service," was the answer. "Robert Price! that is R.P. as sure as I am alive, and the fortune-teller was a witch! it is all out! O the wonderful art of fortune-tellers!"

The little sleep she had that night was disturbed with dreams of graves, and ghosts, and funerals; but as they were morning dreams, she knew those always went by contraries, and that a funeral denoted a wedding. Still a sigh would now and then heave, to think that in that wedding Jacob could have no part. Such of my readers as know the power which superstition has over the weak and credulous mind, scarcely need be told, that poor Sally's unhappiness was soon compleated. She forgot all her vows to Jacob; she at once forsook an honest man whom she loved, and consented to marry a stranger, of whom she knew nothing, from a ridiculous notion that she was compelled to do so by a decree which she had it not in her power to resist. She married this Robert Price, the strange gardener, whom she soon found to be very worthless, and very much in debt. He had no such thing as "money beyond sea," as the fortune-teller had told her; but, alas! he had another wife there. He got immediate possession of Sally's 20l. Rachel put in for her share; but he refused to give her a farthing, and bid her get away, or he would have her taken up on the vagrant act.[16] He soon ran away from Sally, leaving her to bewail her own weakness; for it was that indeed, and not any irresistible fate, which had been the cause of her ruin. To compleat her misery, she herself was suspected of having stolen the silver cup which Rachel had pocketed.

Her master, however, would not prosecute her, as she was falling into a deep decline, and she died in a few months of a broken heart, a sad warning to all credulous girls.

Rachel, whenever she got near home, used to drop her trade of fortune-telling, and only dealt in the wares of her basket. Mr. Wilson, the clergyman, found her one day dealing out some very wicked ballads to some children.[17] He went up with a view to give her a reprimand; but had no sooner begun his exhortation than up came a constable, followed by several people. – "There she is, that is she, that is the old witch who tricked my wife out of the five guineas," said one of them. "Do your office, constable; seize that old hag. She may tell fortunes and find pots of gold in Taunton[18] gaol, for there she will have nothing else to do!" This was that very farmer Jenkins, whose wife had been cheated by Rachel of the five guineas. He had taken pains to trace her to her own parish: he did not so much value the loss of the money, but he thought it was a duty he owed the public to clear the country of such vermin.[19] Mr. Wilson immediately committed her. She took her trial at the next assizes, when she was sentenced to a year's imprisonment. In the meantime, the pawnbroker to whom she had sold the silver cup, which she had stolen from poor Sally's master, impeached her; and as the robbery was fully proved upon Rachel, she was sentenced for this crime to Botany Bay; and a happy day it was for the county of Somerset, when such a nuisance was sent out of it. She was transported much about the same time that her husband Giles lost his life, in stealing the net from the garden wall, as related in the second part of poaching Giles.

I have thought it my duty to print this little history as a kind warning to all you young men and maidens not to have anything to say to CHEATS, IMPOSTORS, CUNNING WOMEN, FORTUNE-TELLERS, CONJURERS, AND INTERPRETERS OF DREAMS. Listen to me, your true friend,[20] when I assure you that God never reveals to weak and wicked women those secret designs of his providence, which no human wisdom is able to foresee. To consult these false oracles is not only foolish, but sinful. It is foolish, because they are themselves as ignorant as those whom they pretend to teach; and it is sinful, because it is prying into that futurity which God, in mercy as well as wisdom, hides from men. God, indeed, *orders* all things; but when you have a mind to do a foolish thing, do not fancy you are *fated* to do it. This is tempting Providence, and not trusting him. It is, indeed, "charging God with folly". Prudence is his gift, and you obey him better when you make use of prudence, under the direction of prayer, than when you madly run into ruin, and think you are only submitting to your fate. Never fancy that you are compelled to undo yourself, or to rush upon your own destruction, in compliance with any supposed fatality. Never believe that God conceals his will from a sober Christian who obey his laws, and reveals it to a vagabond gipsy[21] who runs up and down breaking the laws both of God and man. King Saul never consulted the witch till he had left off serving God.[22] The Bible will direct us what to do better than any conjurer, and there are no days unlucky but those which we make so by our own vanity, folly, and sin.

Z

THE
SUNDAY SCHOOL.

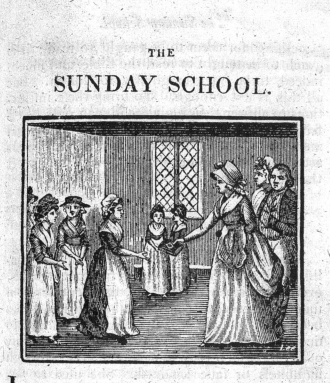

I Promifed, in the Cottage Cook, to give fome account of the manner in which Mrs. Jones fet up her fchool. She did not much fear being able to raife the money; but money is of little ufe, unlefs fome perfons of fenfe and piety can be found to direct thefe inftitutions. Not that I would difcourage thofe who fet them up, even in the moft ordinary manner, and from mere views of worldly policy. It is fomething gained to refcue children from idling away their Sabbath in the fields or the ftreets. It is no fmall thing to keep them from thofe tricks to which a day of leifure tempts the idle and the ignorant. It is

THE HISTORY
OF
HESTER WILMOT: PART ONE

Being the second part of the Sunday School.[1]

HESTER WILMOT was born in the parish of Weston, of parents who maintained themselves by their labour; they were both of them ungodly, it is no wonder, therefore, they were unhappy. They lived badly together, and how could they do otherwise? for their tempers were very different, and they had no religion to smooth down this difference, or to teach them that they ought to bear with each other's faults. Rebecca Wilmot was a proof that people may have some right qualities, and yet be but bad characters, and utterly destitute of religion. She was clean, notable, and industrious. Now I know some folks fancy that the poor who have these qualities need have no other; but this is a sad mistake, as I am sure every page in the Bible would show; and it is a pity people do not consult it oftener. They direct their ploughing and sowing by the information of the Almanack, why will they not consult the Bible for the direction of their hearts and lives?[2] Rebecca was of a violent, ungovernable temper; and that very neatness which is in itself so pleasing, in her became a sin, for her affection to her husband and children was quite lost in an over-anxious desire to have her house reckoned the nicest in the parish. Rebecca was also a proof that a poor woman may be as vain as a rich one, for it was not so much the comfort of neatness, as the praise of neatness, which she coveted. A spot on her hearth, or a bit of rust on a brass candlestick, would throw her into a violent passion. Now it is very right to keep the hearth clean and the candlestick bright, but it is very wrong so to set one's affections on a hearth, or a candlestick, as to make one's self unhappy if any trifling accident happens to them; and if Rebecca had been as careful to keep her heart without spot, or her life without blemish, as she was to keep her fire-irons free from either, she would have been held up in this history, not as a warning, but a pattern, and in that case her nicety would have come in for a part of the praise. It was no fault in Rebecca, but a merit, that her oak table was so bright you could almost see to put your cap on in it; but it was no merit but a fault, that when John, her husband, laid down his cup of beer upon it so as to leave a mark, she would fly out into so terrible a passion that all the children were forced to run to corners; now poor John, having no corner to run to, ran to the alehouse, till that which was at first a refuge, too soon became a pleasure.

Rebecca never wished her children to learn to read, because she said it would only serve to make them lazy, and she herself had done very well without it. She would keep poor Hester from church to stone the space under the chairs in fine patterns and flowers.[3] I don't pretend to say there was any harm in this little decoration, it looks pretty enough; and it is better to let the children do that than do nothing. But still these are not things to set one's heart upon; and, besides, Rebecca only did it as a trap for praise; for she was sulky and disappointed if any ladies happened to call in and did not seem delighted with the flowers which she used to draw with a burnt stick on the white wash of the chimney corners. Besides, all this finery was often done on a Sunday, and there is a great deal of harm in doing even right things at a wrong time, or in wasting much time on things which are of no real use, or in doing any thing at all out of vanity. Now I beg that no lazy slattern of a wife will go and take any comfort in her dirt from what is here said against Rebecca's nicety; for I believe, that for one who makes her husband unhappy through neatness, twenty do so by dirt and laziness. All excesses are wrong, but the excess of a good quality is not so common as the excess of a bad one; and not being so obvious, perhaps, for that very reason requires more animadversion.[4]

John Wilmot was not an ill-natured man, but he had no fixed principle. Instead of setting himself to cure his wife's faults by mild reproof and a good example, he was driven by them into still greater faults himself. It is a common case with people who have no religion, when any cross accident befalls them, instead of trying to make the best of a bad matter, instead of considering their trouble as a trial sent from God to purify them, or instead of considering the faults of others as a punishment for their own sins – instead of this I say, what do they do but either sink down at once into despair, or else run for comfort into evil courses. Drinking is the common remedy for sorrow, if that can be called a remedy, the end of which is to destroy soul and body. John now began to spend all his leisure hours at the Bell. He used to be fond of his children; but when he could not come home in quiet and play with the little ones, while his wife dressed him a bit of hot supper, he grew in time not to come home at all. He who has once taken to drink can seldom be said to be guilty of one sin only; John's heart became hardened. His affection for his family was lost in self-indulgence. Patience and submission, on the part of his wife, might have won much upon a man of John's temper; but instead of trying to reclaim him, his wife seemed rather to delight in putting him as much in the wrong as she could, that she might be justified in her constant abuse of him.[5] I doubt whether she would have been as much pleased with his reformation as she was with always talking of his faults, though I know it was the opinion of the neighbours, that if she had taken as much pains to reform her husband by reforming her own temper, as she did to abuse him and expose him, her endeavours might have been blessed with success. Good christians,[6] who are trying to subdue their own faults, can hardly believe that the ungodly have a sort of savage satisfaction in trying, by indulgence of their own evil tempers, to lessen the happiness of those with whom they have to do. Need we look any further for a proof of our own corrupt nature, when we see mankind delight in sins which offer neither the temptation of profit nor the allurement of pleasure, such as plaguing, vexing, or abusing each other?

Hester was the eldest of their five children; she was a sharp, sensible girl, but at fourteen years old she could not tell a letter, nor had she ever been taught to bow her knee to Him who made her; for John's, or rather Rebecca's house, had seldom the name of God pronounced in it, except to be blasphemed.

It was just about this time, if I mistake not, that Mrs. Jones set up her Sunday School, of which Mrs. Betty Crew was appointed mistress, as was related in the last volume. Mrs. Jones, finding that none of the Wilmots were sent to School, took a walk to Rebecca's house, and civilly told her she called to let her know that a school was opened, to which she desired her to send her children on the Sunday following, especially her eldest daughter, Hester. "Well," said Rebecca, "and what will you give her if I do?" – "Give her!" replied Mrs. Jones;" that is rather a rude question, and asked in a rude manner: however, as a soft answer turneth away wrath, I assure you that I will give her the best of learning; I will teach her to *fear God and keep his commandments.*" – "I would rather you would teach her to fear me, and to keep my house clean," said this wicked woman. "She shan't come, however, unless you will pay her for it." [7] – "Pay her for it!" said the lady; "will it not be reward enough that she will be taught to read the word of God without any expence to you? For though many gifts both of books and clothing, will be given the children, yet you are not to consider these gifts so much in the light of payment as an expression of good-will in your benefactors." – "I say," interrupted Rebecca, "that

Hester shan't go to school. Religion is of no use that I know of but to make people hate their own flesh and blood; and I see no good in learning but to make folks proud, and lazy, and dirty. I cannot tell a letter myself, and, though I say it, that should not say it, there is not a notabler woman in the parish." – "Pray," said Mrs. Jones, mildly, "do you think that young people will disobey their parents the more for being taught to fear God?" – "I don't think any thing about it," said Rebecca: I shan't let her come, and there's the long and short of the matter. Hester has other fish to fry; but you may have some of these little ones if you will." – "No," said Mrs. Jones, "I will not; I have not set up a nursery, but a school. I am not at all this expence to take crying babes out of the mother's way, but to instruct reasonable beings in the road to eternal life; and it ought to be a rule in all schools, not to take the troublesome *young* children, unless the mother will try to spare the *elder* ones, who are capable of learning." – "But," said Rebecca, "I have a young child, which Hester must nurse while I dress the Sunday dinner; and she must iron the rags, and scour the irons and dig the potatoes, and fetch the water to boil them." – "As to nursing the child, that is indeed a necessary duty, and Hester ought to stay at home part of the day to enable you to go to church; and families should relieve each other in this way: but as to all the rest, they are no reasons at all; for the irons need not be scoured so often, and the rags should be ironed, and the potatoes dug, and the water fetched on the Saturday; and I can tell you that neither your minister here, nor your judge hereafter, will accept of any such excuses."

All this while Hester staid behind, pale and trembling, lest her unkind mother should carry her point. She looked up at Mrs. Jones with so much love and gratitude as to win her affection, and this good lady went on trying to soften this harsh mother. At last Rebecca condescended to say, "Well, I don't know but I may let her come now and then when I can spare her, provided I find you make it worth her while." All this time she had never asked Mrs. Jones to sit down, nor had once bid her children be quiet, though they were crying and squalling the whole time. Rebecca fancied this rudeness was the only way she had of showing she thought herself to be as good as her guest, but Mrs. Jones never lost her temper. The moment she went out of the house, Rebecca called out loud enough for her to hear, and ordered Hester to get the stone and a bit of sand to scrub out the prints of that dirty woman's shoes. Hester in high spirits cheerfully obeyed, and rubbed out the stains so neatly, that her mother could not help lamenting that so handy a girl was going to be spoiled by being taught godliness, and learning, and such nonsense.

Mrs. Jones, who knew the world, told her agent, Mrs. Crew, that her grand difficulty would arise, not so much from the children as the parents. These, said she,[8] are apt to fall into that sad mistake, that because their children are poor, and have little of this world's goods, the mothers must make it up to them in false indulgence. The children of the gentry are much more reproved and corrected for their faults, and bred up in far stricter discipline. He was a king who said, *Chasten thy son, and let not thy rod spare for his crying.*[9] But do not lose your patience; the more vicious the children are, you must remember the more they stand in need of your instruction. When they are bad, comfort yourself with thinking, how much worse they would have been but for you; and what a burden they would become to society if these evil tempers were to receive no check. The great thing which enabled Mrs. Crew to teach well was the deep insight she had got into the corruption of human nature. And I doubt if any one can make a thoroughly good teacher of religion and morals, who wants this master-key to the heart. Others, indeed, may teach knowledge, decency, and good manners; but those, however valuable, are not Christianity. Mrs. Crew, who knew that out of the heart proceed lying, theft, and all that train of evils which begin to break out even in young children, applied her labours to correct this root of evil. But though a diligent, she was an humble teacher, well knowing that unless the grace of God blessed her labours, she should but labour in vain.

Hester Wilmot never failed to attend the school, whenever her perverse mother would give her leave; and her delight in learning was so great, that she would work early and late to gain a little time for her book. As she had a quick capacity, she learned soon to spell and read; and Mrs. Crew, observing her diligence, used to lend her a book to carry home, that she might pick up a little at odd times. It would be well if teachers would make this distinction. To give or lend books to those who take no delight in them is an useless expence; while it is kind and right to assist well-disposed young people with every help of this sort. Those who love books seldom hurt them, while the slothful, who hate learning, will wear out a book more in a week than the diligent will do in a year. Hester's way was to read over one question in her catechism, or one verse in her hymn-book, by fire-light, before she went to-bed; this she thought over in the night; and when she was dressing herself in the morning she was glad to find she always knew a little more than she had done the morning before. It is not to be believed how much those people will be found to have gained at the end of the year, who are accustomed to work up all the little odd ends and remnants of leisure; who value time even more than money;

and who are convinced that minutes are no more to be wasted than pence. Nay, he who finds he has wasted a shilling, may by diligence hope to fetch it up again; but no repentance, or industry, can ever bring back one wasted hour. My good young reader, if ever *you* are tempted to waste an hour, go and ask a dying man what he would give for that hour which you are throwing away, and, according as he answers, so do you act.[10]

As her mother hated the sight of a book, Hester was forced to learn out of sight. It was no disobedience to do this, as long as she wasted no part of that time which it was her duty to spend in useful labour. She would have thought it a sin to have left her work for her book; but she did not think it wrong to steal time from her sleep, and to be learning an hour before the rest of the family were awake. Hester would not neglect the washing-tub or the spinning-wheel, even to get on with her catechism, but she thought it fair to think over her questions while she was washing and spinning. In a few months she was able to read fluently in St. John's gospel, which is the easiest. But Mrs. Crew did not think it enough that her children could read a chapter; she would make them understand it also. It is in a good degree owing to the want of religious knowledge in teachers, that there is so little religion in the world. Unless the Bible is laid open to the understanding, children may read from Genesis to the Revelation, without any other improvement than barely learning how to pronounce the words. Mrs. Crew found there was but one way to compel their attention; this was by obliging them to return back again to her the sense of what she had read to them, and this they might do in their own words, if they could not remember the words of Scripture. Those who had weak capacities would, to be sure, do this but very imperfectly; but even the weakest, if they were willing, would retain something.[11] She so managed, that *saying the Catechism* was not merely an act of the memory, but of the understanding; for she had observed formerly, that those who had learned the Catechism in the common formal way, when they were children, had never understood it when they became men and women, and it remained in the memory without having made any impression on the mind. Thus this fine summary of the christian religion is considered as little more than a form of words, the being able to repeat which is a qualification for being confirmed by the bishop, instead of being considered as really containing those grounds of christian faith and practice, by which they are to be confirmed christians.[12]

Mrs. Crew used to say to Mrs. Jones, Those who teach the poor must indeed give line upon line, precept upon precept, here a little and there a little, as they can receive it. So that teaching must be a great grievance to those who do not really make it a *labour of love*. I see so much levity, obstinacy, and ignorance, that it keeps my own forbearance in continual exercise, insomuch, that I trust that I am getting good myself while I am doing good to others. No one, madam, can know till they try, that after they have asked a poor untaught child the same question nineteen times, they must not lose their temper, but go on and ask it the twentieth. Now and then, when I am tempted to be impatient, I correct myself, by thinking over that active proof which our blessed Saviour requires of our love to him when he says, *Feed my lambs.*[13]

Hester Wilmot had never been bred to go to church, for her father and mother had never thought of going themselves, unless at a christening in their own family, or at a funeral of their neighbours, both which they considered merely as opportunities for good eating and drinking, and not as offices of religion.

As poor Hester had no comfort at home, it was the less wonder she delighted in her school, her Bible, and her church; for so great is God's goodness, that he is pleased to make religion a peculiar comfort to those who have no other comfort. The God whose name she had seldom heard but when it was *taken in vain*, was now revealed to her as a God of infinite power, justice, and holiness. What she read in her Bible, and what she felt in her own heart, convinced her she was a sinner; and her catechism said the same. She was much distressed one day on thinking over this promise which she had just made (in answer to the question which fell to her lot), *To renounce the devil and all his works, the pomps and vanities of this wicked world, and all the sinful lusts of the flesh.* I say she was distressed on finding that these were not merely certain words which she was bound to repeat, but certain conditions which she was bound to perform. She was sadly puzzled to know how this was to be done, till she met with these words in her Bible: *My grace is sufficient for thee.* But still she was at a loss to know how this grace was to be obtained. Happily Mr. Simpson preached on the next Sunday from this text, *Ask and ye shall have*, &c. In this sermon was explained to her the nature, the duty, and the efficacy of prayer. After this she opened her heart to Mrs. Crew, who taught her the great doctrines of Scripture, in a serious but plain way. Hester's own heart led her to assent to that humbling doctrine of the catechism, that *We are by nature born in sin*; and truly glad was she to be relieved by hearing of *That spiritual grace by which we have a new birth unto righteousness.* Thus her mind was no sooner humbled by one part, than it gained comfort from another. On the other hand, while she was rejoicing in *a lively hope in God's mercy through Christ,* her mistress put her in mind that that was the only *true* repentance, *by which we forsake sin.* Thus the catechism, explained by a pious teacher, was found to contain *all the articles of the christian faith.*[14]

Mrs. Jones greatly disapproved the practice of turning away the scholars because they were grown up. Young people, said she "want to be warned at sixteen more than they did at six, and they are commonly turned adrift at the very age when they want most instruction; when dangers and temptations most beset them. They are exposed to more evil by the leisure of a Sunday evening than by the business of a whole week: but then religion must be made pleasant, and instruction must be carried on in a kind, and agreeable and familiar way. If they once dislike the teacher they will soon get to dislike what is taught, so that a master or mistress is in some measure answerable for the future piety of young persons, inasmuch as that piety depends on their manner of making religion pleasant as well as profitable."

To attend Mrs. Jones's evening instructions was soon thought not a task but a holiday. In a few months it was reckoned a disadvantage to the character of any young person in the parish to know they did not attend the evening school. At first, indeed, many of them came only with a view to learn for amusement; but, by the blessing of God, they grew fond of instruction, and some of them became truly pious. Mrs. Jones spoke to them one Sunday evening as follows: – "My dear young women, I rejoice at your improvement; but I rejoice with trembling. I have known young people set out well, who afterwards fell off. The heart is deceitful. Many like religious knowledge, who do not like the strictness of a religious life. I must, therefore, watch whether those who are diligent at church and school, are diligent in their daily walk. Whether those who say they *believe* in God, really *obey* him. Whether they who profess to *love* Christ keep his *commandments*. Those who hear themselves commended for early piety may learn to rest satisfied with the praise of man. People may get a knack at religious phrases without being religious; they may even get to frequent places of worship as an amusement, in order to meet their friends, and may learn to delight in a sort of *spiritual gossip,*[15] while religion has no power in their hearts. But I hope better things of you, and things that accompany salvation, though I thus speak."

What becomes of Hester Wilmot, with some account of Mrs. Jones's May-day feast for her school, my readers shall be told next month.

THE HISTORY
OF
HESTER WILMOT: PART TWO:

The New Gown

HESTER WILMOT, I am sorry to observe, had been by nature peevish and lazy: she would, when a child, now and then slight her work, and when her mother was very unreasonable she was too apt to return her a saucy answer; but when she became acquainted with her own heart, and with the Scriptures, these evil tempers were, in a good measure, subdued; for she now learned to imitate, not her violent mother, but *him who was meek and* lowly.[1] When she was scolded for doing ill, she prayed for grace to do better; and the only answer she made to her mother's charge, "that religion only served to make people lazy," was to strive to do twice as much work, in order to prove that it really made them diligent. The only thing in which she ventured to disobey her mother was, that when she ordered her to do week-days' work on a Sunday, Hester cried, and said she did not dare to disobey God; but to show that she did not wish to save her own labour she would do a double portion of work on the Saturday night, and rise two hours earlier on the Monday morning.

Once, when she had worked very hard, her mother told her she would treat her with a holiday the following Sabbath, and take her a fine walk to eat cakes and drink ale at Weston fair, which, though it was professed to be kept on the Monday, yet, to the disgrace of the village, always began on the Sunday evening.[2] Rebecca, who would on no account have wasted the Monday, which was a working day, in idleness and pleasure, thought she had a very good right to enjoy herself at the fair on the Sunday evening, as well as to take her children. Hester earnestly begged to be left at home, and her mother in a rage went without her. A wet walk, and more ale than she was used to drink, gave Rebecca a dangerous fever. During this illness, Hester, who would not follow her to a scene of dissolute mirth, attended her night and day, and denied herself necessaries that her sick mother might have comforts; and though she secretly prayed to God that this sickness might change her mother's heart, yet she never once reproached her, or put her in mind, that it was caught by indulging in a sinful pleasure.

Another Sunday night her father told Hester, he thought she had now been at school long enough for him to have a little good of her learning, so he desired she would stay at home and read to him. Hester cheerfully ran and fetched her Testament. But John fell a laughing, called her a fool, and said, it would be time enough to read the Testament to him when he was going to die, but at present he must have something merry. So saying he gave her a song-book which he had picked up at the Bell. Hester having cast her eyes over it refused to read it, saying, she did not dare offend God by reading what would hurt her own soul. John called her a canting hypocrite, and said, he would put the Testament into the fire; for that there was not a more merry girl than she was before she became religious.[3] Her mother for once took her part, not because she thought her daughter in the right, but because she was glad of any pretence to show her husband was in the wrong; though she herself would have abused Hester for the same thing if John had taken her part. John, with a shocking oath, abused them both, and went off in a violent passion. Hester, instead of saying one undutiful word against her father, took up a Psalter in order to teach her little sisters; but Rebecca was so provoked at her for not joining her in her abuse of her husband, that she changed her humour, said John was in the right, and Hester a perverse hypocrite, who only made religion a pretence for being undutiful to her parents. Hester bore all in silence, and committed her cause to him *who judgeth righteously*. It would have been a great comfort to her if she had dared to go to Mrs. Crew, and to have joined in the religious exercises of the evening at school. But her mother refused to let her, saying, it would only harden her heart in mischief. Hester said not a word; but after having put the little ones to bed, and heard them say their prayers out of sight, she went and sat down in her own little loft, and said to herself, "It would be pleasant to me to have taught my little sisters to read: I thought is was my duty; for David has said, *Come ye children, hearken unto me: I will teach you the fear of the Lord.*[4] It would have been still more pleasant to have passed the evening at school, because I am still ignorant, and fitter to learn than to teach; but I cannot do either without flying in the face of my mother: God sees fit to-night to change my pleasant duties into a painful trial. I give up my will, and I submit to the will of my father; but when he orders me to commit a known sin, then I dare not do it, because in so doing I must disobey my Father which is in heaven."[5]

Now it so fell out, that this dispute happened on the very Sunday next before Mrs. Jones's yearly feast. On May-day all the school attended her to church, each in a stuff gown of their own earning, and a cap and white apron of her giving.[6] After church there was an examination made into the learning and behaviour of the scholars: those who were most perfect in their chapters, and who brought the best character for industry, humility, and sobriety, received a Bible, or some other good book.

Now Hester had been a whole year hoarding up her little savings, in order to be ready with a new gown on the May-day feast. She had never got less than two shillings a-week by her spinning,[7] besides working for the family, and earning a trifle by odd jobs. This money she faithfully carried to her mother every Saturday night, keeping back, by consent, only two-pence a week towards the gown. The sum was complete, the pattern had long been settled, and Hester had only on the Monday morning to go to the shop, pay her money, and bring home her gown to be made. Her mother happened to go out that morning early to iron in a gentleman's family, where she usually staid a day or two,[8] and Hester was busy putting the house in order before she went to the shop.

On that very Monday there was to be a meeting at the Bell of all the idle fellows in the parish; John Wilmot, of course, was to be there. Indeed, he had accepted a challenge of the blacksmith to a batch at all-fours.[9] The blacksmith was flush of money; John thought himself the best player; – and, that he might make sure of winning, he resolved to keep himself sober, which he knew was more than the other would do. John was so used to go upon tick for ale, that he got to the door of the Bell before he recollected that he could not keep his word with the gambler without money, and he had not a penny in his pocket, so he sullenly turned homewards. He dared not apply to his wife, as he knew he should be more likely to get a scratched face than a sixpence from her; but he knew that Hester had received two shillings for her last week's spinning on Saturday, and perhaps she might not yet have given it to her mother. Of the hoarded sum he knew nothing. He asked her if she could lend him half-a-crown, and he would pay her next day. Hester, pleased to see him in good humour, after what had passed the night before, ran up and fetched down her little box, and in the joy of her heart that he now desired something she *could* comply with, without wounding her conscience, cheerfully poured out her whole little stock upon the table. John was in raptures at the sight of three half-crowns and a sixpence, and eagerly seized it, box and all, together with a few hoarded halfpence at the bottom, though he had only asked to borrow half-a-crown. None but one whose heart was hardened by a long course of drunkenness could have taken away the whole, and for such a purpose. He told her she should certainly have it again next morning, and, indeed, intended to pay it, not doubting but he should double the sum. But John over-rated his own skill, or luck, for he lost every farthing to the blacksmith, and sneaked home before midnight, and quietly walked up to-bed. He was quite sober, which Hester thought a good sign. Next morning she asked him, in a very humble way, for the money, which she said she would not have done, but that if the gown was not bought directly it would not be ready in time for the feast. John's conscience had troubled him a little for what he had done, for when he was not drunk he was not ill-natured, and he stammered out a broken excuse, but owned he had lost the money, and had not a farthing left. The moment Hester saw him mild and kind, her heart was softened, and she begged him not to vex; adding, that she would be contented never to have a new gown as long as she lived, if she could have the comfort of always seeing him come home as sober as he was last night. For Hester did not know that he had refrained from getting drunk, only that he might gamble with a better chance of success; and that when a gamester keeps himself sober, it is not that he may practise a virtue, but that he may commit a worse crime. "I am indeed sorry for what I have done," said he: "you cannot go to the feast, and what will Madam Jones say?" – "Yes, but I can," said Hester; "for God looks not at the gown, but at the heart, and I am sure he sees mine full of gratitude at hearing you talk so kindly; and if I thought my dear father would change his present evil courses, I should be the happiest girl at the feast to-morrow." John walked away mournfully, and said to himself, – "Surely there must be something in religion, since it can thus change the heart. Hester was once a pert girl, and now she is as mild as a lamb. She was once an indolent girl, and now she is up with the lark. She was a vain girl, and would do any thing for a new ribbon; and now she is contented to go in rags to a feast at which every one else will have a new gown. She deprived herself of her gown to give me the money; and yet this very girl, so dutiful in some things, would submit to be turned out of doors, rather than read a loose book at my command, or break the Sabbath. I do not understand this; there must be some mystery in it." All this he said as he was going to work. In the evening he did not go to the Bell; whether it was owing to his new thoughts, or to his not having a penny in his pocket, I will not take upon me positively to say; but I believe it was a little of one, and a little of the other.

As the pattern of the intended gown had long been settled in the family, and as Hester had the money by her, it was looked on as good as bought, so that she was trusted to get it brought home, and made in her mother's absence. Indeed, so little did Rebecca care about the school, that she would not have cared any thing about the gown, if her vanity had not made her wish that her daughter should be the best drest of any girl at the feast. Being from home, as was said before, she knew nothing of the disappointment. On May-day morning, Hester, instead of keeping from the feast, because she had not a new gown, or meanly inventing any excuse for wearing an old one, dressed herself out as neatly as she could in her poor old things, and went to join the school in order to go to church. Whether Hester had formerly indulged a little pride of heart, and talked of this gown rather too much, I am not quite sure; certain it is, there was a great hue and cry made at seeing Hester Wilmot, the neatest girl, the most industrious girl in the school, come to the May-day feast in an old stuff gown, when every other girl was so creditably drest. Indeed, I am sorry to say, there were two or three much too smart for their station, and who had dizened themselves out in very improper finery, which Mrs. Jones made them take off before her.[10] "I mean this feast," said she, "as a reward of industry and piety, and not as a trial of skill who can be finest, and outvie the rest in show. If I do not take care, my feast will become an encouragement, not to virtue, but to vanity. I am so great a friend to decency of apparel, that I even like to see you deny your appetites, that you may be able to come decently dressed to the house of God. To encourage you to do this, I like to set apart this one day of innocent pleasure, against which you may be preparing all the year, by laying aside something every week towards buying a gown out of your little savings. But, let me tell you, that meekness and an humble spirit is of more value in the sight of God and good men than the gayest cotton gown, or the brightest pink ribbon in the parish."

Mrs. Jones, for all this, was as much surprised as the rest at Hester's mean garb: but such is the power of a good character, that she gave her credit for a right intention, especially as she knew the unhappy state of her family. For it was Mrs. Jones's way (and it is not a bad way) always to wait, and enquire into the truth, before she condemned any person of good character, though appearances were against them. As we cannot judge of people's motives, said she, we may, from ignorance, often condemn their best actions, and approve of their worst. It will be always time enough to judge unfavourably, and let us give others credit as long as we can, and then we, in our turn, may expect a favourable judgment from others, and remember who has said, *Judge not, that ye be not judged.*[11]

Hester was no more proud of what she had done for her father than she was humbled by the meanness of her garb; and notwithstanding Betty

Stiles, one of the girls whose finery had been taken away, sneered at her, Hester never offered to clear herself by exposing her father, though she thought it right secretly to inform Mrs. Jones of what had passed. When the examination of the girls began Betty Stiles was asked some questions on the fourth and fifth commandments which she answered very well. Hester was asked nearly the same questions, and, though she answered them no better than Betty had done, they were all surprised to see Mrs. Jones rise up, and give a handsome Bible to Hester, while she gave nothing to Betty. This girl cried out rather pertly, "Madam, it is very hard that I have no book: I was as perfect as Hester." – "I have often told you," said Mrs. Jones, "that religion is not a thing of the tongue but of the heart. That girl gives me the best proof that she has learned the fourth commandment to good purpose, who persists in keeping holy the Sabbath-day, though commanded to break it by a parent whom she loves. And that girl best proves that she keeps the fifth, who gives up her own comfort, and clothing, and credit, *to honour and obey her father and mother,* even though they are not such as she could wish. Betty Stiles, though she could answer the questions so readily, went abroad last Sunday when she should have been at school, and refused to nurse her sick mother when she could not help herself. Is this having learnt these two commandments to any good purpose?"[12]

Farmer Hoskins, who stood by, whispered Mrs. Jones, "Well, Madam, now you have convinced even me of the benefit of religious instruction; now I see there is a meaning to it. I thought it was in at one ear and out at the other, and that a song was as well as a psalm; but now I have found the proof of the pudding is in the eating. I see your scholars must *do* what they *hear,* and *obey* what they *learn.* Why, at this rate, they will all be the better servants for being really godly, and so I will add a pudding to next year's feast."[13]

The pleasure Hester felt in receiving a new Bible made her forget that she had on an old gown. She walked to church in a thankful frame; but how great was her joy, when she saw, among a number of working men, her own father going into church! As she passed by him, she cast on him a look of so much joy and affection, that it brought tears into his eyes, especially when he compared her mean dress with that of the other girls, and thought who had been the cause of it. John, who had not been at church for some years, was deeply stuck with the service. The confession with which it opens went to his heart. He felt, for the first time, that he was a *miserable sinner, and that there was no health in him.*[14] He now felt compunction for sin in general, though it was only his ill behaviour to his daughter which had brought him to church. The sermon was such as served to strengthen the impression which the prayers had made; and when it was over, instead of joining the ringers, (for the belfry was the only part of the church John liked, because it usually led to the ale-house,) he quietly walked back to his work. It was, indeed, the best day's work he ever made. He could not get out of his head the whole day the first words he heard at church: *When the wicked man turneth away from his wickedness, and doth that which is lawful and right, he shall save his soul alive.*[15] At night, instead of going to the Bell, he went home, intending to ask Hester to forgive him; but as soon as he got to the door, he heard Rebecca scolding his daughter for having brought such a disgrace on the family as to be seen in that old rag of a gown, and insisted on knowing what she had done with the money. Hester tried to keep the secret, but her mother declared she would turn her out of doors if she did not tell the truth. Hester was at last forced to confess she had given it to her father. Unfortunately for poor John, it was at this very moment that he opened the door. The mother now divided her fury between her guilty husband and her innocent child, till from words she fell to blows. John defended his daughter, and received some of the strokes intended for the poor girl. This turbulent scene partly put John's good resolutions to flight, though the patience of Hester did him almost as much good as the sermon he had heard. At length the poor girl escaped up stairs, not a little bruised, and a scene of much violence passed between John and Rebecca.[16] She declared she would not sit down to supper with such a brute, and set off to a neighbour's house, that she might have the pleasure of abusing him the longer. John, whose mind was much disturbed, went up stairs without his supper. As he was passing by Hester's little room he heard her voice, and as he concluded she was venting bitter complaints against her unnatural parents, he stopped to listen, resolving to go in and comfort her. He stopped at the door, for, by the light of the moon, he saw her kneeling by her bedside, and praying so earnestly that she did not hear him. As he made sure she could be praying for nothing but his death, what was his surprise to hear these words: "O Lord, have mercy upon my dear father and mother; teach me to love them, to pray for them, and do them good; make me more dutiful and more patient, that, adorning the doctrine of God, my saviour, I may recommend his holy religion, and my dear parents may be brought to love and fear thee, through Jesus Christ."

Poor John, who would never have been hard-hearted if he had not been a drunkard, could not stand this, he fell down on his knees, embraced his child, and begged her to teach him how to pray. He prayed himself

as well as he could, and though he did not know what words to use, yet
his heart was melted; he owned he was a sinner, and begged Hester to
fetch the prayer-book, and read over the confession with which he had
been so struck at church. This was the pleasantest order she had ever
obeyed. Seeing him deeply affected with a sense of sin, she pointed out
to him the Saviour of sinners; and in this manner she passed some hours
with her father, which were the happiest of her life; such a night was
worth a hundred cotton, or even silk gowns.[17] In the course of the week
Hester read over the confession, and some other prayers to her father so
often, that he got them by heart, and repeated them while he was at work.
She next taught him the fifty-first psalm.[18] At length he took courage to
kneel down and pray before he went to bed. From that time he bore his
wife's ill-humour much better than he had ever done, and as he knew her
to be neat, and notable, and saving, he began to think, that if her temper
was not quite so bad, his home might still become as pleasant a place to
him as ever the Bell had been: but unless she became more tractable, he
did not know what to do with his long evenings after the little ones were
in bed, for he began, once more, to delight in playing with them. Hester
proposed that she herself should teach him to read an hour every night,
and he consented. Rebecca began to storm, from the mere trick she had
got of storming: but finding that he now brought home all his earnings,
and that she got both his money and his company (for she had once
loved him), she began to reconcile herself to this new way of life.[19] In a
few months John could read a psalm. In learning to read it he also got
it by heart, and this proved a little store for private devotion; and while
he was mowing or reaping he could call to mind a text to cheer his labour.
He now went constantly to church, and often dropped in at the school
on a Sunday evening to hear their prayers. He expressed so much pleasure
at this, that one day Hester ventured to ask him if they should set up
family prayer at home? John said he should like it mightily; but as he
could not yet read quite well enough, he desired Hester to try to get a
proper book, and begin next Sunday night. Hester had bought, of a pious
hawker, for three halfpence, the Book of Prayers, printed for the Cheap
Repository, and knew she should there find something suitable.[20]

When Hester read the exhortation at the beginning of this little book,
her mother, who sat in the corner, and pretended to be asleep, was so much
struck that she could not find a word to say against it. For a few nights,
indeed, she continued to sit still, or pretended to rock the young child while
her husband and daughter were kneeling at their prayers. She expected John
would have scolded her for this; and so perverse was her temper, that she

was disappointed at his finding no fault with her. Seeing at last that he was very patient, and that though he prayed fervently himself, he suffered her to do as she liked, she lost the spirit of opposition for want of something to provoke it. As her pride began to be subdued, some little disposition to piety was awakened in her heart. By degrees she slid down on her knees, though at first it was behind the cradle, or the clock, or in some corner, where she thought they would not see her. Hester rejoiced even in this outward change in her mother, and prayed that God would at last be pleased to touch her heart as he had done that of her father.

As John now spent no idle money, he had saved up a trifle by working over-hours; this he kindly offered to Hester to make up for the loss of her gown. Instead of accepting it, Hester told him, that as she herself was young and healthy, she should soon be able to clothe herself out of her own savings, and begged him to make her mother a present of this gown, which he did. It had been a maxim for Rebecca, that it was better not to go to church at all than go in an old gown. She had, however, so far conquered this evil notion, that she had lately gone pretty often. This kindness of the gown touched her not a little; and the first Sunday she put it on, Mr. Edwards happened to preach from this text, *God resisteth the proud, but giveth grace to the humble.*[21] This sermon so affected Rebecca that she never once thought she had her new gown on, till she came to take it off when she went to bed, and that very night, instead of skulking behind, she knelt down by her husband, and joined in prayer with much fervour.

There was one thing sunk deep in Rebecca's mind; she had observed, that since her husband had grown religious he had been so careful not to give her any offence, that he was become scrupulously clean: took off his dirty shoes before he sat down, and was very cautious not to spill a drop of beer on her shining table. Now it was rather remarkable, that as John grew more neat, Rebecca grew more indifferent to neatness. But both these changes arose from the same cause, the growth of religion in their hearts. John grew cleanly from the fear of giving pain to his wife, while Rebecca grew indifferent from having discovered the sin and folly of an over-anxious care about trifles. When the heart is once given up to God, such vanities in a good degree die of themselves.

Hester continues to grow in grace, and in knowledge. Last Christmas-day she was appointed an under-teacher in the school; and many people think that some years hence, if any thing should happen to Mrs. Crew, Hester may be promoted to be head-mistress.[22]

PATIENT JOE;

Or, The NEWCASTLE COLLIER.

HAVE you heard of a Collier of honest renown,
Who dwelt on the borders of Newcastle Town?
His name it was Joseph—you better may know
If I tell you he always was call'd patient JOE.

Whatever betided he thought it was right,
And Providence still he kept ever in sight;
To those who love GOD, let things turn as they wou'd
He was certain that all work'd together for good.

He prais'd his Creator whatever befel;
How thankful was Joseph when matters went well!
How sincere were his carols of praise for good health,
And how grateful for any increase in his wealth!

PATIENT JOE: OR, THE NEWCASTLE COLLIER

HAVE you heard of a Collier[1] of honest renown,
Who dwelt on the borders of Newcastle Town?
His name it was Joseph – you better may know
If I tell you he always was call'd Patient JOE.

What ever betided, he thought it was right,
And Providence still he kept ever in sight;
To those who love GOD, let things turn as they wou'd,
He was certain that all work'd together for good.

He prais'd his Creator whatever befell;
How thankful was Joseph when matters went well!   10
How sincere were his carols of praise for good health,
And how grateful for any increase in his wealth!

In trouble he bow'd him to GOD's holy will;
How contented was Joseph when matters went ill!
When rich and when poor be alike understood
That all things together were working for good.

If the Land was afflicted with war, he declar'd
'Twas a needful correction for sins which *he* shar'd;
And when merciful Heaven bid slaughter to cease,
How thankful was Joe for the blessing of peace!   20

When Taxes ran high, and provisions were dear,
Still Joseph declar'd he had nothing to fear;
It was but a trial he well understood,
From HIM who made all work together for good.

Tho' his wife was but sickly, his gettings but small,
A mind so submissive prepar'd him for all;
He liv'd on his gains were they greater or less,
And the GIVER he ceas'd not each moment to bless.

When another child came he receiv'd him with joy,
And Providence bless'd who had sent him a boy;   30
But when the child dy'd – said poor Joe, I'm content,
For GOD had a right to recall what he lent.[2]

It was Joseph's ill fortune to work in a pit
With some who believ'd that profaneness was wit;
When disasters befell him much pleasure they shew'd,
And laugh'd and said – Joseph, will this work for good?

But ever when these would profanely advance
That *this* happen'd by luck, and *that* happen'd by chance;
Still Joseph insisted no chance could be found,[3]
Not a sparrow by accident falls to the ground.   40

Among his companions who work'd in the pit,
And made him the butt of their profligate wit,
Was idle Tim Jenkins, who drank and who gam'd,
Who mock'd at his Bible, and was not asham'd.[4]

One day at the pit his old comrades he found,
And they chatted, preparing to go under ground;
Tim Jenkins as usual was turning to jest
Joe's notion– that all things which happen'd were best.[5]

As Joe on the ground had unthinkingly laid
His provision for dinner of bacon and bread,   50
A dog on the watch seized the bread and the meat,
And off with his prey ran with footsteps so fleet.

Now to see the delight that Tim Jenkins express'd!
"Is the loss of thy dinner too, Joe, for the best?"
"No doubt on't," said Joe; "but as I must eat,
"'Tis my duty to try to recover my meat."

So saying, he follow'd the dog a long round,
While Tim laughing and swearing went down under ground.
Poor Joe soon return'd, tho' his bacon was lost,
For the dog a good dinner had made at his cost.   60

When Joseph came back, he expected a sneer,
But the face of each Collier spoke horror and fear:
What a narrow escape hast thou had, they all said,
The pit is fall'n in, and Tim Jenkins is dead!

How sincere was the gratitude Joseph express'd!
How warm the compassion which glow'd in his breast!
Thus events great and small, if aright understood,
Will be found to be working together for good.

"When my meat," Joseph cry'd, "was just now stol'n away,
"And I had no prospect of eating to-day,   70
"How cou'd it appear to a short-sighted sinner,
"That my life would be sav'd by the loss of my dinner?" 6

                                                          Z.

THE RIOT;

Or, HALF a LOAF is better than no BREAD.

In a Dialogue between *Jack Anvil* and *Tom Hod*.

To the Tune of " A Cobler there was," &c.

TOM.

COME neighbours, no longer be patient and quiet,
   Come let us go kick up a bit of a riot;
I am hungry, my lads, but I've little to eat,
So we'll pull down the mills, and seize all the meat:
I'll give you good sport, boys, as ever you saw,
So a fig for the Justice, a fig for the law.

                   Derry down.

THE RIOT:

Or, Half a Loaf is better than no Bread.
In a dialogue between Jack Anvil and Tom Hod.[1]

To the Tune of "A Cobler there was."

TOM

COME neighbours, no longer be patient and quiet,
Come let us go kick up a bit of a riot;
I am hungry, my lads, but I've little to eat,
So we'll pull down the mills, and seize all the meat:[2]
I'll give you good sport, boys, as ever you saw,
So a fig for the Justice, a fig for the law.
Derry down.

Then his pitchfork Tom seiz'd – Hold a moment, says Jack,
I'll shew thee thy blunder, brave boy, in a crack,
And if I don't prove we had better be still,   10
I'll assist thee straitway to pull down every mill;
I'll shew thee how passion thy reason does cheat,
Or I'll join thee in plunder for bread and for meat.
Derry down

What a whimsey to think thus our bellies to fill,
For we stop all the grinding by breaking the mill!
What a whimsey to think we shall get more to eat
By abusing the butchers who get us the meat!
What a whimsey to think we shall mend our spare diet
By breeding disturbance, by murder and riot!   20
Derry down.

Because I am dry, 'twould be foolish, I think,
To pull out my tap and to spill all my drink;
Because I am hungry and want to be fed,
That is sure no wise reason for wasting my bread:
And just such wise reasons for mending their diet
Are us'd by those blockheads who rush into riot.
Derry down.

I would not take comfort from others distresses,
But still I would mark how God our land blesses;   30
For tho' in Old England the times are but sad,
Abroad I am told they are ten times as bad;
In the land of the Pope there is scarce any grain,
And 'tis worse still, they say, both in Holland and Spain.[3]
Derry down.

Let us look to the harvest our wants to beguile;
See the lands with rich crops how they every where smile!
Mean time to assist us, by each Western breeze –
Some corn is brought daily across the salt seas.
Of tea we'll drink little, of gin none at all,   40
And we'll patiently wait and the prices will fall.
Derry down.

But if we're not quiet, then let us not wonder
If things grow much worse by our riot and plunder;
And let us remember, whenever we meet,
The more Ale we drink, boys, the less we shall eat.
On those days spent in riot *no* bread you brought home,
Had you spent them in labour you must have had *some*.
Derry down.

A dinner of herbs, says the wise man, with quiet,   50
Is better than beef amid discord and riot.[4]
If the thing can't be help'd, I'm a foe to all strife,
And I pray for a peace every night of my life;
But in matters of state not an inch will I budge,
Because I conceive I'm no very good judge.
Derry down.

But though poor, I can work, my brave boy, with the best,
Let the King and the Parliament manage the rest;
I lament both the War and the Taxes together,
Tho' I verily think they don't alter the weather.   60
The King, as I take it, with very good reason,
May prevent a bad law, but can't help a bad season.
                              Derry down.

The parliament men, altho' great is their power,
Yet they cannot contrive us a bit of a shower;
And I never yet heard, tho' our Rulers are wise,
That they know very well how to manage the skies;[5]
For the best of them all, as they found to their cost,
Were not able to hinder last winter's hard frost.

Besides I must share in the wants of the times,
Because I have had my full share in it's crimes;[6]
And I'm apt to believe the distress which is sent
Is to punish and cure us of all discontent.
– But harvest is coming – potatoes are come!
                              Derry down.

And tho' I've no money, and though I've no lands,
I've a head on my shoulders, and a pair of good hands;
So I'll work the whole day, and on Sundays I'll seek   80
At church how to bear all the wants of the week.
The Gentlefolks, too, will afford us supplies,
They'll subscribe – and they'll give up their puddings and pies.[7]
                              Derry down.

Then before I'm induced to take part in a Riot,
I'll ask this short question – What shall I get by it?
So I'll e'en wait a little till cheaper the bread,
For a mittimus[8] hangs o'er each Rioter's head;
And when of two evils I'm ask'd which is best,
I'd rather be hungry than hang'd, I protest.   90
                              Derry down.

Quoth Tom, thou art right; if I rise, I'm a Turk,
So he threw down his pitchfork, and went to his work.
                                        Z.

THE STORY OF
SINFUL SALLY,
THE
Hampshire Tragedy,
THE
BAD BARGAIN,
AND
ROBERT & RICHARD.

SOLD BY HOWARD & EVANS,
(Printers to the CHEAP REPOSITORY for Moral and Religious
Tracts) No. 41, and 42, *Long-lane, West-smithfield,*
and J. HATCHARD, 190, *Piccadilly,* London; by
J. BINNS, *Bath:*—And by all Booksellers, Newsmen,
and Hawkers in Town and Country.

*** *Great allowance will be made to Shopkeepers and Hawkers.*

PRICE ONE PENNY or 6s. *per Hundred.*

Entered at Stationer's-Hall.

THE STORY OF SINFUL SALLY

told by herself, shewing
How from being SALLY of the GREEN she was first led to become
SINFUL SALLY, and afterwards, DRUNKEN SAL, and how at last she
came to a most melancholy and almost hopeless End; being therein a Warning
to young Women both in Town and Country.

Come each maiden lend an ear,
　　Country Lass and London Belle!
Come and drop a mournful tear
　　O'er the tale that I shall tell!

I that ask your tender pity,
　　Ruin'd now and all forlorn,
Once, like you, was young and pretty,
　　And as cheerful as the morn.

In yon distant cottage sitting,
　　Far away from London town,　　　　　　　10
Once you might have seen me knitting
　　In my simple Kersey Gown.[1]

Where the little lambkins leap,
　　Where the meadows look so gay,
Where the drooping willows weep,
　　Simple Sally used to stray.

Then I tasted many a Blessing,
　　Then I had an honest fame;
Father Mother me caressing,
　　Smil'd, and thought me free from blame.　　20

Then, amid my friends so dear,
  Life it speeded fast away;
O, it moves a tender tear,
  To bethink me of the day!

From the villages surrounding,
  Ere I well had reach'd Eighteen,
Came the modest youths abounding,
  All to Sally of the Green.

Courting days were thus beginning,
  And I soon had prov'd a wife;   30
O! if I had kept from sinning,
  Now how blest had been my life.

Come each maiden lend an ear,
  Country Lass and London Belle!
Come ye now and deign to hear
  How poor sinful Sally fell.

Where the Hill begins inclining,
  Half a furlong from the Road,
O'er the village white and shining
  Stands Sir William's great abode.   40

Near his meadow I was tripping,
  Vainly wishing to be seen,
When Sir William met me skipping,
  And he spoke me on the Green.

Bid me quit my cloak of scarlet,
  Blam'd my simple Kersey Gown;
Ey'd me then, so like a Varlet,[2]
  Such as live in London town.

With his presents I was loaded,
  And bedeck'd in ribbons gay;   50
Thus my ruin was foreboded,
  O, how crafty was his way!

Vanish'd now from Cottage lowly,
  My poor Parents' hearts I break;
Enter on a state unholy,
  Turn a Mistress to a Rake.

Now no more by morning light
  Up to God my voice I raise;
Now no shadows of the night
  Call my thoughts to prayer and praise.   60

Hark! a well-known sound I hear!
  'Tis the Church's Sunday Bell;
No; I dread to venture near:
  No; I'm now the Child of Hell.

Now I lay my Bible by,
  Chuse that impious book so new,
Love the bold blaspheming lie,
  And that filthy novel too.[3]

Next to London town I pass
  (Sinful Sally is my name)   70
There to gain a front of brass,
  And to glory in my Shame.

Powder'd well, and puff'd and painted,
  Rivals all I there out-shine;
With skin so white and heart so tainted,
  Rolling in my Chariot fine.

In the Park I glitter daily,
  Then I dress me for the play,
Then to masquerade so gaily,
  See me, see me tear away.   80

When I meet some meaner Lass[4]
  Then I toss with proud disdain;
Laugh and giggle as I pass,
  Seeming not to know a pain.

Still at every hour of leisure
  Something whispers me within,
O! I hate this life of pleasure,
  For it is a Life of Sin.

Thus amidst my peals of laughter
  Horror seizes oft my frame: 90
Pleasure now – Damnation after,
  And a never-dying flame.

Save me, Save me, Lord, I cry,
  Save my soul from Satan's chain!
Now I see Salvation nigh,
  Now I turn to Sin again.

Is it then some true Repentance
  That I feel for evil done?
No; 'tis horror of my sentence,
  'Tis the pangs of Hell begun.   100

By a thousand ills o'ertaken
  See me now quite sinking down;
'Till so lost and so forsaken,
  Sal is cast upon the town.

At the dusk of evening grey
  Forth I step from secret cell;
Roaming like a beast of prey,
  Or some hateful Imp of Hell.

Ah! how many youths so blooming
  By my wanton looks I've won;   110
Then by vices all consuming
  Left them ruin'd and undone!

Thus the cruel spider stretches
  Wide his web for every fly;
Then each victim that he catches
  Strait he poisons till he die.

Now no more by conscience troubled,
  Deep I plunge in every Sin:
True; my sorrows are redoubled,
  But I drown them all in Gin.   120

See me next with front so daring
  Band of ruffian Rogues among;
Fighting, cheating, drinking, swearing,
  And the vilest of the throng.

Mark that youngest of the thieves;
  Taught by Sal he ventures further;
What he filches Sal receives,
  'Tis for Sal he does the murther.

See me then attend my victim
  To the fatal Gallows Tree;   130
Pleas'd to think how I have nick'd him,
  Made him swing while I am free.

Jack I laughing see depart,
  While with Dick I drink and sing;
Soon again I'll fill the cart,
  Make this present Lover swing.

But while thus with guilt surprising,
  Sal pursues her bold career,
See God's dreadful wrath arising,
  And the day of vengeance near!   140

Fierce disease my body seizes,
  Racking pain afflicts my bones;
Dread of Death my spirit freezes,
  Deep and doleful are my groans.

Here with face so shrunk and spotted
  On the clay-cold ground I lie;[6]
See how all my flesh is rotted,
  Stop, O Stranger, see me die!

Conscience, as my breath's departing,
  Plunges too his arrow deep,   150
With redoubled fury starting
  Like some Giant from his sleep.

In this Pit of Ruin lying,
  Once again before I die,
Fainting, trembling, weeping, fighting,
  Lord to thee I'll lift mine eye.

Thou can'st save the vilest Harlot,
  Grace, I've heard is free and full,
Sins that once were "red as scarlet"
  Thou can'st make as "white as wool."⁷   160

Savior, whom I pierc'd so often,
  Deeper still my guilt imprint!
Let thy mighty Spirit soften
  This my harden'd heart of flint.

Vain, alas! is all my groaning,
  For I fear the die is cast;
True, thy blood is all-atoning,
  But my day of Grace is past.⁸

Savior! hear me or I perish!
  None who *lives* is quite undone;   170
Still a Ray of Hope I'll cherish
  'Till Eternity's begun.

CHEAP REPOSITORY.

THE
SORROWS of YAMBA;

OR, THE

Negro Woman's Lamentation.

Sold by J. MARSHALL,
(PRINTER to the CHEAP REPOSITORY for
Religious and Moral Tracts) No. 17, Queen-Street,
Cheapfide, and No. 4, Aldermary Church-Yard,
and R. WHITE, Piccadilly, LONDON.
By S. HAZARD,
PRINTER to the CHEAP REPOSITORY, at Bath;
and by all Bookfellers, Newfmen, and Hawkers,
in Town and Country.—Great Allowance will be
made to Shopkeepers and Hawkers.
Price an Halfpenny each, or 2s. 3d. per 100—1s. 3d. for 50.—
6d. for 25.
Entered at Stationers Hall.

THE SORROWS OF YAMBA;

or, the Negro Woman's Lamentation[1]
To the tune of Hosiers Ghost

"In St. Lucie's distant isle,
  Still with Afric's love I burn;[2]
Parted many a thousand mile,
  Never, never to return.

Come, kind death! and give me rest;
  Yamba has no friend but thee;
Thou can'st ease my throbbing breast;
  Thou can'st set the Prisoner free.

Down my cheeks the tears are dripping,
  Broken is my heart with grief;   10
Mangled my poor flesh with whipping,
  Come, kind death! and bring relief.

Born on Afric's Golden Coast,
  Once I was as blest as you;
Parents tender I could boast,
  Husband dear, and children too.

Whity man he came from far,
  Sailing o'er the briny flood;
Who, with help of British Tar,[3]
  Buys up human flesh and blood.   20

With the Baby at my breast
  (Other two were sleeping by)
In my Hut I sat at rest,
  With no thought of danger nigh.

From the Bush at even tide,
  Rush'd the fierce man-stealing Crew;
Seiz'd the Children by my side,
  Seiz'd the wretched Yamba too.

Then for love of filthy Gold,
  Strait they bore me to the Sea,   30
Cramm'd me down a Slave Ship's hold,
  Here were Hundreds stow'd like me.[4]

Naked on the Platform lying,
  Now we cross the tumbling wave;
Shrieking, sickening, fainting, dying,
  Deed of shame for Britons brave.[5]

At the savage Captain's beck;
  Now like Brutes they make us prance;
Smack the Cat[6] about the Deck,
  And in scorn they bid us dance.   40

Nauseous horse-beans they bring nigh,
  Sick and sad we cannot eat;
Cat must cure the Sulks, they cry,
  Down their throats we'll force the meat.

I in groaning pass'd the night,
  And did roll my aching head;
At the break of morning light,
  My poor Child was cold and dead.

Happy, happy, there she lies,
  Thou shalt feel the lash no more,   50
Thus full many a Negro dies
  Ere we reach the destin'd shore.

Thee, sweet infant, none shall sell,
  Thou has't gained a wat'ry Grave;
Clean escap'd the Tyrants fell,
  While thy mother lives a Slave.

Driven like Cattle to a fair,
  See they sell us young and old;
Child from Mother too they tear,
  All for love of filthy Gold   60

I was sold to Massa hard,
  Some have Massas kind and good;
And again my back was scarr'd,
  Bad and stinted was my food.

Poor and wounded, faint and sick,
  All expos'd to burning sky;
Massa bids me grass to pick,
  And I now am near to die.

What and if to death he send me,
  Savage murder tho' it be,   70
British Law shall ne'er befriend me,
  They protect not Slaves like me.[7]

Mourning thus my wretched state,
  (Ne'er may I forget the day)
Once in dusk of evening late
  Far from home I dar'd to stray;

Dar'd, alas! with impious haste
  Tow'rds the roaring Sea to fly;
Death itself I long'd to taste,
  Long'd to cast me in and Die.   80

There I met upon the Strand
  English Missionary Good,
He had Bible book in hand,
  Which poor me no understood.[8]

Led by pity from afar
  He had left his native ground;
Thus if some inflict a scar,
  Others fly to cure the wound.

Strait he pull'd me from the shore,
  Bid me no self-murder do;   90
Talk'd of state when life is o'er,
  All from Bible good and true.

Then he led me to his Cot,
  Sooth'd and pity'd all my woe;
Told me 'twas the Christian's lot
  Much to suffer here below.

Told me then of God's dear Son,
  (Strange and wond'rous is the story)
What sad wrong to him was done,
  Tho' he was the Lord of Glory.   100

Told me too, like one who knew him,
  (Can such love as this be true?)
How he died for them that slew him,
  Died for wretched Yamba too.

Freely he his mercy proffer'd,
  And to Sinners he was sent;
E'en to Massa pardon's offer'd:
  O if Massa would repent!

Wicked deed full many a time
  Sinful Yamba too hath done   110
But she wails to God her crime,
  But she trusts his only Son.

O ye slaves whom Massas beat,
  Ye are stain'd with guilt within:
As ye hope for mercy sweet,
  So forgive your Massas' sin[9]

And with grief when sinking low,
  Mark the Road that Yamba trod;
Think how all her pain and woe
  Brought the Captive home to God.   120

Now let Yamba too adore
  Gracious Heaven's mysterious Plan;
Now I'll count my mercies o'er,
  Flowing thro' the guilt of man.

Now I'll bless my cruel capture,
  (Hence I've known a Saviour's name)
Till my grief is turn'd to Rapture,
  And I half forget the blame.

But tho' here a Convert rare,
  Thanks her God for Grace divine;   130
Let not man the glory share,
  Sinner, still the guilt is thine.

Here an injur'd Slave forgives,
  There a Host for vengeance cry;
Here a single Yamba lives,
  There a thousand droop and die.

Duly now baptiz'd am I,
  By good Missionary Man:[10]
Lord, my nature purify
  As no outward water can!   140

All my former thoughts abhorr'd,
  Teach me now to pray and praise;
Joy and Glory in my Lord,
  Trust and serve him all my days.

Worn indeed with Grief and Pain,
  Death I now will welcome in:
O, the Heavenly Prize to gain!
  O, to 'scape the power of Sin!

True of heart, and meek, and lowly,
  Pure and blameless let me grow!   150
Holy may I be, for Holy,
  Is the place to which I go.

But tho' death this hour may find me,
  Still with Afric's love I burn,
(There I've left a spouse behind me)
  Still to native land I turn.

And when Yamba sinks in Death,
  This my latest prayer shall be,
While I yield my parting breath,
  O, that Afric might be free.   160

Cease, ye British Sons of murder!
  Cease from forging's Afric's chain
Mock your Saviour's name no further,
  Cease your savage lust of gain.[11]

Ye that boast "*Ye rule the waves*,"
  Bid no Slave Ship soil the sea,
Ye, that "*never will be slaves*,"
  Bid poor Afric's land be free.[12]

Where ye gave to war it's birth,
  Where your traders fix'd their den,   170
There go publish *"Peace on Earth*,"
  Go proclaim "good-will to men."

Where ye once have carried slaughter,
  Vice, and Slavery, and Sin;
Seized on Husband, Wife, and Daughter,
  Let the Gospel enter in.

Thus, where Yamba's native home,
  Humble Hut of Rushes stood,
Oh if there should chance to roam
  Some dear Missionary good;   180

Thou in Afric's distant land,
  Still shalt see the man I love;
Join him to the Christian band,
  Guide his Soul to Realms above.

There no Fiend again shall sever
　Those whom God hath join'd and blest;
There they dwell with Him for ever,
　There *"the weary are at rest."*[13]

NOTES

For general details of the texts used for this edition, see the **Note on Texts** in the Introduction.

Notes for *Tom White, Part One*

First published in 1795, probably in March. Spinney notes its registration at Stationer's Hall on 24 February.

1. Title changed from 'Postilion' to the more modern 'Postboy' in More's *Works*, though the old title is retained in many later chapbook issues. A postilion rides on the near horse of a pair which is drawing a coach without a coachman (*SOED*); he is, in effect, the driver.

2. *Sunday school.* Sunday schools were founded by Robert Raikes in 1780 and developed by others, such as Sarah Trimmer, who were anxious to save young souls and to improve the religious tone of society. Hannah More and her sister Martha established and maintained a number of Sunday Schools in the Mendip region (see Introduction). Details of local resistance to their enterprise and the methods by which they overcame suspicion and apathy are given in Martha's journals, edited by Arthur Roberts in 1859 as *Mendip Annals*.

3. *poor beasts.* More's comments on cruelty to animals reflects a late-eighteenth century sensibility and awareness of human responsibility to the 'brute creation'. The subject is often treated in instructive books written for children during this period, for example, by Mary Wollstonecraft and Ann and Jane Taylor.

4. *travel ... on a Sunday.* This reprimand to gentlefolks illustrates the changing concept of appropriate behaviour on Sundays which Evangelical writers put forward in tracts and sermons. In a passage added in later editions. More also lectures the upper classes: 'and it is still more inexcusable in the great who have every day at their command.' Unnecessary travel is Sabbath-breaking; it diverts attention from religious observance. The Sabbath is recorded in the Book of Genesis as the seventh day, on which God rested from the labour of Creation; as a day of rest, its observance should benefit the labouring classes.

5. *long out of place.* Out of work. Added in some later editions: 'and nobody ever cared to be driven by him.' An example of More's underlining of points when revising for publication; space is too limited in this edition to give more than a few instances of the many minor changes to her texts.

6. *never was an hospital ... Christian religion.* This sentence is set in capital letters, not italics, in the 1818 edition. More's expression of pride in

the social improvements of the later Enlightenment period reveals some historical ignorance of Jewish, Islamic and other medical traditions in the 'heathen world' which she contrasts with the Christian world. Following the words *Christian religion* in the 1818 edition is this comment:

> A religion which, like its Divine Founder, while its grand object is the salvation of men's souls, teaches us also to relieve their bodily wants. It directs us never to forget that He who forgave sins, healed diseases, and while he preached the Gospel, fed the multitude.

7. *all-fours.* Card game with four points at stake: High, Low, Jack, Game.
8. *next temptation.* Added later: 'He thought that amendment was a thing to be set about at any time; he did not know that *it is the grace of God which bringeth us to repentance.* (Allusion to Romans 2: 4: 'the goodness of God leadeth thee to repentance'.)
9. *his strength was perfect weakness.* 2 Corinthians 12: 9: 'my strength is made perfect in weakness'
10. *cast his bread … waters.* Ecclesiastes 11: 1: 'Cast thy bread upon the waters: for thou shalt find it after many days'. Added in later editions after 'his own good time': 'and in his own way, but *our* zeal and *our* exertion are the means by which he commonly chooses to work'.
11. *catechism.* The words *'to do our duty in that state of life in which it shall please God to call us'* refer to the Catechism. At Sunday School children were made to learn the Catechism, a sequence of questions and answers on the Christian religion printed in the Book of Common Prayer. Its heading describes it as 'an Instruction to be learned of every Person, before he be brought to be confirmed by the Bishop'. In a later addition to the paragraph, More stresses its importance: 'It is, if I may so speak, the very grammar of Christianity and of our church; and they who understand every part of their catechism thoroughly will not be ignorant of any thing which a plain Christian needs to know'. Many of her Tracts make reference to catechism; in *Black Giles, Part* 2 the process of questioning children on sin is dramatized.
12. *prayers and provender.* Added later: 'and I beg leave to recommend Tom's maxim to all travellers, whether master or servant, carrier or coachman'.
13. *linch-pins.* These connect the wheel to the axle of the carriage
14. *wanton stroke inflicted.* This paragraph makes approximate reference to the following verses in the Bible: Proverbs 12: 10: 'A righteous man regardeth the life of his beast but the tender mercies of the wicked are cruel'; Jonah 4: 11: 'And should I not spare Nineveh, that great

city, wherein are more than sixscore thousand persons ... and also much cattle?'. Later More adds, "Doth God care for horses," said he, and shall man be cruel to them?"; see 1 Corinthians 9: 9: 'Doth God take care for oxen?'.

15. *life which is to come.* 1 Timothy 4: 8: 'for bodily exercise profiteth little: but godliness is profitable unto all things, having promise ...'

16. *from the parish.* From destitution and the need to apply for parish relief.

17. *new parishioner.* Dr Shepherd is one of many models of religious zeal in the Tracts; More instructs the local clergy and magistrates in their responsibilities to the poor, but as we see later in this tale, a benevolent interest in parishioners is liable to become intrusive. Tom White has been promoted by More to the rank of 'Mr' on account of his industry and virtue; those who take the advice of their betters respectfully will be given encouragement to make a modest advance in social status. The term 'condescending', often found in the Tracts, has the same unpleasant overtones as 'patronizing' to our ears, but a more neutral reading would be possible at the time.

18. *mistress of a family.* The subject of educating women and preparing them for their domestic responsibilities, both moral and practical, appears throughout More's work. For the upper and middle classes her views were set out in the treatise *Strictures on the Modern System of Female Education* (1799) and in *Coelebs in Search of a Wife* (1808). In *The Two Wealthy Farmers* – one of the *Stories for the Middle Ranks of Society* – she gives a lively account of the defective education, which turns the daughters of Farmer Bragwell into the 'tawdry, vain, dressy' girls Tom White must avoid.

19. *she shall be praised.* Proverbs 31: 30.

20. *saved fifty pounds.* Worth about £1,500 in 2000.

21. *cares and strifes.* More's footnote in 1795 read: *See Dodd's Sayings'.* John Dod (1549? - 1645) was a puritan preacher. *Old Mr Dod's Sayings* was published in 1667.

22. *troubles from which you cannot save one another.* Added later: 'misfortunes which no human prudence can avoid'. More embellishes sentences when revising, echoing Biblical parallelism.

23. *good man ... sin against God?* By 1818 'good' is changed to 'well disposed'. *'How shall I do this great wickedness ... ':* Genesis 39: 9: 'How then can I do this great wickedness, and sin against God?'.

24. *vile trash.* This final paragraph and the Hymn printed after it in 1795 is omitted in the *Works.* For the 'vile trash' sung in stable yards see collections of ballads, such as *Later English Broadside Ballads,* ed. John

Holloway and Joan Black. London, 1975, which draws on the Madden Collection, and *The Common Muse,* ed. V. de Sola Pinto and A.E. Rodway, London, 1957.

25. *HYMN ON DIVINE PROVIDENCE.* Joseph Addison (1672-1719), *The Spectator* 453, 9 August 1712. The first of thirteen verses printed in the 1795 chapbook is quoted here:

> When all thy mercies, O my God,
> My rising soul surveys.
> Transported with the view I'm lost
> In wonder, love and praise ...

Notes for *The Way to Plenty, or Tom White, Part Two*
First published in September 1795.

1. The title-note 'Written in 1795, the Year of Scarcity' is added in later editions, but printed here for clarity.

2. *GOD maketh his sun to shine on the just and the unjust.* Matthew 5: 45: ' he maketh his sun to rise on the evil and on the good, and sendeth rain on the just and on the unjust'. The use of capitals for the name of God is not consistent in early issues of the Tracts; this might be More's choice of emphasis, or it might result from compositors' errors and the relative piety of the printers.

3. *battle to the strong.* Ecclesiastes 9: 11. More inserts 'always' ('not always to the swift ... ')

4. *blight ... fire ... distemper.* The plight of farmers in the bad winter of 1795 is related here to the misfortunes inflicted on Job, 'a perfect and an upright man', as God allows Satan to test his faith by fire, destruction, and the 'sore boils' of disease; see Job 1.

5. *bread of carefulness.* Ezekiel 12: 19: 'They shall eat their bread with carefulness ... that her land may be desolate ... '

6. *by the great.* 'Of work done: At a fixed price for the whole amount; by task; by the piece. Now *dialect.' (SOED)*

7. *seven shillings.* More's creative arithmetic can be translated into modern terms by reference to the 'Note on Money, 1790-1800' in the Introduction. Her advice in this paragraph forms part of a prolonged campaign to get men out of the ale-house and back in the home. See *Hester Wilmot, Part 2.*

8. Added in later editions: 'The barn was thatched, the mutton bought, the beer brewed, the friend invited, and the holiday enjoyed'. More, when revising, tends to sum up and round off. This spoils the quick movement of 'And so Tom was upon the roof in a twinkling'.

9. *barns ... fruits of the earth in due season.* Psalms 65: 11: '*Thou crownest the year with thy goodness...*'; Book of Common Prayer: the Litany: 'that it may please thee to give and preserve to our use the kindly fruits of the earth' and Galatians 6: 9: 'in due season we shall reap, if we faint not'.

10. *adorn the horns of the ram ... innocent.* The communal harvest supper is one of the old village ceremonies recorded in Hardy's novels; he might have found pagan echoes in this ritual. More's comment is probably based on Old Testament references to the sacrifice of rams.

11. *But thou, when thou makest a feast ... just.* Luke 14: 13-14: 'But when thou makest a feast, call the poor, the maimed, the lame, the blind'.

12. *sixty-fifth psalm.* See note 9 above. Psalm 65 begins: 'Praise waiteth for thee, O God'.

13. *THE HARD WINTER.* More adds a footnote in later editions: 'Written during the scarcity of 1795'. See Introduction for comments on the threat of famine and unrest in that year, and note 23 below.

14. *tired of manna, he sent them quails.* Reference to the 'murmurs' of the Chosen People in the wilderness. God's gift of manna to eat is not to their taste; they want flesh. He sends them a flock of quails. Numbers 11: 5-9, 31-33.

15. *seed-time and harvest time to the end.* Genesis 8: 22: 'While the earth remaineth, seed-time and harvest, and cold and heat, and summer and winter, and day and night shall not cease'.

16. *head lands.* Headland: the unploughed strip at the end of a field where the horses turn.

17. *sea-port town.* Possibly Bristol, where More spent her youth.

18. *charity begins at home ... end there.* The tail-piece to the familiar saying adapts a line in Sheridan's *The School for Scandal*, Act 5, 1 (1777): '[his charity] is of that domestic sort which never stirs abroad at all'.

19. *qualified.* Licensed according to the game laws, which are examined by More in *Black Giles the Poacher, Part 1*.

20. *the Subscription.* A form of communal self-help in parishes; either the better-off subscribed to a fund for the poor, or parishioners contributed to a insurance system against sudden misfortune. More and her sister Martha set up such funds in their Sunday Schools; she made sure that even the poor paid up according to their means in order to enjoy some security, independence, and self-respect.

21. *the vestry.* Thomas Pearce, in *The Compleat Justice of the Peace and Parish Officer*, London, 1756, states that 'a vestry is the assembly of the whole parish met together in some convenient place for the dispatch

of the business of the parish'. The word 'vestry' comes from the part of the church in which the priest's vestments were stored.

22. *last month's ... Cheap Repository.* A convenient advertising hook; there are other examples of sales promotion or the promise of sequels in the series. Each month three Tracts were issued: a History (i.e. a tale or story), a Poem or ballad, and a Sunday Reading, a more soberly didactic piece of writing. This passage describes the Sunday school master reading the Tract *Hints* ... aloud after the evening service, when parents slip in to listen; it shows the method by which More's precepts were disseminated even among the illiterate.

23. *BAD MANAGEMENT.* More's recipes for the cottage cook (throw in a sheep's head, grey pease, turnip, and any garden stuff) are written in the shadow of famine. They are based on more appetizing models set down earlier by Sarah Trimmer in her *Family Magazine.* Even food is subject to the boundaries of class: the poor should not 'fly in the face of [their] betters' by eating white bread while they, setting an example, are making do with coarser brown. Cobbett was at first impressed by More's Tracts, though he later turned against her values. Compare his *Cottage Economy* (7 parts, 1821-2; 1822). She reminds the middle classes of their social responsibilities in much sterner terms when addressing them directly in the tract 'A Cure for Melancholy'.

24. *a poor man gets seven or eight shillings a week.* Worth roughly £12-14 in 2000.

25. *baked it at home.* Many families, having only a fire, would prepare food to be baked in a communal oven.

26. *difficulty of getting a little milk.* The image of the milkmaid is so familiar in idealized visions of rural life that it is surprising to learn how the poor suffered in this way from the commercial enterprise of farmers' wives, who earned money by turning their milk into butter and selling it at market. An early broadside tract by More suggests that some gave short measure.

27. *one-way beer.* I have not been able to trace this term; the context suggests that it refers to milder home-brewed beer as opposed to beer sent for to the alehouse; see the earlier argument between Mr White and Tom Brick about the cost of brewing or buying ale.

28. *modest complaints ... redress them.* Betty Plane has the right degree of deference to reassure the middle ranks and gain their help ('begging your pardon, sir'; 'kind gentlefolks'; 'for indeed the rich have been very kind ... what we should have done without them'). The words 'with all humility' and 'modest complaints' reinforce More's points.

29. *RIOT.* The fear of social disorder and revolution is constant in More's
    work. *Village Politics* (1792) is her most famous anti-Jacobin tract; its
    theme is reworked in 'The Riot', a Cheap Repository ballad printed
    in this edition.

Notes for *The Shepherd of Salisbury Plain, Part One*
First published in 1795, probably on 3 March
    The text of both parts is taken from the annual selection of Tracts
    'published in 1795' probably printed or reprinted in 1796. I have
    not listed minor variations in the early issues, but as this is More's
    most famous Cheap Repository Tract it seems necessary in this case
    to show the extent of her later revisions. In some chapbooks (e.g.
    in 1795) the title includes a hyphen: 'Salisbury-Plain'.

1. *Salisbury Plain.* The plain on which Stonehenge stands. In the literature
    of the Romantic period it is regarded as a primitive landscape, relatively
    uninhabited, bleak and treeless. See Wordsworth's poem 'Guilt and
    Sorrow, or Incidents upon Salisbury Plain', written 1791-4, part of
    which was published in 1798 as 'The Female Vagrant'.

2. *visible:* 'wonderful' (1801*).* Inserted later in More's *Works* and the 2-
    volume *Stories and Tales* (1818) is the paragraph printed below. This is
    one of several extensive additions to the tale in the Cadell and Davies
    editions which disturb the balance between the narrative and didactic
    content. Cheap separate reprints of the tract keep to the original shorter
    text, with minor variations, into the 1820s.

> As this serene contemplation of the visible heavens insensibly lifted
> up his mind from the works of God in nature to the same God as
> he is seen in revelation, it occurred to him that this very connection
> was clearly intimated by the royal prophet in the nineteenth psalm; that
> most beautiful description of the greatness and power of God exhibited
> in the former part plainly seeming intended to introduce, illustrate, and
> unfold the operations of the word and Spirit of God on the heart in
> the latter. And he began to run a parallel in his own mind between
> the effects of that highly poetical and glowing picture of the material
> sun in searching and warming the earth, in the first six verses, and the
> spiritual operation attributed to the "law of God" which fills up the
> remaining part of the psalm. And he persuaded himself that the Divine
> Spirit which dictated this fine hymn had left it as a kind of general
> intimation to what use we were to convert our admiration of created
> things; namely, that we might be led by a sight of them to raise our
> views from the kingdom of nature to that of grace, and that the

contemplation of God in his works might draw us to contemplate him in his word.

In the midst of these reflections, Mr. Johnson's ...

3. *notable.* More often applies this adjective to women who make their mark in household management. The word is listed in dictionaries as archaic, meaning 'capable, bustling, housewifely'.

4. *out of the abundance ... mouth speaketh.* Matthew 12: 34.

5. *Yours ... life, said he.* From this point More – or the printer – omits all inverted commas to indicate speech in this 1795 tract, though they reappear in Part 2 and in later editions. This inconsistent punctuation is also found in an earlier issue of 1795 with a different title-page, showing Hazard as Printer. To clarify the dialogue for the reader, they are restored here.

6. *David.* The Old Testament Book of Psalms was thought to have been composed by King David, once a poor shepherd-boy. The Shepherd's speech echoes the psalms in many details; he finds the twenty-third Psalm ('The Lord is my Shepherd') particularly appropriate for spiritual guidance.

7. *King Saul.* For the narrative of Saul and David, which contrasts worldly power with the strength of simple virtue, see the First Book of Samuel 17, 18 ff.

8. *Moses was a shepherd ... Midian:* Exodus 2: 15. The following comments on the appearance of angels to the shepherds of Bethlehem refer to Luke 2: 8.

9. *Shepherds ... Carpenters:* For these Biblical references to trades, see Luke 2: 8; John 10:11 ('I am ... the good shepherd'); Matthew 4: 18-19 ('I will make you fishers of men'); Matthew 13: 55 ('Is this not the carpenter's son?'); Acts 18: 3 (Paul as tentmaker).

This paragraph, which follows the words 'carpenters have had' in the *Works,* does not appear in the 1795 version:

> Besides, it seems as if God honoured industry also. The way of duty is not only the way of safety, but it is remarkable how many in the exercise of the common duties of their calling humbly and rightly performed, as we may suppose, have found honours, preferment, and blessing; while it does not occur to me that the whole sacred volume presents a single instance of a like blessing conferred on idleness. Rebekah, Rachel, and Jethro's daughters, were diligently employed in the lowest occupations of a country life, when Providence, by means of those very occupations, raised them up husbands so famous in history, as Isaac, Jacob, and the prophet Moses. The shepherds were neither playing nor sleeping, but 'watching their flocks,' when they received the news of a Saviour's birth; and the woman of Samaria, by

the laborious office of drawing water, was brought to the knowledge
of Him who gave her to drink of 'living water.'

10. *tap a shoe:* the Shepherd makes profitable use of 'leisure' time in his
    work by cobbling shoes for his family as he recites the Bible. Time
    for reflection might lead shepherds, like weavers, to dangerous political
    conclusions.

11. *best part of the Bible by heart.* In some later editions of this tract the
    Shepherd's remarkable memory has shrunk; he has the 'best part of
    the New Testament', not of the whole Bible, by heart.

12. *wife and eight children:* More based this tale on the life of a real shepherd,
    David Saunders. Renowned for stoical piety, he had sixteen children
    to feed and had suffered from leprosy in his youth. More leaves out
    these striking details, perhaps to make her shepherd more representative
    of the common man.

13. *no man maketh me afraid.* Job 11: 19: 'none shall make thee afraid'.

14. The following passage does not appear in the 1795 text:

> "I am afraid," said Mr. Johnson, "that your difficulties may
> sometimes lead you to repine."
>
> "No, sir," replied the shepherd, "it pleases God to give me two ways
> of bearing up under them. I pray that they may be either removed or
> sanctified to me. Besides, if my road be right I am contented, though
> it be rough and uneven. I do not so much stagger at hardships in the
> right way, as I dread a false security, and a hollow peace, while I may
> be walking in a more smooth, but less safe way. Besides, sir, I strengthen
> my faith by recollecting what the best men have suffered, and my hope,
> with the view of the shortness of all suffering. It is a good hint, sir,
> of the vanity of all earthly possessions, that though the whole Land of
> Promise was his, yet the first bit of ground which Abraham, the father
> of the faithful, got possession of, in the land of Canaan, was a *grave.*"

15. *shilling a day … five years old.* In *The Way to Plenty/ Tom White 2*
    More says that a poor man 'gets seven or eight shillings a week',
    about £12-14 in 2000, so the Shepherd's lot is far from the pastoral
    ideal. See 'Note on Money, 1790-1800' for an estimate of equivalent
    values in 2000.

16. *'pothecary's … 'natomy:* apothecary or chemist; skeleton. The Shepherd
    is later shown to be in debt to the doctor.

17. More's footnote, 1795: 'This piece of frugal industry is not
    imaginary, but a real fact, as is the character of the shepherd, and
    his uncommon knowledge of the Scriptures.'

18. *knitting … which helps to pay our rent.* This paragraph illustrates the co-operative methods of cottage industry, even at the level of subsistence; contrast accounts of the confinement and regulation of factory workers in the cities as the Industrial Revolution developed. The sickly wife disentangles ('cards') with a strong comb the fleece collected by the infants; the eldest daughter is the spinster. The next stage should be dyeing, but plain folk need no colour in their homespun stockings, which are knitted by the boys. Skilled workers, the wife and daughters produce better work for sale. More is aware of the social stigma of 'barefoot'; for self-respect the wearing of shoes and stockings is essential. She herself knitted many dozen pairs of white stockings to give to Sunday School pupils.

19. *pride is a great sin.* Pride is the first of the Seven Deadly Sins. Apocrypha: Ecclesiasticus 10: 13: 'pride is the beginning of sin'.

20. *lying-in.* Childbirth.

21. *she might have had the palsy.* Before 'the palsy' (paralysis, tremor) More adds in later editions 'her hands lame, as well as her feet'.

22. At this point More inserted a passage which appears neither in the Tracts of 1795 nor in the later separate issues and reprints which I have seen. It is included here to show the expanded treatment of applied theology in her *Works.* She had been criticised by stricter Evangelicals for not giving more explicit religious instruction in the narrative tracts. The Shepherd's political comment on 'that nonsensical wicked notion about equality' flatters his middle-class questioner.

> "I fear, shepherd," said Mr. Johnson, "you have found this to be but a bad world."
>
> "Yes, sir," replied the shepherd; "but it is governed by a good God; and, though my trials have now and then been sharp, why then, sir, as the saying is, if the pain be violent, it is seldom lasting; and if it be but moderate, why then we can bear it the longer; and, when it is quite taken away, ease is the more precious, and gratitude is quickened by the remembrance. Thus, every way, and in every case, I can always find out a reason for vindicating Providence."
>
> "But," said Mr. Johnson, "how do you do to support yourself under the pressure of actual want. Is not hunger a great weakener of your faith?"
>
> "Sir," replied the shepherd, "I endeavour to live upon the promises. You who abound in the good things of this world are apt to set too high a value on them. Suppose, sir, the king, seeing me hard at work, were to say to me, that, if I would patiently work on till Christmas, a

fine palace and a great estate should be the reward of my labours. Do
you think, sir, that a little hunger, or a little cold, or a little wet would
make me flinch, when I was sure that few months would put me in
possession? Should I not say to myself frequently, –'cheer up, shepherd,
'tis but till Christmas!' Now, is there not much less difference between
this supposed day and Christmas, when I should take possession of the
estate and palace, than there is between time and eternity, when I am
sure of entering on a kingdom not made with hands? There is some
comparison between a moment and a thousand years, because a thousand
years are made up of moments, all time being made up of the same
sort of stuff, as I may say; while there is no sort of comparison between
the longest portion of time and eternity. You know, sir, there is no way
of measuring two things, one of which has length and breadth, which
shows it must have an end somewhere, and another thing, which being
eternal, is without end and without measure."

"But," said Mr. Johnson, "is not the fear of death sometimes too
strong for your faith?"

"Blessed be God, sir," replied the shepherd, "the dark passage
through the valley of the shadow of death is made safe by the power
of Him who conquered death. I know, indeed, we shall go as naked
out of this world as we came into it, but an humble penitent will not
be found naked in the other world, sir. My Bible tells me of garments
of praise and robes of righteousness. And is it not a support, sir, under
any of the petty difficulties and distresses here, to be assured by the
word of Him who cannot lie, that those who were in white robes came
out of great tribulation? But, sir, I beg your pardon for being so
talkative. Indeed, you great folks can hardly imagine how it raises and
cheers a poor man's heart, when such as you condescend to talk
familiarly to him on religious subjects. It seems to be a practical
comment on that text which says, *The rich and poor meet together; the Lord
is the maker of them all.* And so far from creating disrespect, sir, and
that nonsensical wicked notion about equality, it rather prevents it. But
to return to my wife."(*Works*, 1830)

23. *rich empty away.* Rewording of Luke 1: 53.

24. *heart smote him.*1 Samuel 24: 5. David's remorse.

25. *all the days of my life.* Psalms 23: 6. The 23rd Psalm begins: 'The LORD
is my Shepherd'.

26. *midnight hours defend.* In the early chapbook issues of the tracts the last
few pages are sometimes filled in with hymns or advertisements for
other titles, or both, as in the 1795 *Shepherd, Part 1.* "The Shepherd's
Hymn" is a metrical version of Psalm 23 (see note 25 above). Only
one of the four stanzas is given here.

Notes for *The Shepherd of Salisbury Plain, Part Two*

First published June 1795. See introductory note to Part I for comment on text and More's revisions.

1. *never travelled on a Sunday*. Added after 1795: 'without such a reason as he might be able to produce at the day of judgment'. See note 3: *Tom White 1*.

2. *trencher*. Wooden platter.

3. *goods ... three generations*. Genre-painting of the working-class interior. More's style here is plain and vivid, even colloquial, in its turn of phrase ('pretty clear'). The passage shows close observation of detail and a degree of sympathy for the way in which objects express the lives of their owners. These qualities are also found in poetry of the period. Compare Wordsworth's later description of the shepherd's cottage in 'Michael' (1800). Elizabeth Gaskell's *Mary Barton* (1848) pays similar attention to the value of common things in the lodgings of the poor, transplanted from country to city. Even the Shepherd's Bible, saved from dog's-ears and dirt, is in sharp focus; More forgets to switch back to the abstract language of piety.

4. *a True Book*. The Bible. This is one of the Tracts, pasted with others to the Shepherd's wall. More understands the value of advertising; she takes every opportunity to promote the series by such reflexive reference.

5. *crown*. Five shillings.

6. *contented Mind ... continual feast*. Proverbs 15: 15: 'he that is of a merry heart hath a continual feast.'

7. *Woman of Samaria ... world*. Jacob's well. See Genesis 29: 2-3, 10; also John 4: 6-15 (Jesus at Jacob's well, speaking to the Woman of Samaria who drew water for him to drink). The name is changed to 'the Woman at the well of Sychar' in some editions.

8. *little round of daily customs*. Wordsworth's long poem 'Michael' (1800) records the stoicism of a shepherd in adversity, though from a different spiritual perspective. He had probably read this famous tract, and others, before publishing the first edition of the *Lyrical Ballads* in 1798. His high vision of 'humble and rustic life' in the *Preface* (1800, 1802) should be contrasted with More's bleaker view of untrained human nature, though in this tract she allows the Shepherd to achieve nobility through self-denial and fortitude. Following the words '*allows himself in*', More inserts an extensive passage which appears in the *Works*, but not in any of the separate tracts which I have seen. The two different versions were available for many years, but the longer one would be found in middle-class family libraries.

"I should like," said Mr. Johnson, "to know how you manage in this respect."

"I am but a poor scholar, sir," replied the shepherd, "but I have made myself a little sort of rule. I always avoid, as I am an ignorant man, picking out any one single difficult text to distress my mind about, or to go and build opinions upon, because I know that puzzles and injures poor unlearned Christians. But I endeavour to collect what is the *general* spirit of meaning of Scripture on any particular subject, by putting a few texts together, which though I find them dispersed up and down, yet all seem to look the same way, to prove the same truth, or hold out the same comfort. So when I am tried or tempted, or any thing happens in which I am at a loss what to do, I apply to my rule–to the *law and the testimony*. To be sure I can't always find a particular direction as to the very case, because then the Bible must have been bigger than all those great books I once saw in the library at Salisbury palace, which the butler told me were acts of parliament; and had that been the case, a poor man would never have had money to buy, nor a working man time to read, the Bible; and so Christianity could only have been a religion for the rich, for those who had money and leisure; which, blessed be God! is so far from being the truth, that in all that fine discourse of our Saviour to John's disciples, it is enough to reconcile any poor man in the world to his low condition to observe, when Christ reckons up the things for which he came on earth, to observe, I say, what he keeps for last. *Go tell John,* says he, *those things which ye do hear and see; the blind receive their sight, and the lame walk, the lepers are cleansed, and the deaf hear, and the dead are raised up.* Now, sir, all these are wonders, to be sure, but they are nothing to what follows; They are but like to lower rounds of a ladder, as I may say, by which you mount to the top – *And the poor have the Gospel preached to them!* I dare say, if John had had any doubts before, this last part of the message must have cleared them up at once. For it must have made him certain sure at once, that a religion which placed preaching salvation to the poor above healing the sick, which ranked the soul above the body, and set heaven above health, must have come from God."

"But," said Mr. Johnson, "you say you can generally pick out your particular duty from the Bible, though that duty be not fully explained."

"Indeed, sir," replied the shepherd, "I think I can find out the principle at least, if I bring but a willing mind. The want of that is the great hinderance. *Whoso doeth my will, he shall know of the doctrine.* You know that text, sir. I believe a stubborn will makes the Bible harder to be understood than any want of learning. 'Tis corrupt affections which blind the understanding, sir. The more a man hates sin, the clearer he will see his way, and more he loves holiness, the better he will understand his Bible. The more practical conviction will he get of that pleasant truth, that *the secret of the Lord is with them that fear him.* Now, sir, suppose I had time and leaning, and possessed all the books I saw at the Bishop's where could I find out a surer way to lay the axe to the root of all covetousness, selfishness, and injustice, than the plain and ready rule, – *to do unto all men as I would they should do unto me?* If my neighbour does me an injury, can I be at any loss how to proceed with him, when I recollect the parable of the unforgiving steward, who refused to pardon a debt of an hundred pence, when his own ten thousand talents had been remitted to him? I defy any man to retain habitual selfishness, hardness of heart, or any other allowed sin, who daily and conscientiously tries his own heart by this touchstone. The straight rule will show the crooked practice to every one who honestly tries the one by the other."

"Why, you seem to make Scripture a thing of general application," said Mr. Johnson, "in cases to which many, I fear, do not apply it."

"It applies to every thing, sir," replied the shepherd. "When those men who are now disturbing the peace of the world, and trying to destroy the confidence of God's children in their Maker and their Saviour; when those men, I say, came to my poor hovel with their new doctrines and their new books, I would never look into one of them; for I remembered it was the first sin of the first pair to lose their innocence for the sake of a little wicked knowledge; besides, *my own Book* told me – *To fear God and honour the king, – To meddle not with them who are given to change, – Not to speak evil of dignities, – To render honour to whom honour is due.* So that I was furnished with a little coat of mail, as I may say, which preserved me, while those who had no such armour fell into the snare." [*Works, 1830.*]

9. *plead difference of clocks.* There was no common time across the country until the coming of the railways made it necessary to standardize the setting of clocks.

10. *to catechise.* This is the skill which qualifies him for Sunday School teaching. Many of the Tracts refer to or illustrate the work done in these schools; see the histories of Black Giles and Hester Wilmot in this edition.

11. *comfort me.* This is a patchwork of Biblical allusions:
   – *the Heavens declare the glory of God*: Psalms 19: 1.
   – *the vallies standing thick with Corn*: Psalms 65: 13. 'The valleys also are covered over with corn; they shout for joy, they also sing.'
   – *giveth me all things richly to enjoy*: I Timothy: 6,17. 'God who giveth us all things to enjoy.'

— *the ox knoweth his owner, and the ass his master's crib.* Isaiah 1. 3.

— *feedeth me in green* pastures: Psalms 23 ('The LORD is my Shepherd'): 'feedeth me in green pastures, and maketh me to lie down beside the still waters, and whose rod and staff comfort me.'

The paragraph ends in some later editions with the following passage (1830 text): 'A religion, sir, which has its seat in the heart, and its fruits in the life, takes up little time in the study. And yet in another sense true religion, which from sound principle brings forth right practice, fills up the whole time, and life too, as one may say'.

12. *irreligious Parish Clerk.* The Clerk was chosen by the Minister to help with the administration of the church and parish, but he had also to make formal responses in the church service; being irreligious should have disqualified him for this office.

13. *Sunday School Society.* Set up in 1785 with Henry Thornton as Treasurer; he was later Treasurer for the Cheap Repository. The experiment of More and her sister in founding a number of Sunday schools illustrates a growing public interest in moral education.

14. *Fifty shillings a Year.* The financing of the Shepherd's new life is carefully worked out in terms of rent and income; philanthropists must not make gestures and forget practicalities. Only the shortfall in rent will be covered by the benefactor, as true charity teaches self-help and the skills of survival.

15. *not ... rich, but useful.* The Shepherd's improved cottage will cost him hard, though congenial, labour. He is to keep to his week-day work, act as Parish Clerk, and run the Sunday School on his only day of rest. Mary's health is weak, but she is assigned to the task of training a class of girls in practical skills; she is also running a family. Readers who find their tearful gratitude hard to stomach might enjoy Rebecca's hostile response to benevolent middle-class intervention in *Hester Wilmot I.*

16. *those visits ... instruction or amusement.* Although Mr Johnson's annual call sounds informal, More established rotas for the annual visitation and inspection of Sunday Schools; the intention was to halt backsliding and to reward virtue and industry. Such 'feasts', or outdoor tea-parties for hundreds of Sunday School children from a ring of parishes, were held throughout the nineteenth century.

Notes for *Betty Brown, The St. Giles's Orange Girl*

First published August 1796.

1. *charitable Society ... all his mercies.* In the 1799 edition and in later collections, More adds a footnote identifying this society as 'The Philanthropic'. Its first Report in 1788 was on the prevention of crime. By 1799 a note of patriotic gratitude is added after 'mercies': 'who has ordered the bounds of our habitation, and cast our lot in such a country'. These words refer to Acts 17: 26 and Isaiah 34: 17.

2. *first of May ... both parties.* Date of the annual chimney-sweepers' festival; they wore ribbons and flowers to dance in the streets or on the green. The girls take part in a separate May-Day tradition, described by I. & P. Opie in *The Lore and Language of Schoolchildren,* Oxford, 1959, xii, p.258. This is not the plaited maypole of revivalists; the girls made garlands and set them on short poles carried over the shoulder. They visited houses, danced and displayed the garlands competitively for reward – in this case 'a few scraps'.

3. *Seven Dials.* A place in the parish of St Giles in the Fields, Holborn where seven streets converged. From the late 17th century, when the area was developed, to 1773 there stood a column with six (not seven) dials facing the roads. Brewer says, 'The district came to be notorious for vice, crime and degradation ... and was long the headquarters of the ballad printers and ballad-mongers.' (*Dictionary of Phrase and Fable,* 1870, rev. I. H. Evans, London, 1981.) Thirty-nine years after More's tract was published, Dickens describes in 'Seven Dials' an argument between two gin-sodden women in the maze of dirty streets. His lodging-house tenants, like Betty, need 'a floating capital of eighteen-pence or thereabouts' for trade. The 'shabby-genteel' man in the back attic shows how More's preoccupation with precise social distinctions has survived. In another Sketch (and in later novels like *Bleak House*) he satirizes the charitable intervention of middle-class ladies. (*Sketches by Boz,* 1835, 1836: 'Seven Dials' and 'The Ladies' Societies'.)

4. *into the bargain.* Added in 1799 edition: 'I never could hope for such a rise in life'.

5. *mouldy ones under.* 'Oranges' lose their capital letter in the 1799 text. The tone of Mrs Sponge's immoral advice ironically echoes More's rhetoric of virtue.

6. *nice ... natural good-nature.* 'Nice': 'fastidious, precise'. By 1799 'good-nature' has become 'good-temper'; the change probably reflects More's theological anxiety about the essential corruption of human nature and the restorative effects of taught religious principles.

7. *genteel ... generosity*. 'Genteel': 'ladylike,' 'behaving as if in a superior social class'. The original sense of 'generosity' has similar connotations. Both words are given ironic overtones here.

8. *died much seldomer*. The 1799 text adds: 'than when they were close shut in'. Dickens later records the effects of 'the fever' in the airless slums of these city underworlds, e.g. in *Bleak House* (1852-3). See also Henry Mayhew: *London Labour and the London Poor* (1851) for a later account of the hard lives of street-traders.

9. *Justices of the new Police*. More studied the influential work of Patrick Colquhoun, magistrate and reformer, on crime and poverty in London, on the reorganization of the police and judicial system, and on the need for reform in the cause of humanity and social stability. She refers to his *Treatise on the Police of the Metropolis*, published early in 1795. He later issued *A General View of the National Police System*, London, 1799.

10. *capital ... your own*. An early version of the credit trap. The landlady sponges off the friendless and ignorant. She has made 7*l*. 10*s* (seven pounds ten shillings), or 30 crowns, out of the one invested in Betty. More offers the common reader practical help with arithmetic as well as religious guidance

11. *abstain ... easy to her*. Added 1799: ' She therefore, at present, said little about the *sin* of drinking, and only insisted on the *expence* of it'. The spelling of '*expence*' is retained by More through many editions.

12. *bad management ... help themselves*. There are no wholly innocent victims in More's view; the term 'bad management' recurs in the tales where no superior sin can be found. Half a century before Samuel Smiles published *Self-Help* in 1859, More insisted that even the poorest members of society should practise this primary virtue.

13. *sinners ... to Tyburn*. The place of public execution until 1783; site of the gallows, at the meeting of Edgware Road and Bayswater Road in London.

14. *Rules for Retail Dealers*. Five new – and secular – Commandments. She also devised a simpler Catechism for children.

15. *no such thing as chance ... distress*. To blame fate or chance is seen by More as a pagan refusal to acknowledge God's right to test us; he permits us to grow spiritually, shaped by suffering.

16. *Sausage Shop ... Second Part*. Betty's shop is mentioned in a separate Tract, which gives an account in ballad form of her husband's work. More has set the verse to the music of a popular song. The full title is 'The Hackney Coachman; or The Way to get a good Fare, to the tune of "I wish I was a Fisherman"'. It begins:

I am a bold Coachman and drive a good Hack,
With a coat of five capes that quite covers my back;
And my wife keeps a sausage-shop not many miles
From the narrowest alley in all Broad St Giles.

Tho' poor we are honest, and very content,
We pay as we go for meat, drink and for rent ...

Notes for *Black Giles, Part One*
First published November 1796.
1. *And I myself.* In this tale the authorial voice confides in a middle-class readership; 'ladies and gentlemen' are urged not to reward the undeserving poor; the upright Magistrate makes similar distinctions in the treatment of prisoners after just sentence. The assumption in this passage seems to be that God has put the poor man at the rich man's gate to open it for his carriage.
2. *tumbling.* Performing acrobatics. More dismisses such unproductive activity; the 'idle' children should be knitting stockings; they would be eager to do so in the Shepherd's family.
3. *right of Common.* Legal term: 'right over land owned by others' (OED), for example, grazing rights.
4. *long-headed fellow.* Shrewd; having foresight.
5. *rats under Parson Wilson's barn-door.* Apart from a woodcut on the title-page there are few illustrations in the tracts, but this ingenious wickedness is shown graphically in some issues.
6. *Rachel ... bottle of gin.* This is the first appearance of one of More's best-known and most controversial figures; for her full history see *Tawney Rachel* in this edition. Pawning her child's *shoes* for gin is doubly shocking to More; a mother should know the social stigma of going barefoot. Other tracts (such as *The Shepherd* and *Betty Brown*) stress the symbolic status of shoes.
7. *antipathy ... Church.* 'Black' Giles seems to be set up here, and in Part 2, to represent the forces of darkness working against the light of Christianity. The adjective 'tawney' (used once to describe Rachel in the 1799 edition of this tract) gives symbolic colouring to his wife; the modern spelling 'tawny' is found in some chapbook issues.
8. *This sort of work.* Added later: 'I hate your regular day-jobs, where one can't well avoid doing one's work for one's money.' (1799 text)
9. *season of their harvest.* Inversion of religious values, as shown in note 7 above. Although More disapproves of Black Giles, she allows herself

more freedom in describing such villains; the virtuous are treated with appropriate sobriety. She is licensed to echo their speech in dialogues, and she catches their casual values in the lighter rhythm and word-play of 'a stray duck was clapped under the smock frock'.

10. *ironing ... ; leisure day ... wicked songs.* From the evidence in this paragraph it might be argued that Rachel deserves a day of rest on secular grounds, but More discounts her labours in the alternative economy and defines Sunday as 'her idle day'. The disgraceful songs might have included ballads such as 'The Rover', a late-eighteenth century broadside ballad in the Madden Collection:

> Then I heard a d — noise,
> Who should it be but her mother,
> Caught me between her daughter's thighs;
> The gallows old whore sung out murder ...
> [John Holloway and Joan Black, eds., *Later English Broadside Ballads*, London, 1975]

11. *wretched manager ... distilled water.* Rachel's domestic priorities conflict with the conventional view that a woman should put husband and children first. She pursues her career as a trickster, taking on the old role of the wise woman, though her fraudulent bottles of peppermint water will cure no indigestion. Chapbooks on the interpretation of dreams were as saleable as improper ballads; see *Tawney Rachel* for an account of how she deceives the gullible by making predictions.

12. *UPRIGHT MAGISTRATE.* This section heading is not in the 1795 version of the tract used for this edition, but it appears in a 1799 text. I have included it to show the structure of More's argument. The old term 'Justice' (i.e. Justice of the Peace) is often replaced by 'Magistrate' in later editions.

13. *unqualified person.* Unlicensed.

14. *game laws ... obey them.* More's hint of dissatisfaction with the harsh game laws at a time of great scarcity shows humane concern in conflict with her usual respect for the legal system, though she does not mention here the snares and man-traps which were often set to deter poachers.

15. *plundering of warrens.* A piece of land enclosed and preserved for the breeding of rabbits for food.

16. *All property is sacred.* This sounds like a quotation, but if it is I have not been able to trace it. Perhaps the ear is tricked by a later assertion: 'Property is theft' ['La propriete c'est le vol'], P-J Proudhon, 1840.

17. *Hulks.* Old war-ships moored in the Thames and used as prisons. See

the opening chapters of Dickens's *Great Expe*[for a] later account of their use.

18. *prevent ... prison ... debt.* British law must be [hout] favour, but after sentence there is room for le[rit is] humble, grateful and deserving; those who are [iles,] will find none. The farmers who benefit from th[bute] loans towards the ignorant poacher's fine in a [e. It] should be noted that Church and State work [the] Vicar is also the Justice.

19. *triumphing of the wicked ... ; Apple Tree.* The ref[. 5.] The advertising of the Second Part – and the pr[ent] rather than instruction – is a typical ploy to mai[ies.]

Notes for *Black Giles, Part Two*

First published December 1796.

1. *instructing them.* The narrative voice is unusuall[rst] paragraph; More uses the first-person pronour[ng] the reader's sympathy for her distasteful task [en] world. This might excuse her in the eyes of sev[rs] for promising an 'entertaining Story' at the end

2. *woman an hurt.* The following sentence appears[in] the 1799 text: 'With what a touching simplicity is [re] of the youth whom our blessed Saviour raised f[he] was the only son of his mother, *and she a widow*

3. *garden ... Apple-tree ... Redstreak.* Contemporary rea[ze] the Biblical symbolism in this tale; The Book of[he] Fall of Man in the Garden of Eden after Adam [uit] of the tree of the knowledge of good and evi[as] traditionally thought to be an apple, the choice o[ms] appropriate, suggesting the ingrained mark of sin.

4. *dirty boy by the hand.* In later collected editions (e[me] issue of 1818) More adds 'in the most condescend[ch] is clearly used as a term of approbation to describ[to] one's inferiors, however resentful or ungrateful the

5. *whose eye ... sinner.* Job 34: 21: 'for his eyes are [of] man, and he seeth all his goings'. Added later (not[799] texts): 'for he is about our bed, and about our path[out] all our ways.'

6. *useful story ... profitable.* The master's cautionary tales s[day] School teaching was made relevant to the lives [ers.]

:' suggests prudent investment in religion.

nts. Exodus 20: 3-17 lists God's Ten Commandments,
own from Mount Sinai by Moses. These Old Testament rules
 were recited by children in Sunday Schools; they formed
e Catechism, or series of set questions and answers about
ian faith, as published in the Church of England Book of
 Prayer. This tale shows a more informal version of
g in Sunday School, better adapted to the children's
ding.
 Giles ... decay. See note 3 above on the symbolism of this

enemies ... hate you. A New Testament commandment: Luke
atthew 5: 44.
eat misery. The 1799 text is more alarming to sinners:

e mercy on them, sir; let me not meet them in the place of
t to which I am going. Lord grant them that time for repentance
 have thrown away!" He languished a few days, and died in great
– a fresh and sad instance that people who abuse the grace of
d resist his Spirit find it difficult to repent when they will.

awney **Rachel**
ed April 1797 as *Tawny Rachel.*
used for this edition is that of the 1799 collection published
n in three volumes; this 'new edition' was a reprint with
 the 1798 collection, which I have not seen. As More has
tracts for this collection, I have left unchanged her spellings
, 'chesnut', 'conjurer', [text], 'compleat', 'tawney'). However, I
d the single inverted commas to double, since that is the form
 other early tracts printed here and in the Cadell and Davies
 1799 collection has only a few woodcuts: the title-page of a
g of *Tawney Rachel* (c.1810) is used to illustrate the tale.
 life. For the tales of country criminals like Black Giles and
 More appears to have referred to *The Compleat Justice of the*
d Parish Officer, by Thomas Pearce (1756). He lists the penalties
ling game, robbing orchards, etc. He explains that a 'vagrant'
 who has no legal settlement in the parish, who should
re be sent back to his or her own parish or the last place
ch he or she was found begging, or set to hard labour before
expelled. But a 'vagabond', like Rachel, is 'one who, without
ll passport, wanders about from his legal place of settlement,

and liveth idly and loitering'. He states that, among others, 'minstrels, jugglers, gipsies, fortune-tellers, players ... hawkers without licence, and wandering beggars, are deemed rogues and vagabonds' (Pearce, 1756, pp. 408-414.)

2. *her wickedness.* More rationally insists that Rachel has no supernatural power; her art is deception, based on shrewd psychological insight; however, the later references to witchcraft in the story suggest a fear of the outsider which verges on superstition.

3. *as she directed.* Rachel's deception of Mrs Jenkins is an example of the simple tricks recorded in old *fabliaux* and contemporary chapbooks; her next fraud is more sophisticated.

4. *ignorant and superstitious.* In later editions More adds 'credulous' before this phrase, which emphasizes the victim's own responsibility. She believes that to be superstitious is to display a pagan belief in the power of Fate instead of resigning oneself to the control of an all-knowing Providence.

5. *Midsummer men.* This is a plant of the sedum family; Brewer names it 'orpine or Live-long'. On Midsummer Eve it was the custom for girls to test the loyalty of their lovers by hanging up the plant in a pot in the house. If it bent to the right the man was faithful; if it turned left he was untrue.

6. *twenty pounds.* Approximately £820 today; a considerable fortune for a country girl of the working class.

7. *Honest Jacob . . . love he bore her.* This refers to an Old Testament story of love and deception. Laban has two daughters, Leah and Rachel. Jacob serves him for seven years for the hand of Rachel in marriage, but is given Leah instead. After protest he wins Rachel but must work another seven years. (Gen. 29: 16-28)

8. *some very loose words.* The woodcut on the title-page shows Rachel's basket of wares for sale. Hanging over the edge are the long 'slip' ballads which arouse More's wrath in many of these tracts. Sally will 'rummage the basket for those songs which had the most tragical pictures'; there are some suitably melodramatic scenes of despairing deaths, hangings, etc. in the Cheap Repository series to catch the customer's eye. For an example of 'very loose words' in unregenerate ballads, see note 10, *Black Giles 1,* and note 17 below.

9. *ague.* An acute fever. Willow bark might have been prescribed as a remedy; it has properties similar to aspirin.

10. *beaufet . . .* buffet: sideboard, side-table.

11. *black art.* Magic or necromancy; used metaphorically here, as Rachel is

said to have no supernatural powers. But such allusions to witchcraft produce a note of uncertainty about her evil acts. (See notes 2 and 22.)

12. *posy of pinks and southernwood in his bosom.* Southernwood is *Artemisia abrotanum*, commonly known as Old Man, a bitter aromatic plant. In some chapbook issues this chuchyard encounter is shown on the title-page.

13. *whey into the vats.* Sally's distraction ruins her dairy produce. According to the *SOED*, rennet is curdled milk from the stomach of a calf, used to curdle milk in the process of making cheese; whey is 'the watery part of the milk which remains after the separation of the curd by coagulation'.

14. *red ribbon ... Lammas fair.* Lammas (August 1st) was originally 'loaf-mass', a harvest service, often followed by a fair. Brightly-coloured ribbons were carried round the villages by pedlars and sold at such fairs; they were important to young women, providing cheap and instant decoration at a time when new clothes were home-made, practical, and seldom affordable. (See *Hester Wilmot 2: The New Dress.*) Moralists condemned ribbons as female frippery, a sure sign of vanity. In the 1830 *Works*, More prefers the spelling 'riband'.

15. *shoulders as round as a tub.* More allows us to see through Sally's eyes; her images are drawn from the dairy.

16. *vagrant act.* See note 1 above.

17. *wicked ballads to some children.* As a bad moral example for the young, these traditional lines might be quoted:

> For I am a Maid and a very good Maid,
>   and sixteen years of age am I,
> And fain would I part with my Maidenhead,
>   if any good fellow would with me lye . . .
> ['The Maid's Complaint for want of a Dil Doul', in *The Common Muse*,
> ed. V. de Sola Pinto and A.E. Rodway, London, 1957, pp. 548-550.]

18. *Taunton gaol.* In Somerset, More's knowledge of the West Country leads her to put local references into tracts which were printed in Bath as well as London. Place-names were sometimes altered by publishers; for example, the two wealthy farmers in a tract of that name who meet at Wey-hill fair are transported to Ireland in a Dublin version issued by William Watson.

19. *such vermin.* Rachel, seen through the eyes of villagers, is an 'old witch' and 'old hag'. Farmer Jenkins dismisses her from the human race in this phrase; it should, perhaps, be remembered that her husband Black

Giles is a rat-catcher who puts vermin in the farmers' barns, which he is then paid to clear.

20. *warning*. In the 1818 and 1830 editions 'kind of warning' becomes 'kind warning', which seems more appropriate for this oracular denunciation. The list of dangerous outsiders, in small capitals here, is put into italics in the 1830 *Works*.

21. *vagabond gipsy*. See note 1 above. Since Rachel lives in 'that Mud Cottage' (see *Black Giles 1*), she is not a true Romany; the term 'gipsy' reflects prejudice against her appearance and irregular way of life. Her skin is tanned and tawny; she is a 'sun-burnt oracle'. Although Rachel might deserve transportation to Botany Bay as punishment for her crimes, More shows persistent anxiety in the tracts about the Other who will not conform to the established social order.

22. *King Saul never consulted the witch till he had left off serving God.* For this reference to Saul's visit to the Witch of Endor, see 1 Samuel 28: 7-20. At the king's request she conjures up the spirit of Samuel. More denies the supernatural power of 'false oracles' like Rachel, though she allows one of the villagers to follow a dangerous tradition in denouncing her as 'old witch'.

Notes for *Hester Wilmot, Part One*
First published June 1797.

This text is taken from the two-volume edition titled *Stories for the Middle Ranks of Society and Tales for the Common People* which was issued separately from the *Collected Works* in 1818 by T. Cadell and W. Davies. Both parts of *Hester Wilmot* appear in vol. II (*Tales*). As the 1818 edition, like the *Works*, is unillustrated, I have chosen to use a woodcut related to the narrative from a copy of *The Sunday School* reprinted c.1812. More refers to *Hester Wilmot*, rather confusingly, as the second part of this earlier tract. The tale was one of the latest issued in the Cheap Repository series.

1. As explained above, the sub-title refers to an earlier tract, *The Sunday School*, which appears in *Stories for the Middle Ranks*, vol.1 of the 1818 edition. There is a note by More at the end of that tract explaining why it has been parted from its sequel:

> It was thought proper to separate them in this collection; as the two preceding numbers rather tend to enforce the duties of the higher and middle class, and the two subsequent ones [i.e. *Hester Wilmot*] those of the poor.

2. *They direct their ploughing ... Almanack.* An almanac is a calendar with

astronomical and other information. This sentence is not in the 1797 chapbook edition. As variations between early and late editions of *Hester Wilmot* are minor in comparison with those in *The Shepherd of Salisbury Plain*, only a few have been noted below.

3. *stone the space ... flowers.* 'patterns and whim-whams' in the 1797 text. She scours designs with the stone used for cleaning or polishing.

4. *and not being so obvious ... animadversion.* Not in the 1797 text; an example of the unnecessary emphasis which weighs down sentences in later versions of the Tracts.

5. *Patience and submission ... wife.* These are the virtues expected of a wife. On the evidence given in the text, Rebecca's bad temper might seem justified, but as her independent spirit threatens patriarchal order in the family and community More will not condone her transgressions.

6. *Good christians.* In this edition the word 'Christian' often loses its capital letter, either in error or in a gesture of humility. Capital 'C' is used in the 1797 text and restored in the 1830 version.

7. *wicked woman ... pay her for it.* Rebecca, illiterate and heretical, is rejecting her child's chance to learn the Catechism ('*fear God and keep his commandments*') and thus to improve her position in this world and the next. When setting up Sunday Schools in the Mendips, More and her sister encountered the resistance of women who could not afford to lose their useful older girls in this domestic economy. A compromise is reached here. To fit learning into their other duties, girls must save time, i.e. sleep less and work harder.

8. *These, said she.* There are no speech marks to help the reader in this or in the later exchange between Mrs Crew and Mrs Jones on human nature and education. The illusion of dialogue is restored by inverted commas in the 1830 edition.

9. *Chasten thy son ... his crying.* Proverbs 19: 18: 'Chasten thy son while there is hope and let not thy soul spare for his crying'. More has either misremembered or adapted the quotation, replacing 'soul' with 'rod', which gives a less compassionate meaning.

10. *My good young reader ... ask a dying man.* Another example of More's attitude to time: waste not want not; invest for eternity. The financial metaphor is sustained in a later speech by Mrs Jones: she speaks of 'making religion pleasant as well as profitable'.

11. *even the weakest ... retain something.* The teaching methods outlined here are advanced for their time, relying on patience, kindness and repetition. But winning minds and hearts is a relentless 'labour of love'; one pities the 'poor untaught child' who is asked the same

question nineteen times.

12. *christianity.* See note 6 on capitalization.

13. *Feed my lambs.* In John 21: 15 Jesus says to his disciple Simon Peter, 'Feed my lambs'. In verse 16 he says, 'Feed my sheep'. More uses the former version in 1797 and 1818 and the latter in 1830.

14. *To renounce the devil ... articles of the christian faith.* This paragraph makes particular reference to the Catechism which has been quoted in previous tracts. The Catechism is defined in the Book of Common Prayer as 'an instruction to be learned of every Person, before he be brought to be confirmed by the Bishop.' The promises are those made at baptism by godparents on behalf of the child, who is now old enough to renew them. Other quotations come from 2 Corinthians 12: 9: 'My grace is sufficient for thee', and John 16: 24: 'Ask, and ye shall receive'.

15. *a sort of spiritual gossip.* The later tales offer the reader a more sophisticated account of the dangers of self-deception, complacency and cant in the newly converted; compare the simpler treatment of Tom White's salvation.

Notes for *Hester Wilmot, Part Two*
First published July 1797.

See introductory note to Part 1 for the relationship between the tales of Hester Wilmot and an earlier Tract, *The Sunday School* (May 1797).

1. *peevish and lazy ... meek and lowly.* Some lack of continuity here: in Part I Hester seemed cheerful and willing enough even before her conversion. The Biblical reference to Matthew 11: 29 introduces the theme of this tale: 'learn of me, for I am meek and lowly in heart: and ye shall find rest in your souls'.

2. *Sunday evening.* More adds a footnote on Sunday fairs:

> 'This practice is too common. Those fairs which profess to be kept on Monday commonly begin on the Sunday. It is much to be wished that magistrates would put a stop to it, as Mr. Edwards did at Weston, at the request of Mrs. Jones. There is another great evil worth the notice of justices. In many villages, during the fair, ale is sold at private houses, which have no license, to the great injury of sobriety and good morals.'

3. *a song-book ... canting hypocrite ... merry girl ... before she became religious.* This argument reflects awareness of a social change in sensibility under the influence of the Evangelicals which was not universally welcome. The immoral songs, repeatedly attacked in the tales printed here, are

denounced more explicitly in *The Sunday School,* where the clergyman confronts a ballad-singer; she is poisoning the souls of innocent girls; they may be 'eternally ruined by this vile trash'.

4. *who judgeth righteously … ; Come ye children … fear of the Lord.* The first quotation shows Christ as example: 'who, when he was reviled, reviled not again … but committed himself to him that judgeth righteously' (1 Peter 2: 23). The second sentence comes from Psalms 34: 11.

5. *I submit to the will of my father … Father which is in heaven.* The reference is to the Lord's Prayer and to Christ's Sermon on the Mount. See Matthew 7: 21 'Not everyone that saith unto me, Lord, Lord, shall enter into the kingdom of heaven; but he that doeth the will of my Father which is in heaven'. This quotation hardly justifies all paternal authority, but seems to endorse it in More's text. For an extensive discussion of women's response to the patriarchal system at this time, see Elizabeth Kowaleski-Wallace, *Their Father's Daughters,* New York: Oxford University Press, 1991.

6. *stuff gown … apron of her giving.* 'Stuff' means 'material for making up garments' but the connotations differ; it often refers to plainer woollen or cotton cloth as opposed to fine silk. The tale records the ceremony of a Sunday School Feast for a group of parishes; it is based on More's experience of organizing these annual events for her own schools and distributing stockings, etc. of her own making, as recorded in her sister's *Mendip Annals.* ed. A. Roberts, second edition, 1859.

7. *two shillings a-week by her spinning … two-pence a-week.* Out of her earnings of about £4.10 in 2000 values, Hester sets aside 34 pence for the new dress. She is later shown to have saved eight shillings (approx. £16.50) towards it in her box.

8. *to iron in a gentleman's family.* More discounts Rebecca's industry because her motives are not correct. In addition to looking after the children and an idle gambler, Rebecca spends several nights away from home, ironing for richer households. Perhaps this is to be read as a dereliction of family duty rather than a contribution to the budget. Earlier in the 18th century Mary Collier complained in verse about the burden of laundry outwork in addition to her other tasks (*The Woman's Labour,* 1739).

9. *all-fours.* Card-game: see note 7, *Tom White 1*

10. *improper finery … take off before her.* Although the old sumptuary laws, which forbade the lower orders to wear fine apparel, had been out of use for centuries, some degree of class distinction in clothing is still thought appropriate by More ('too smart for their station'). This view,

combined with religious scruples about vanity and pride, leads Mrs Jones to strip the frippery off misguided girls.

11. *Judge not that ye be not judged.* Matthew 7: 1

12. *religion is not a thing of the tongue ... good purpose.* The anecdote here illustrates the principles set out in More's *Practical Piety* (1811), which became a popular religious handbook. Control over minds is strengthened by moral appraisals of the girls and denunciation of uncooperative parents in a public ceremony. Material rewards no doubt reinforce her teachings.

13. *better servants ... feast.* In her Tales More offers reassurance to the middle-classes who fear that education of the poor might upset the social order, or at least distract servants and labourers from their duties. *Mendip Annals* (see note 6) records some real arguments with suspicious farmers on this theme.

14. *miserable sinner ... no health in him.* Adapted from the Confession in the Church of England Morning Service (Book of Common Prayer).

15. *When the wicked man ... save his soul alive.* Ezekiel 18: 27. This is the first of the Sentences printed in the Book of Common Prayer (Cambridge, 1771 ed.) for both the Morning and Evening Service. Although the minister might read 'one or more' of the Sentences, these would usually be the first words heard in church by the converted.

16. *fell to blows ... much violence.* Domestic violence, especially when committed by the woman, distorts More's ideal of holy family life as achieved by the Shepherd of Salisbury Plain.

17. *hours with her father ... silk gowns.* These words illustrate not only the pleasures of filial piety but the sense of spiritual power and control More promises women in exchange for trifling material desires

18. *the fifty-first psalm.* Psalm 51 starts with the words: 'Have mercy upon me, O God, according to thy loving-kindness: according unto the multitude of thy tender mercies blot out my transgressions'.

19. *new way of life.* This passage shows the practical application of piety and duty in making the house into the home, which will become the social ideal (often imprisoning for women) as the nineteenth century progresses. Boredom leads the husband to the alehouse; literacy will help to fill the evenings with devotional reading and family prayers. And More's Tracts will be very suitable for this purpose – see the advertisement below.

20. *bought, of a pious hawker ... Book of Prayers ... Cheap Repository.* More adds a footnote on this Tract: 'These prayers may be had also divided into two parts, one fit for private persons, the other for families, price

one halfpenny'.

21. *God resisteth the proud ... to the humble.* James 4: 6 ('unto the humble').

22. *promoted to be head-mistress.* Dedication to piety is the qualification which offers working-class women the approved method of bettering the self – in terms of status and finance as well as morality – with the help of middle-class patronage. Teaching is a safer career for women than writing. After an unsuccessful experiment as patron of the milkwoman poet Ann Yearsley, who showed, in More's view, an ungrateful independence of spirit and sinful pride, she does not encourage authorship among the poor.

Notes for *Ballads*

These ballads formed part of the Cheap Repository Series, but they were not reprinted in the *Stories ... and Tales ...* (1818); that edition includes only the prose narratives. 'Patient Joe' and 'The Riot' were reprinted in her *Works* from 1801 on.

'Patient Joe'

First published July 1795.

1. *a Collier.* Mining is the subject of another Tract, 'The Lancashire Collier Girl', which is probably written by More, though not signed.

2. *recall what he'd lent.* Patient Joe's resignation to the will of God exceeds even that of the Shepherd of Salisbury Plain. The popular survival of tracts like this into the 1830s and later might have suggested a name for two long-suffering characters in Dickens's novels. The old narrative of 'Patient Grissel' was published in ballad form in the 18th century.

3. *no chance could be found.* See comment on fate and chance in *Betty Brown,* note 15 ('no such thing as chance'), and on Providence in *Tawney Rachel,* note 4.

4. *idle Tim Jenkins ... ashamed.* Since publishing the pamphlet *Village Politics* in 1792 More has dramatized moral arguments in this way, setting up opposing types to act out a cautionary tale.

5. *all things ... best.* It seems unlikely that More would quote from Voltaire's *Candide* (1759): 'tout est au mieux ... / 'all is for the best ...' The reference is probably to Milton's *Samson Agonistes* (1671), line 1745: 'All is best, though oft we doubt'.

6. *loss of my dinner?* These double rhymes and the insistent metre of the ballad combine to produce a flat-footed effect. Since More had written and published metrically skilful verse in earlier years, it seems likely that the poem is consciously contrived to imitate some familiar ballads

of the time. The bathos of these last lines might be half-humorous; her poem echoes a popular song which starts: 'A Cobler there was, and he lived in a stall, / Which served him for Kitchen, for Parlour, and Hall'. More refers to this song in the heading of 'The Riot'.

'The Riot'

First published August 1795. More's heading suggests that the ballad should be sung to the tune of 'A Cobler there was'. See comment above ('Patient Joe', note 6).

1. *Jack Anvil ... Tom Hod.* See 'Patient Joe', note 4. More's adversarial dialogues are seen to better advantage in *Village Politics* (1792); here the radical side of the argument is swiftly suppressed. See *The Way to Plenty/ Tom White 2* for an account of the food-shortages in time of war, which provoked unrest in the working class and the fear of revolution in the upper social orders. The pitchfork mentioned in the text and shown in the woodcut becomes a dangerous symbol of labour turned to hellish disorder.
2. *seize all the meat.* Problems in distributing meat are discussed in *The Way to Plenty,* where the well-off suggest garden recipes and kindly agree to buy only prime cuts and give up gravy soup, so that the poor can afford at least the cheap meat from which it is made.
3. *Holland and Spain.* Refers to the early stages in the war against France. Holland and Spain were allies of Britain, but they surrendered to France, and became her allies in 1795. See Jennifer Mori, *Britain in the Age of the French Revolution 1785-1820,* Harlow: Longman, 2000, for a study of British politics and the war in Europe. The reference to the Pope might reflect an old suspicion of Catholicism, given new political edge.
4. *dinner of herbs ... riot.* Proverbs 15: 17: 'Better is a dinner of herbs where love is, than a stalled ox and hatred therewith'.
5. *Rulers ... manage the skies.* More avoids questions of political accountability; the English weather is to blame for famine.
6. *full share in it's crimes.* More, or the printer, often uses an old form 'it's', now incorrect, for the possessive.
7. *puddings and pies.* See *The Way to Plenty* for other examples of self-denial by the middle classes for the benefit of the poor.
8. *mittimus.* Legal term: warrant for arrest, from the Latin word at the start of the writ: 'mittimus' ('We send').

'Sinful Sally'

First published February 1796. The early text is not signed, and the ballad does not appear in More's *Collected Works*. The authorship is uncertain, but Spinney refers to it in a paragraph on More, and I have seen a later issue signed Z. It shares the characteristic of some other ballads by More, being both entertaining and grimly didactic. She might have thought it improper to claim authorship of a ballad in which the first-person voice belongs to a diseased prostitute, even though such confessions and complaints are familiar in the genre. In some chapbooks Sally is shown dying, but this woodcut comes from a later edition. c.1810, in which she is pointing out a wine-shop to her lover. It appears to be a variant of an original printed in 1796; blocks eventually wore out and had to be re-cut. In some early issues there is a set of small cuts showing the stages of her degeneration.

1. *kersey gown.* 'A kind of coarse woollen cloth' (*SOED*)
2. *Varlet.* Rogue, rascal.
3. *filthy novel.* Country girls are corrupted by cheap ballads, but the rake's mistress completes her loss of innocence with the help of fiction.
4. *meaner Lass.* Thomas Hardy's poem 'The Ruined Maid' (1866) records a similar encounter, providing a contrast between innocence and experience:

   > And whence such fine garments, such prosperi-ty?'
   > 'O didn't you know I'd been ruined?' said she.

5. *ruined and undone.* Ironically, the man is 'ruined' here. The phrase is conventionally applied to a seduced and abandoned woman; the man's complaint is of venereal disease.
6. *clay-cold ground I lie.* More made a collection of traditional ballads before starting work on the Tracts, and studied them carefully. The words 'clay-cold' are found in laments by dead or mourning lovers, for example: 'I crave one kiss of your clay-cold lips'.
7. *red ... white ... wool.* Isaiah 1: 18: 'though your sins be as scarlet, they shall be as white as snow: though they be red like crimson, they shall be as wool'.
8. *day of Grace is past.* For the theological concept of grace, see Romans 3: 24: 'being justified freely by his grace, through the redemption that is in Jesus Christ'.

'The Sorrows of Yamba'

First published November 1795. The authorship of this tract is disputed, though several critics have attributed it to More. It is unsigned and not included in her *Collected Works*. It was reprinted as More's work in at least two works published in her lifetime: a Religious Tract Society pamphlet, Newcastle, 1823, and an Anti-Slavery Collection, 1828, with poems by Cowper, Montgomery, Pringle and others. However, the text in the 1828 book is heavily cut and appears without editorial comment, so it can hardly be taken as proof of authorship. More was so firmly identified in the public mind with the series of Tracts that a distinction between what she edited and what she wrote might not have been made. Her poem 'Slavery' (1788) confirms her commitment to the abolitionist movement, and the didactic religious tone in 'Yamba' seems authentic. As I argued in relation to 'Sinful Sally' she might not have wished to identify herself with the first-person narrator. Yamba is given a voice; her speech is a curious blend of literary and evangelical diction, but at times she recounts her sufferings more graphically and movingly in broken English. Although the experiment is patronizing in effect, it precedes by several years Wordsworth's representation of common speech in the *Lyrical Ballad*s.

In *Subject to Others: British Women Writers and Colonial Slavery* 1670-1834, (London: Routledge, 1992) Moira Ferguson accepted More's authorship. Alan Richardson subsequently attributed the poem jointly to More and to Eaglesfield Smith, a minor poet, since it appears in a shorter version under his pseudonym, E.S.J., in the *Universal Magazine* in 1797 and in variant forms in his *Poetical Works* (1802 and 1822). Richardson points out that the conversion narrative and the use of dialect do not occur in any of Smith's versions, which suggest that these elements, at least, might have been written by More, perhaps being added editorially (*Slavery, Abolition and Emancipation: Writings in the British Romantic Period*, Vol.4: *Verse*, London: Pickering and Chatto, 1999). I have not read Smith's poems, but if, as Richardson notes, he has titled his 1802 version, 'Ianda (Not Wholly Original)', it seems possible he is drawing on More's unsigned text, so using her Repository, as it names invites, as a common resource for the creation of literary ballads.

1. *or the Negro Woman's Lamentation.* This sub-title does not appear in some 1795 issues.
2. *St. Lucie's distant isle … Afric's love.* St Lucia is one of the Windward Islands in the Caribbean; the ship has transported slaves from Africa to the West Indies.

3. *British Tar.* Colloquial term for a sailor. Some sea-faring clothes were made waterproof by the application of tar.

4. *Hundreds stowed like me.* The early chapbook version of the ballad has a set of small but expressive woodcuts in the text; these show, among other scenes, the capture of the slaves, their appalling treatment on the ship, and their public sale.

5. *shame for Britons brave.* Given More's patriotic views, this denunciation might seem out of character, but the castigation of those responsible for inhumanity shows her determination to correct and develop the national character.

6. *the Cat.* The-cat-o'-nine tails. A lash for flogging.

7. *British Law ... slaves like me.* As a result of prolonged campaigning by the Evangelicals and other humanitarians, the British slave-trade was abolished partially in 1806 and fully in 1807.

8. *poor me no understand.* See passage heading these notes for comment on the representation of Yamba's speech

9. *Massas' sin.* As usual in the tracts, the victim is advised to consider herself a sinner as she prays for her oppressor. The sin is not specified, but is probably an Evangelical version of original sin, shared by all humanity since Adam's Fall.

10. *Missionary Man.* Although Roman Catholic missionaries had for centuries travelled the world to save souls, Protestant missionary work developed mainly from the late 18th century, expanding greatly in the time of empire.

11. *lust of gain.* Social problems must be addressed in moral terms; the materialism and greed of the 'British Sons of Murder' is to be cured by conversion and salvation. Here a collective act of the reformed will seems to overtake the slow process of legislation.

12. *never will be slaves.* From 'Rule, Britannia' by James Thomson (1704-48). The song appears in his *Alfred; A Masque* (1740). The original lines are: 'And guardian angels sung this strain: "Rule Britannia, rule the waves, /Britons never will be slaves"'.

13. *weary are at rest.* Job 3:17: 'There the wicked cease from troubling; and there the weary be at rest'.